ReInventing
The University

ReInventing
The University
Literacies and Legitimacy in the
Postmodern Academy

CHRISTOPHER L. SCHROEDER

UTAH STATE
UNIVERSITY PRESS
Logan, Utah

Utah State University Press
Logan, Utah 84322-7800

Manufactured in the United States of America.
Cover design by Barbara Yale-Read.
Cover art from a collage by Carly Doan. Used by permission.

03   02   01   3   2   1

Library of Congress Cataloging-in-Publication Data

Schroeder, Christopher L., 1970-
  Reinventing the university : literacies and legitimacy in the
postmodern academy / Christopher L. Schroeder.
      p. cm.
Includes bibliographical references (p.) and index.
  ISBN 0-87421-409-2 (alk. paper)
  1. Education, Higher—United States—Curricula. 2. Postmodernism and
education—United States. 3. Student participation in curriculum
planning—United States. I. Title.
  LB2361.5 .S38 2001
  378.1'99'0973--dc21
                            00-012955

CONTENTS

ACKNOWLEDGMENTS

Thanks, first, to the students, colleagues, and friends who have given generously of their time to talk with me about literacies, cultures, and education in the United States. In addition, I want to thank all of those who contributed pieces to this text, whether they appeared in the final version or helped me to think through some of the questions, including Jean Wasko, Constantine Santas, and each of the students whose work appears here under their own name or by pseudonym.

I want especially to thank Helen Fox, Carl Williams, Peter Elbow, Victor Villanueva, Patricia Bizzell, and Ann Dobie, all of whom read my manuscript at various stages in the process and provided unwavering support and insightful suggestions. Also, I want to thank Sherri Condon and Jim McDonald, who read pieces of an earlier version. Thanks, too, to Edmund Miller and Richard McNabb, who offered their perspectives at crucial moments while I was finishing the manuscript, and to Karen Ogulnick, Rose Collins, and Shaireen Rasheed, who have recently agreed to carry these conversations outside of English departments to other departments across the curriculum.

A big thanks goes to Michael Spooner at USU press for his support, belief and encouragement, and to Michael's assistant, Adi Broberg, who helped to finalize many of the particulars.

A bigger thanks goes to Mahal and Mateo who, at the end of each long day in the academy, never fail to remind me of meaning and priorities. In many ways, this book reads and writes a future that I hope you will know.

And the biggest thanks goes to Ranimarie, the greatest woman I have ever known. From the first day we met, your unconditional acceptance has been the greatest experience I have ever had. *Mahal kita ngayon at magpakailanman.*

These, and others, deserve credit for the parts that work; I alone am responsible for what does not.

PROLOGUE
Reread(writ)ing the Contemporary Crisis in Literacy

The student has to appropriate (or be appropriated by) a specialized discourse, and he has to do this as though he were easily and comfortably one with his audience, as though he were a member of the academy or an historian or an anthropologist or an economist; he has to invent the university by assembling and mimicking its language while finding some compromise between idiosyncrasy, a personal history, on the one hand, and the requirements of convention, the history of a discipline, on the other hand. He must learn to speak our language. Or he must dare to speak it or to carry off the bluff, since speaking and writing will most certainly be required long before the skill is "learned." And this, understandably, causes problems.

David Bartholomae
"Inventing the University"

Education may well be, as of right, the instrument whereby every individual in a society like our own, can gain access to any kind of discourse. But we well know that in its distribution, in what it permits and in what it prevents, it follows the well-trodden battle-lines of social conflict. Every educational system is a political means of maintaining or of modifying the appropriation of discourse, with the knowledge and the powers it carries with it.

Michel Foucault
"The Discourse of Language"

On March 29, 2000, a headline on the front page of *The New York Times* announced "Citing a Crisis, Bush Proposes Literacy Effort." Above the fold—interspersed with articles about the failures of NASA's management, the conflicts facing Haitian immigrants in the United States, the efforts of nonprofit groups to exploit a loophole in the tax law, and decisions of OPEC nations to increase oil production despite Iran's resistance—is an article about politics and literacy. It opens with this paragraph: "Once again mooring traditionally Democratic issues to the agenda of his Republican presidential campaign, Gov. George W. Bush of Texas today proposed a five-year, $5 billion program to address what he termed a national literacy crisis among children" (Levy A1). "America must confront a national emergency," the article quotes Bush as saying in a speech to a coalition of Asian-American groups.

> Too many of our children cannot read. In the highest-poverty schools—I want you to hear this statistic—in the highest-poverty schools in America, 68 percent of fourth graders could not read at a basic level in 1998. . . . [W]e will not tolerate illiteracy amongst the disadvantaged students in the great country called America. . . . [M]ore and more we are divided into two nations: one that reads and one that can't, and therefore one that dreams and one that doesn't. Reading is the basis for all learning, and it must be the foundation for all other education reforms.(A1; A18)

What was candidate (now President) Bush's solution? According to his aides, "his plan would help roughly 900,000 children with poor reading skills, at a cost of $1,000 per child per year for tutoring and other assistance," and "[b]esides that $900 million, an additional $100 million a year would go to testing and teacher training" (A1). Literacy crises, however, soon disappear in the machinations of election-year politics, as aides to Vice President Al Gore "quickly dismissed" the "Bush plan" by attempting "to shift attention to Mr. Bush's tax-cut proposal," a cut that, Gore's aides claim, "would leave no money for new education initiatives" (A1, A18).

What is interesting to me is neither Bush's reductive definition of literacy nor that the way he narrates a literacy crisis to an audience comprised largely of minorities serves as a political strategy in a campaign that is eager to rebuild its image after a bloody primary. Nor is it the amount of money that he suggests will solve the problem, nor the political language of defining a problem, nor the Republican Party's new-found concern with minorities, poverty, and education, nor the way that literacy is situated as the central function of education in America. What is interesting to me first is the fact that Bush is willing to identify the existence of a literacy crisis at all, and second, his implied suggestion that such a crisis breaks along cultural lines.

Why is the fact that Bush is willing to acknowledge the existence of literacy crisis surprising to me? After all, we're due to begin talking again about a literacy crisis and a back-to-basics movement, as we do every so often in America[1] (though a cursory survey of the public discourse over the past twenty years suggests that, despite Governor Bush's assertions, there are decidedly mixed opinions about the existence of a literacy crisis at all[2]). I suppose there are several reasons that I am surprised—including the mere fact that Bush and I agree on something. At this point, I'll limit myself to two. First, similar to many teachers and textbooks, Bush invokes a universalized definition of literacy, as if what it means to be literate can be separated from the contexts in which literate practices are meaningful. Second, even in connecting literacy and culture, Bush's proposed solutions to the cultural biases in literacy leave the educational institutions relatively unchanged, thereby perpetuating cultural biases, albeit different ones, in the name of addressing what he is calling the crisis in literacy. If, in an effort to respond to any literacy crisis, we are to get clear about the conditions of literacy in America and if we are to generate legitimate alternatives, then we must come to terms with both the ways that particular definitions of literacy have been universalized in an effort to speak of literacy for all people in every situation, and we must be willing to change our academic institutions, which historically have served to prepare and certify Americans for and in literacy.

Whenever issues of language and literacy surface, as Antonio Gramsci argues, a reorganization of cultural hegemony is about to occur.[3] This book is an effort to participate in the current discussions of language and literacy and in the emerging reorganization of cultural hegemony. It is about reinventing the university, about reorganizing and reconfiguring the institutions that play such a significant role in the conditions of literacy in America. It does not propose a different model of literacy instruction, but argues that we need a different model of literacy itself—a collaborative, context-specific model that emerges from the conflicts between competing cultures, including the culture of the academy and the culture of the students and teachers who comprise it. *ReInventing the University* does not suggest, naively, that we can escape a cultural hegemony, but suggests instead that we can collaborate on a cultural hegemony that, in the end, will meet more of the literacy needs of students, teachers, and American society itself.

At the same time, this is a story of my efforts to participate in this new cultural hegemony and to legitimize others to participate in the conversations that give rise to the cultural hegemony. It is a story of failures and successes, dead ends and promising paths. Also, it is a story of my efforts to reinvent the university even as I am searching for my place in it and working within its confines. And as is often the case with stories, it concludes as an aporia, without a clear solution or resolution, a story that rereads and rewrites without offering surefire solutions, only some suggestions.

As we know, critics have been identifying literacy crises since 1870,[4] which, not incidentally, was shortly after the institutionalization of the German model of education and the emergence of English departments in American colleges and universities. And the coupling of literacy crises and American educational institutions is not surprising. In their introduction to *Contending with Words*, Patricia Harkin and John Schilb argue that this literacy crisis was defined by critics as a failure on the part of American colleges and universities to teach writing and reading in ways that were consistent with conventional values (3). What is surprising and new, I think, is what social and historical contexts for education and literacy suggest about both the condition of literacy in the United States and U. S. educational institutions today. In a recent survey of first-year students, researchers at UCLA discovered that students increasingly view education as a means to higher incomes rather than a way of expanding their experiences and perspectives. According to this large survey, 74.9 percent of first-year students identified their primary goal in college as economic success, while 40.8 percent indicated personal growth and development. For their peers twenty years ago, the numbers were almost reversed. According to the director of the survey, the trend is more significant in light of "unprecedented levels of academic and political disengagement,"[5] a lack of engagement that can also be seen in dropout and graduation rates in America. According to ACT, Inc., the national college-drop-out rate for first-year students increased consistently from 1983 until 1996 (though it decreased slightly in 1997), and the graduation rate had reached a new all-time low in 1997.[6] If we consider cultural variables, then the numbers from the same period are even more revealing: though the average composite ACT score of female students increased four times between 1990 and 1996 as the average score of males remained constant, this average score for females (20.8) is still below the national average; further, the increases in the scores of both females and minorities occurred predominantly in mathematics and not in English, reading, or reasoning abilities.[7]

In light of these and other conditions, Mark Edmundson seems to have it right when he explains the seemingly contradictory mix of boredom and ambition in contemporary students by suggesting that the problem lies with the educational system itself, and specifically with its increased emphasis on training and entertaining and not on transformation.[8] Students (and their parents) have become consumers, Bill Readings argues, in contemporary academic institutions that are busy transforming themselves into "bureaucratically organized and relatively autonomous consumer-oriented corporation[s]" (11). The implications for education have been dramatic and far-reaching. In American colleges and universities, education has become immersed in what bell hooks calls a "crisis of engagement," a condition in which knowledge has been "commoditized" and "authentic learning" has ceased. This crisis in education, she maintains, is also "a crisis in meaning" that affects students and teachers alike, both of whom are uncertain about the purpose of education, as well as "unsure about what has value in life" (51). Some have gone so far as to argue that if the social crises of meaning in America continue, the end of education may be forthcoming.[9]

Along with the social contexts of education, the social contexts for literacy help to complete the picture of literacy in America. Currently in America, forty million adults sixteen or older have what the National Institute of Literacy has designated as "significant literacy needs." Historically, according to Jan Nespor, literacy instruction has undergone three distinct phases that have increasingly separated literacy practices from their social contexts:

> Literacy instruction, which had at first been part of an apprenticeship in certain forms of complex social activities and had later become part of a routinized form of social practice (religious observance), had now become routinized and embedded in a hermetic context: the public school. Formal literacy instruction was no longer grounded in everyday contexts of use (even of the ritualistic-religious variety). Instead, children were placed in particular institutional contexts whose sole function was to impart "skills" abstracted from contexts of use. Instead of learning to do things that entail reading and writing, one learned to "read" and "write" in courses designed to teach nothing but reading and writing. (176-77)

As the practices of literacy instruction shifted from invoking context-specific abilities to universalized skills situated within their own classrooms, the cultural values that these versions of literacy represented shifted from communal values and towards increasingly institutionalized cultures, first of the church and then of the state. Along with an increasingly decontextualized understanding of literacy came an increasingly institutionalized version of culture, which, more and more, became the purview of experts.[10]

Together, the practices of literacy instruction and the institutionalization of cultures produced a cultural capital, or what Bill Readings (drawing upon Pierre Bourdieu) calls "the confluence of symbolic and sociocultural capital" (105 ff), as the standard for certification by experts. In this way, the means of social reproduction had been textualized within classrooms designed to provide socialization into the dominant cultural values through developing competencies in the sanctioned versions of literacy.[11] Drawing upon Gramsci, Louis Althusser explains that social reproduction in the public domain occurs through repression and violence, yet in the private domain—in which he includes educational institutions and cultural formations—social reproduction occurs through what he calls ideology, or consent.[12] In spite of the oversimplification between public and private domains, I believe the distinction is helpful in understanding the ways that education and literacy contribute to social reproduction in contemporary American society.

Within the contexts that I have constructed, the act of becoming literate amounts to being certified in certain social practices and, through them, in particular cultural values. My reading of the crisis goes something like this:

particular versions of cultural capital have been institutionalized within American colleges and universities as the standards for certification. As such, these cultural values have formed the basis for full-fledged admission into social and economic credibility and authority. Or, to flip it, particular versions of what it means to write and read have been situated within U. S. colleges and universities as a way of ensuring the currency of particular cultural capital and as a way of exerting social control. This control occurs primarily through consent but also through repression, and some, such as Keith Gilyard and J. Elspeth Stuckey, would even argue, it occurs through cultural suicide and violence. In being situated so in the acadamy, sanctioned versions of literacy—not only certain ways of writing and reading but also, through these practices, versions of who to be and how to see the world—come to serve as the cultural capital of U. S. society at large. After all, academic writing, according to a best-selling textbook in composition classrooms, "has wide-ranging implications for the way we think and learn as well as for our chances of success, our personal development, and our relationships with other people" (*St. Martins* 2).

What I want to suggest is that the narratives of education that dominate U. S. colleges and universities are inextricably tied to the dominant versions of literacy in society, and to the versions of cultural capital that make these literacy practices meaningful. For example, school-based literacies, as Ron Scollon and Suzanne B. K. Scollon have demonstrated, privilege syntax and sequential relations among sentences, the ability to fictionalize writers and readers as rational minds, and truth values over rhetorical and social conditions.[13] These are the literacy practices and the cultural capital of white, middle class America,[14] the same practices and capital that, in part, have given rise to the narratives of education, literacy, and meaning in U. S. schools. However, the coupling of education, literacy, and social control is not, on the face of it, necessarily new or different. John Trimbur has argued that, in fact, this crisis is more the result of the appropriation of literacy by educational institutions and a meritocratic social order and less an actual decline, whatever that may look like, in the literacy practices in America (294). What is different about my reading of the situation has to do with what I believe to be an increasing social illegitimacy of these institutionalized versions of literacy and the cultural capital they endorse, especially in an increasingly different America. One could say this reading is not new, for Victor Villanueva, Helen Fox, and others have made similar cases about these conditions for minority, or world majority, students. However, I would like to argue that, even for traditional mainstream students—white, middle class, often male—the sanctioned versions of literacy in the academy are suffering from what Jean François Lyotard has called (in *The Postmodern Condition*) the mercantilization of knowledge and the legitimation crisis, a condition in which the standards for literate performance have ceased to hold meaning for an increasing majority of students, including those whom these literacy practices and cultural capital have historically represented.[15]

In the increasing differences between the literacies that students are bringing to the classroom and the literacy of the "traditional college curriculum" that Maureen Hourigan writes about (50), we can see what I believe to be the cultural conflicts that have given rise to the contemporary crisis in literacy and education. As part of larger social crises of education and meaning in American society, these conflicts cannot be resolved by institutional response from American colleges and universities, which in the past has meant new conferences, journals, books, and other institutional formations designed to address increasingly specialized aspects of literacy and education.[16] For not only has this modernist trend failed to address the conditions of literacy in American society, but it has also contributed to larger crises of meaning and education in postmodern America by institutionalizing a version of culture that is more and more irrelevant to students.[17]

According to Readings, in *The University in Ruins*, there are three options: reaffirming a national cultural identity, reinventing cultural identities that are relevant to American society, and abandoning the "social mission" of academic institutions, at least in terms of representing cultures (90). Though Readings's sense of the shift from reason and culture to excellence provides insight into the contemporary conditions that are being called the literacy crisis, his position— that academic institutions need to abandon their social function—is not just unnecessary but will only exacerbate the contemporary conditions. And Richard Miller's optimistic pessimism in *As If Learning Mattered* (202), though helpful, ends up selling short the efforts of committed teachers towards educational and cultural reform. Though I will take up Readings and Miller again the epilogue, let me mention briefly my position that it is impossible for literacy practices *not* to endorse particular versions of cultural capital. Abandoning the social mission of academic institutions will merely deny this intertextuality, thereby increasing the degree to which sanctioned literacies in the academy ensure social reproduction. It is not necessary to sacrifice widespread change in order to praise the local.

Within this context, I hope *ReInventing* serves Readings's second option—a redefinition of the institutionalized cultures, a redefintion that contingent, local, and on-going, that legitimizes students and teachers to engage institutions and history in conversations over the practices of literacy and their relations to classrooms and institutions.

If culture in a postmodern society is a highly contested term, then trying to understand the culture(s) of classrooms is an effort that is doomed almost before it begins. Conventional definitions of culture, such as "a vast structure of language, customs, knowledge, ideas, and values . . . which provide . . . people with a general design for living and patterns for interpreting reality" (qtd. in Evans 273), lead critics and theorists to focus upon traditional variables— gender, class, and ethnicity—as the boundaries along which cultures break. With conventional definitions such as this one, we can talk about a culture of a particular group of people, as Henry Evans does when he argues that, "[b]ecause a people's sociopolitical condition dictates its educational needs, multicultural education for African Americans is necessarily different from multicultural education for European Americans and other emigrant cultural groups" (276). However, the cultural dimensions of gender, class, and ethnicity rarely exist in isolation from each other, and as Maureen Hourigan argues throughout *Literacy as Social Exchange*, the confluence of class, gender, and ethnicities often gives rise to competing literacies (125-27). In classrooms, the situation is complicated even more when the cultures of specific disciplines and individual teachers are superimposed upon the competing cultures and literacies that are already present in classrooms.

What I propose to examine in *ReInventing* is the culture of the academy. I want to argue that the extent to which people—students and teachers, in this case—share particular practices (and, in so doing, assume particular positions and accept specific versions of the world) is the extent to which they share a literacy and a culture that makes it meaningful. In so doing, I want to talk about the cultures of classrooms and cultures of particular classrooms. I want to talk about how they may be similar to and different from the cultures of classrooms constructed by other sections of the same course or, more obviously, from classrooms constructed by other disciplines. And the degree to which classrooms sanction different practices and, through them, different positions for people to assume and versions of the world to accept, is the degree to which we can distinguish among competing literacies within the academy. It is this tension between the social and the individual that give rise to the ways that I am using literacy and culture throughout this book.

For me, the most salient conflicts within literaci(es) practices center upon issues of legitimacy and authority and the ways that these have been appropriated within academic institutions in America.[18] Within American colleges and universities, the naturalization of literacy practices in English departments has resulted in a widespread alienation and lack of engagement through the privileging of an academic cultural capital and denying alternatives. This is so, in part, because of the ways that the sanctioned literacy practices have been decontextualized from the social and cultural contexts that make them mean-ingful. If I can construct historical and social contexts, perhaps I can clarify my reading of the contemporary conditions of education and literacy in America. One context for understanding what I am calling the contemporary crises in literacy and meaning is to see it in relation to what John Trimbur calls a "the rise of mass public education" and an institutionalization of "a meritocratic educational order" (280). With the appropriation of an elective model of edu-cation in the late nineteenth century, American colleges and universities shifted their social function from serving an aristocratic social class to provid-ing a means for social mobility for a developing American middle class.[19] As such, American colleges and universities appropriated the American Dream of equality and individualism—a dream that, as we all know, presupposes a uni-versal culture and a egalitarian society. Nevertheless, the new elective colleges and universities, in the absence of the sorting mechanism of social class, needed a method for certifying eligible students for admission into the newly elite status of the educated middle class, and this process, as Susan Miller argues in *Textual Carnivals*, came to be situated within English departments and specifically in literature and composition classrooms (51). Together, litera-ture and composition classrooms were the sites where students were socialized into the cultural capital of the academy and by virtue of their certification entered into the newly forming middle class.

Within the new American colleges and universities, the ensuing specializa-tion that was part and parcel of the elective model of education only served to decontextualize the certificatory function of schools and the standards for cer-tification in the cultural capital of the academy. Given how well known this history is, I will merely hit some highlights. In what seems like a contradiction to its contemporary function in American colleges and universities, the disci-pline of English studies originated in the Dissenting Academies of England during the late seventeenth and eighteenth centuries,[20] a period during which rhetoric, as the production of discourse, still possessed a significant social function. In America, the development of English studies occurred in such a way that separated the rhetorical from the poetic[21] in a process that ultimately denied the role of rhetoric within the larger social context.[22] In order to main-tain the legitimacy of the new discipline of English studies in American col-leges and universities, English departments denied the intellectual status of the rhetorical, now limited predominantly to composition, in order to preserve the privileged status of the poetic and, ultimately, the shape of future departments and the discipline.[23] In terms of literacy and legitimacy, one of most significant results was the decontextualization of a social literacy as interdependent prac-tices of discursive production and consumption and the institutionalization of a decontextualized academic literacy that restricted the production of discourse to nonliterary texts and privileged the consumption of literary works.

In contemporary American colleges and universities, the function of English departments is still the same—to certify students. The problem is that, within these departments, historical, class-based versions of literacy have been naturalized and legitimized. For a number of reasons that had equally as much to do with the history of literary studies as with the social mission of educational institutions in America and the discipline of composition studies itself, American colleges and universities have reduced the official role of literature classrooms in this process of certification to the point that, now (according to administrators, faculty members in other departments, and many composition specialists)[24] composition classrooms, more than literature classrooms, serve as the site where students are certified in the standards for literate performance and, through them, in the cultural capital of the academy, though literature's presence can still be seen (or felt).[25]

As defined by composition studies under the auspices of the English departments, the discursive practices of the sanctioned academic literaci(es) colonialize students into the cultural capital of the academy. The problem, however, is less with the skills and abilities of the students and more with the cultural capital that the sanctioned literacies invoke. This is so not merely in the "classrooms filled with the children of color," as Villanueva explains, whose cultural capital "differs from the white middle class"[26] but also in those classrooms filled predominantly, and often exclusively, with children of an increasingly fragmented and different white middle class. My contention is that the cultural capital of the academy is increasingly less relevant to even the children of the white middle class, those purportedly mainstream students whose literacies are being shaped by sit-coms and MTV, by email and the Internet, by mega-malls and market-driven advertising—in short, by the realities of postmodern America. To be sure, white, middle-class communities have historically been the recipients of the cultural legacy legitimized by conventional academic literaci(es); I would never try to argue that the personal and educational histories of many of the students who appear in these pages have not predisposed them towards the culture of the academy, or, on the other hand, that their experiences are the same as those that the world-majority students from Helen Fox's *Listening to the World* have. What I would argue is that, even for the prototypical white, middle-class student, the cultural capital of the academy can be, and increasingly is, foreign and other.

These conflicts emerge most evidently in the issues of authority and credibility. For example, while students in Fox's *Listening* struggle to understand the authority of "original"—as in the original source or the original thought (which dialogic literacies would deny)—the students with whom I have worked, coming from a society that privileges cultural equality and individualism, struggle to understand that authority and credibility within conventional academic literacies come more from scholarly books and numerical studies, as well as from their opinions and experiences, and not from their opinions and perspectives alone. In these and other ways, the cultural values that students bring to classrooms are different from those of the academy. If, even for competing reasons, the cultural capital of the academy is foreign to the students who comprise American colleges and universities today, then the answer to the current conditions that have been called the literacy crisis is not more fragmentation or specialization, nor is it the denial of these differences implicit in the calls for back-to-basics movements. Instead, we must begin to consider alternatives to the conventional literacies of the academy, alternatives that reflect legitimate versions of cultural capital, legitimate for students, teachers, institutions, and disciplines. Only in addressing students' literacy needs, and not solely the needs of institutions, can these alternatives can escape the current crises of legitimacy and meaning in American education and American society.

The read(writ)ing I am making emerges from the conflicts and historical conditions that comprised my experiences within various English departments across the country. First as a student, then a student-teacher, and later a teacher, I found myself increasingly disillusioned with the dominant cultural capital of the American academies and American society, with the currency that others have called a cultural Calvinism. According to Lester Faigley, cultural Calvinism requires that "children of the professional middle class often must go to school twenty years or more and serve an apprenticeship after that . . . just to achieve their parents' status" (*Fragments* 54). In order to succeed, cultural Calvinism demands of us "the self-discipline and faith in deferred gratification that [our] parents possessed," and yet "the terms of success for the professional middle class exacerbate [our] anxiety because affluence threatens to lead to self-indulgence," which undermines "the Protestant ethic of hard work and delayed gratification" (54). For me, it was more, however, than simply the amount of investment that was necessary; it included the prevailing definitions of success (i.e. affluence) and the concomitant anxiety and uncertainty. In short, cultural Calvinism appeared to me, as it did to others,[27] to be mentally, emotionally, and spiritually bankrupt. As I successively acquired my (provisional) institutional legitimacy by earning degrees and experiences, I found myself initially alienated from, and then increasingly uninterested in, the sanctioned literaci(es) of the academy, in spite of my historical and social background that would suggest otherwise. Nevertheless, my growing distaste for the dominant cultural capital of the academy and society did not interfere with my success in the classroom—at least in the terms defined by my teachers and the institutions in which I studied. As a white, male, middle class European-American student, I found it relatively easy to participate in the cultural capital of the academy by accommodating and assimilating the literacies as defined by classrooms, teachers, and institutions and by making the necessary adjustments along the way. When I took a theory course from a professor who despised social constructivism, I wrote a paper attacking the relativism of Stanley Fish and his interpretive communities. When I wrote for a professor who privileged social constructivism, I used Fish et al. to legitimize positions that lauded provisionality and contingency. I could demonstrate proficiency in the sanctioned literaci(es) of the academy. Clearly, I had learned my lesson.

Well, some might say I hadn't. When it came time to write the dissertation, I had begun to explore literacies, culture, and the academy in earnest, and I was determined to make the experience both satisfying and rewarding, in and of itself, by centering upon these very issues that I had been working through (implicitly at least until the latter stages of graduate school) in my experiences within the academy. What I discovered, however, was that I had not learned my lesson. I had not expected that, even in the latter stages of being a student, at the point at which I was more like my professors than ever, I would still be expected to perform the dominant literaci(es) of the academy. This insight came the hard way: after literally seven drafts, my dissertation was accepted (my dissertation director did much penance that year), and I was finally legit, or so I thought, and I could move on to the intellectual work that I found most satisfying. Again, I was wrong. Over and over, I would still be expected to acquire a legitimacy through institutionally specific forms and discourses, as recognized by department chairs and academic deans.

All the while, not only were academic literaci(es) unable to meet my intellectual needs, they were also unable to provide for material needs. As everyone knows, it is virtually impossible to live upon T.A. and adjunct salaries. As a teaching assistant, I earned $3,750 plus tuition remission each semester, and later as an adjunct, I would be paid $500 a credit hour, which meant that, if I taught the maximum load allowed by that institution—three courses—for the semester, I would earn $4,500 each term. To make matters worse, I learned that, upon graduating, I would be entering into a job search in which, only 35.7% of new Ph.D.s in the classics, modern languages, and linguistics were obtaining tenure-track appointments (the lowest percentage, incidentally, in twenty years). Furthermore, only 61.4% of these same graduates would find full-time teaching appointments (ADE). Even after I began to earn a full-time salary, I discovered other problems, such as the loan officer's assurance that, if I were a medical doctor, she would be able to obtain much better interest rates for me.

The conclusion that I reached—the same conclusion that many of us, I'm sure, have reached—was that, if legitimacy was going to require such a constant investment of time and energy, then some other return would be needed, an intellectual compensation, perhaps, that would make the expenditures worthwhile. So I began to search for literacies that would satisfy both the academy, in which I had chosen to work and my intellectual needs. One could say I began to look for ways to integrate my literacy needs with the literacy needs of my discipline and my profession. To my surprise (though, in retrospect, it shouldn't have surprised me), I discovered that there were others, such as Victor Villanueva, who were writing about similar issues of legitimacy throughout graduate school and beyond and who were searching for more satisfying alternatives. What was different, though, was our context.

Obviously, literacies and crises are contingent terms. Some argue that what is being called the literacy crisis has less to do with the educational system and more to do with changing public values,[28] and others assert that there is no literacy crisis, that what is being called the literacy crisis is the symptom of a shift in understandings of literacy in which simply writing and reading are not enough.[29] Regardless, the advantages of being literate have been described in context-free and universal terms. The benefits attributed to being literate have been numerous: intellectual achievement; rational thinking; abstract language; critical attitudes; awarenesses of time and space; political freedom and democracy; complex governmental formations; economic security; upward mobility; better citizenship with middle-class values; personal fulfillment; lower crime rates; urbanization; and others.[30] When resituated within historical and social contexts, the benefits that have been ascribed to literacy—what Beth Daniell calls "the modernist promise of literacy"—are actually the results of culturally-based discourses and literacy practices, not, in fact, intrinsic to a universal literacy itself, and are, in Daniell's words, "inequitably fulfilled" (404).

A closer look at the grand literacy narratives in the academy will reveal the ways in which these versions of literacy are wedded to modernist practices and modernist discourses. In "Literacy and Politics of Education," C. H. Knoblauch identifies four competing versions of literacy in American schools, which sanction "fundamentally different perceptions of social reality; the nature of language and discourse; the importance of culture, history, and tradition; the

function of schools, as well as other commitments, few of which are nego-
tiable" (76). The first two versions of literacy are what Knoblauch calls functional literacy and cultural literacy, both of which, in his words, "dominate the
American imagination" (76-77). As represented by basic and technical writing
programs and by business, industrial, and military training programs, functional literacy defines literacy as a set of minimal mechanical skills designed to
communicate information (76). Cultural literacy, on the other hand,
exchanges a mechanistic version of skills for purportedly transcendent cultural
values, usually the values of Western European societies (77). The remaining
versions of literacy are what Knoblauch calls personal growth literacy and critical literacy. Drawing upon the American narratives of unlimited freedom and
individualism, personal growth literacy, as endorsed by subjective theories of
writing and the whole language movement, posits language as expressive of
individual imagination through writing, reading, and speaking (78). Finally,
critical literacy posits a connection between the practices of writing and reading and the awareness of social conditions in the ways that it recognizes the
ability of those with authority to name the world for others (79).

In spite of the surface differences among competing versions that Knoblauch
provides, all of them are situated within modernist discourses, which efface difference in their agendas towards unity and totalization, and reflect a Eurocentrism,
which, as Danny Weil points out, depends upon a universalization of the world
(96). As for functional and cultural literacies, it is fairly easy to recognize their cultural and linguistic biases.[31] Many have dismantled the cultural presuppositions
behind them.[32] Imbued with conventional dualities and predicated upon an artificial orality-literacy binary, functional literacies privilege the practices of standard English and Eurocentric subjectivities and exclude other discursive practices
and subject positions, such as those of African-American English, that fail to conform to these standards. In doing so, functional literacies simultaneously reinforce dominant cultures, histories, and traditions and maintain the marginalized
status of the functionally illiterate.[33] In a not wholly dissimilar way, cultural literacies endorse universalized practices and engage in cultural discrimination, not by
overtly endorsing standard discourses but by privileging the cultural capital they
bear. In some ways, personal growth and critical literacies are only now beginning
to receive the same critical attention. Though these literacies are generally seen as
liberal and/or radical alternatives designed to alter or transform society,[34] they,
too, are legitimized by and, in turn, legitimize modernist narratives. For example,
personal growth literacies tend to deny conflict and posit a nonexistent social
equality.[35] Also, personal growth literacies fail to acknowledge the ways that the
stories that people can tell are those that are culturally available to them, the conventions of which are constructed and constrained by the contexts in which they

appear.[36] For another example, critical literacies have been criticized for their use of binary oppositions and false dichotomies, for their reductive understandings of social class, for their blatant sexism, and for their belief in false and correctable ideologies,[37] much of which reflects their dependence upon foundational understandings of the world based upon a belief in the ultimate accessibility of reality and the existence of universal truths.

Clearly, literacy is a contested term, one that, in the ways it is defined, has significant intellectual, social, and moral implications. For these insights, we have postmodernism to thank. By the end of the twentieth century, the ways that poststructuralism and postmodernism had problematized the modernist project had a significant impact upon the study of literacy. Around the same time as critics were championing the most recent crisis in literacy, a group of likeminded scholars and intellectuals turned their attention to the versions of literacy that dominated American schools and American society, and they began talking about the literacy myths, to use Harvey Graff's term, that these hegemonic versions of literacy engendered. In doing so, they relied upon an interdisciplinary approach to the study of literacy, an approach that came to be called the new literacy studies.[38] Assuming a social approach to literacy, these researchers (who ranged from Graff, James Paul Gee, Ron Scollon and Suzanne B. K. Scollon to Shirley Brice Heath, Jennifer Cook-Gumperz and John Gumperz, and many others from a variety of disciplines) argued that the literacy myths were actually the results of historical and social literacy practices, and not inherent within literacy itself. Furthermore, they suggested that the dominant versions of literacy denied their social and historical conditions and the interrelations among writing, reading, and power in the ways that they situated literacy within individuals rather than communities. As an alternative, these researchers argued that all definitions of literacy—including critical literacy—are inherently political in the ways that they establish power relations among people and naturalize particular versions of reality. In regard to classroom practices, they suggested that school-based literacies endorse certain values and versions of culture that are important to the hegemony of those currently in power. Though perhaps relying upon an oversimplified understanding of hegemony in their early work, the proponents of this new literacy studies emphasized the political dimensions of being literate and the role of literacies in social reproduction.

Within the contexts generated by the new literacy studies, what critics have called the literacy crisis becomes less about declining skills or rising standards for reading and writing and more about the standards and legitimacy of sanctioned literacies themselves.

❦

In the acts of reread(writ)ing the narrative of literacy in the academy, I have legitimized my own narrative, a narrative that bespeaks my own histories and cultures, my experiences in classrooms, as both a student and a teacher, and in institutions, as colleague and faculty member, and my experiences in the world beyond classrooms in all its forms—husband, father, friend, etc. As much as I might want or as much as I might be expected to do so, I cannot escape this situatedness, my situatedness, within the world; consequently, what I have done is legitimize a contingent narrative within a sea of contingent narratives, a narrative that is provisional and incomplete, a provisionality and incompleteness that, in the end, I cannot escape or avoid. However, such a recognition does not vitiate the rereading and rewriting that I do here, for all readings and writings are, in the end, provisional and incomplete.

Neither are these acts of rereading and rewriting an attempt to give rise to an alternative literacy construct that can be imported into classrooms and imposed upon students and teachers, for doing so would make it no different from conventional literacies that deny the difference of classrooms and students, institutions and disciplines. Rather, it is an attempt to negotiate the positionality and provisionality of literacy classrooms and my own situatedness within the discipline of English studies in American colleges and universities.

As is always the case, my reading and writing of the wor(l)d will privilege particular dimensions and overlook others. What makes it different, however, is that it attempts to recognize its own history, the contributions that people and experiences have made to it, the ways that it has been changed and transformed in its encounters with others and with the world.

As such, this narrative, in the act of reading and writing, is an effort to read and write itself, to construct its own literacy of literacies and education, of teaching and learning in America.

For some time, it has become something of a truism in contemporary intellectual circles that schools are powerful and persuasive social institutions. In the act of educating, schools situate students within specific social practices, and in doing so, they naturalize and legitimize particular discourses and cultures, along with the cultural capital that accompanies a proficiency in these discourses and values. One of the ways that this process of socialization occurs is through the literacy instruction, both tacit and explicit, that students receive in the course of the programs. In classrooms, instruction in the practices of literacy, or the acts that are considered to be writing, reading, thinking, etc., conducts students into the discourse communities of the academy and, to borrow Lester Faigley's pun,[39] offers them conduct upon which to model their discursive practices and their discourses. As such, the discourses of the academy "discipline" students, as well as their teachers, through the practices and the versions of literacy that they sanction, less by coercion, though there is plenty of that, and more by consent.[40] Even in many ostensibly radical classrooms, students cannot escape the tendency of academic literaci(es) to privilege a naturalized version of academic culture at the expense of the literacies and cultures that lie beyond it. More specifically, academic literaci(es) denie(s) the difference of subjectivities and versions of the world in the literacies that students bring with them (constructed-inscribed within their primary and popular discourses) in favor of a universalized (academic) subject position and uniform versions of the (academic) world—that is, in favor of the cultural capital of the academy. From the perspective that I have assumed, this denial is responsible for the contemporary crisis in literacy and meaning. And I see in this crisis, as I have suggested earlier, a condition in which learning to write, read, speak, think, value, etc. *academically* amounts to acceding to institutionally sanctioned discursive practices, subject positions, and versions of the world that maintain the current social relations and institutional formations and that alienate writers and readers from themselves and their experiences.

As such, the contemporary crises in literacy and meaning are actually crises in the cultural capital of the academy itself. Critiques of the academy, of course, are expected from those who are elided in the cultural histories of the academy. However, at the same time, there is a growing discontent, I believe, even within the dominant academic cultures, and it can be seen, for example, in the currency that subjectivist literacies have within the academy. Within the contexts I have established, one way to understand the popularity of expressivist theories of writing and reader-response theories of reading is to construct them as reactions to the dissatisfactions of the dominant literacies of the academy, with their universalized practices and uniform cultures, by more mainstream theorists and practioners. In the ways that the academy has accepted, for example, the contraries of Peter Elbow's doubting-believing game or the contingencies of Wolfgang Iser's textual gaps and indeterminacy, we can see a desire for alternatives to the universality of the dominant literacies of the academy. (In some ways, the reactions to expressivist and reader-response theories suggest the threat that these approaches potentially hold for the dominant literacies of the academy.) Unfortunately, the degree to which expressivist theories of writing or reader-response theories of reading privilege the individual is the degree to which these potentially transformative practices have been constructed within institutional formations and colonialized by these institutions. In denying the social implications of such practices and restricting them at the level of the individual, being constructed and colonialized within institutions have robbed these practices of their potential for change. If these individual practices can be resituated within historical and social contexts, then these practices, as some have suggested,[41] could transform classrooms and institutions through dialogue and difference, not unlike the dialogic classrooms that Kay Halasek describes in *A Pedagogy of Possibility*.

If it is true that the dominant standards for literate performance in American colleges and universities (and, by extension, in American society) are failing to satisfy the literacy needs of American students and American society, then such dissatisfaction represents potential sites of power that can enable us to reinvent the academy. Moreover, they enable us to do so in ways that go beyond merely assimilationist explanations of reconciling personal histories with institutional discourses, as I would argue David Bartholomae offers in "Inventing the University," to enacting classrooms in ways that lead to mutually satisfying literacies, literacies that satisfy both writers and readers and the academy itself. Of all the obstacles that such reinventings must overcome, one of the biggest is the issue of institutional legitimacy. Without this legitimacy, alternative literacies will remain in conversations at conferences or in print without transforming classroom practices, or, perhaps worse, they will be assimilated within institutions before they can produce any changes within the narratives of education that dominate American colleges and universities.

In *The New Literacy*, Paul Morris and Stephen Tchudi have documented the failure of conventional literacies and traditional discourses to respond to the cultural and linguistic needs of a postmodern United States. However, these insights into language and culture are not new to the academy. For example, scholars in applied linguistics and contrastive rhetorics, such as Ilona Leki and Ulla Conner, have long argued over the relationship between culture and language. Furthermore, others, such as Geneva Smitherman, Tony Crowley, and Rosina Lippi-Green, have argued that standard literacies reinforce cultural biases and social discrimination, and in so doing, these and other scholars have ushered in what James Comas has argued goes beyond a political turn in language studies to the "recasting of our disciplinary infrastructure in the mode of 'the political,' that is, the infrastructure of canons, curricula, pedagogy, and modes of research" (190).

His accusation of political essentialism notwithstanding, it is clear that the politicized contexts of literacy studies, composition studies, contrastive rhetorics, applied linguistics, literary studies, and related disciplines have given rise to challenges to conventional literacies and traditional discourses within the academy and have sought to legitimize alternatives. Perhaps most recently, Patricia Bizzell, in "Hybrid Discourses," argues that these alternative, or "hybrid," discourses have had a currency within academic institutions since the late 1980s and the early 1990s, at least within the disciplines of composition and rhetoric. Turning to the work of Keith Gilyard, Helen Fox, bell hooks, Mike Rose, Victor Villanueva, and others, Bizzell argues that these alternatives have certain features in common—nonstandard versions of English, nontraditional cultural references, personal experiences, offhand refutations, appropriative histories, humor, indirection, and textual reproduction. Beyond those whom Bizzell cites, others in composition and rhetoric who have experimented with alternatives to conventional academic literacies include Scott Lyons (mixed blood rhetorics) and Winston Weathers (narrative rhetorics). In addition to scholars in composition and rhetoric, scholars and intellectuals in other disciplines, such as Gloria Anzaldúa (anthropology/chicana-women's studies), Marilyn Cochran-Smith (education), Lemuel Johnson (comparative literature), Anne Sullivan (biology), and Jane Tompkins (literary studies), have experimented with alternative discourses in their intellectual work.

At the same time that alternative literacies and discourses are surfacing in scholarship, they are also appearing in composition classrooms across the United States. Bizzell, in her article on hybrid discourses, argues that teacher's composition cannot ignore these alternative discourses if they are going to prepare students for success in other classrooms and other contexts, and in a related way, Peter Elbow, in "Inviting the Mother Tongue," advocates for the legitimacy of students' primary discourses in classrooms conventionally dominated exclusively by academic literacies. Even before Bizzell and Elbow, however, others, such as Lillian Bridwell-Bowles, Xin Liu Gale, and Derek Owens, were calling for alternatives to conventional academic literacies as legitimate ways of learning and knowing in classrooms. In a similar way, essay collections, such as *Elements of Alternative Style* and *Writing in Multicultural Settings*, had begun to challenge conventional academic discourses and to recognize the importance of cultural literacies in writing classrooms.

ReInventing falls within both of these traditions. However, there are several differences. One of the biggest is that *ReInventing* extends these challenges beyond the composition classroom to include literature classrooms, English departments, and the institutions in which they exist. In doing so, I hope to bring together the interrelated practices of producing and consuming discourses under the heading of literacy. As a result, these challenges are not simply to conventional ways of producing discourses but also to ways of consuming them. Another difference includes the manner in which I try to reread and rewrite what critics are calling the contemporary crisis in literacy, not as a deficiency in students' abilities but as a lack of legitimacy of academic culture. Still another difference is the way in which I don't limit myself to authorizing cultural conflicts within the conventionally recognized differences—class, gender, and ethnicity—but include additional differences, differences that cut across these conventional fault lines (to play on Miller's article "Fault Lines in the Contact Zone"). In yet another way, I am trying to reconceive our business as teaching students to control discourses and as engaging in intellectual work to reread and rewrite culture and society, and I am speculating on what, in an ideal world, this revisioning would look like at departmental and institutional levels. One of the purposes of this text, then, is to contribute to the process that Patricia Bizzell, Helen Fox, Xin Liu Gale, Keith Gilyard, Derek Owens, Victor Villanueva, and others have begun in acquiring an institutional legitimacy for these alternative literacies.

Over the years, I considered myself to be a fairly competent teacher of writing and reading. As is the case for many who experiment with engaged pedagogies, I believed that my efforts in classrooms encouraged and empowered students in ways that led to satisfying learning for them, and in part, the responses from students seemed to confirm my impressions. For example, one writer from an introductory composition course I taught wrote in a student evaluation that the instructor "Definately[42] knows the subject, personality is open to our level. Can make you think when you really didn't want to." Another student noted that I am "Knowledgable about all areas of the subject being taught and always willing to help with writing problems." One student from a contemporary American literature course wrote that "The learning atmosphere was comfortable and casual" in spite of cramming an entire semester into eight meetings, and this same student goes on to cite my "level of knowledge and enthusiasm for the subject" and characterizes me as a "very bright person" who "loves the material that he teaches."

In addition to responses from students, I was encouraged in my efforts by Patricia Bizzell, Peter Elbow, Victor Villanueva, and others in the profession. In spite of the frustrations that accompany teaching, I always found myself excited about the prospects of each new semester—different writers and readers, different ideas and understandings, and a different subjectivity as a teacher, one that had been changed by the experiences with other writers and readers and with my own writing and reading. From my perspective, I believed that I was growing as a writer, reader, and teacher, if only because I had written more, read more, and taught more at the beginning of each semester than I had at the beginning of the previous semester. Along the way, I began to construct my own literacies. For example, I recognized the ways that Paulo Freire's emphasis upon the cognitive dimensions of learning enabled students to transcend the social passivity that can accompany expressivism, and yet I saw merit in the feminist desire of bell hooks and others to teach the whole person, not just the mind, and I struggled to bring these two together in the literacies I was constructing. And I assumed all along that others in the academy, both students and teachers, would also be interested in negotiating the differences between the literacies of the academy, with their cultural capital, and the popular and private literacies that we brought into the classroom.

As more experienced teachers might have told me, that assumption is not necessarily true.[43] In what came as a surprise to me, some responses from students and colleagues suggested that my efforts to construct literacies might not be as productive as I had thought or hoped. One student in a second semester composition course wrote of me in a course evaluation that "[the instructor] was confusing when he taught and I wondered where he was going with his teaching method." Another student from an American literature survey wrote in the course evaluation that "Mr. Schroeder had an approach to this class that I have never encountered before. The class was very loosely structured and, at times, decisions regarding its direction were made by the students. Quite honestly, in taking a class I look to the instructor to share with me the knowledge he/she possesses on the topic." In the course evaluation of the same class, another student wrote that "Although the group work was very productive, I would have enjoyed more lecture. It was very apparent that the instructor was highly knowledgeable and I would have liked him to share more of his knowledge with the class" and, later, that "While I have learned a tremendous amount from this class, its 'loose' structure made me a bit uneasy from time to time. Being an English major lends itself to the discipline that critical thinking skills foster. Perhaps this is why I wanted a bit more discipline." Still another student, this time from an Introduction to Literature course, asks what she believes to be a rhetorical question in her course evaluation: "Do you really even want to be here? It's like you don't even want to be a teacher—as if you just settled for this profession," which couldn't be farther from the truth. Something wasn't working.

Not unlike these responses from students, some responses from colleagues and administrators were disconcerting. After I suggested in a faculty meeting that one of the problems with conventional academic essays might be the limits of linear reasoning, a colleague asked, "What other ways are there to think besides linear?" In response to a set of my student evaluations from one summer, the chair of the department wrote that "The numerical ratings for the final item—the overall rating—are more positive than negative, although they are not outstanding," and, in response to the next fall's set, that "In terms of the numbers" the students had assigned to the prompt "Overall, I rate this instructor . . ." I was "certainly doing well" and that "it is important to keep this in perspective." Nevertheless, she continued, in the large picture of student evaluations—and I see a lot of these—yours are not particularly outstanding, and I know you are striving for excellence in your teaching. The positives that come through consistently in the narrative comments are exactly the things that I value most—knowledge and a willingness of help. The students are very appreciative of your personal interest in them, and that interest is much in keeping with what [the institution] wants to offer. The single consistent comment on the critical side seems to be a lack of clarity, and I wish I understood more about what the students mean. It seems as if it is less about a lack of clarity in explaining literature and more about a lack of clarity in explaining the course and your expectations. Do you think I'm right about this? If you are interested, we can talk about some of your assignments and your mode of presenting them, if that is the source of some confusion.

Near the end of the evaluation, she wrote, "At any rate if you'd like to talk further, I'm here. From my end, as an employer, I see absolutely no reason for concern; my only interest is as a colleague." Though my material existence might not be at stake, my practices and methods clearly were.

Perhaps the best example of the conflicts over the legitimacy of my classrooms is a letter that students in a second semester writing course submitted to the chair of the English department:

This letter is regarding the Tue-Th COMP2 class taught by Chris Schroeder. We understand that some members of our class came to you to complain about Chris's teaching methods, and we would like to counter those complaints. We feel that Chris is an interested, positive, and generally a good teacher. He is obviously dedicated to really teaching us about writing and how to think about language. His method is one that we really appreciate because it involves treating us as thinking adult individuals who are responsible for our own learning. Chris trusts us to be able to have our own ideas, and some members of the class seem to resent having to think and not being spoon-fed knowledge.

When I received a copy of this letter from the chair, I had mixed feelings. Here was a classroom divided against itself. Something, perhaps even something from our semester, authorized a contingent of students to offer their readings of the classroom to the department chair, in an example of students using their literacy skills in order read and write the classroom. At the same time, a different group of students felt compelled to challenge the reading offered by the first group—again another literacy act. Unfortunately, the issue at hand was the legitimacy of my classroom practice, the very practice that had been encouraging students to use their literacies to reread and rewrite their worlds.

These experiences, and others, play an important role in this narrative that I am trying to tell.

Literacies exist as historical and social constructions that comprise specific discursive practices, which, in turn, legitimize particular versions of who to be and how to see the world. In other words, becoming literate, or what James Paul Gee defines as learning to control a discourse,[44] involves acquiring and/or learning specific discursive practices and the skills and/or abilities to use these practices in such a way as to construct sanctioned versions of the self and the world.

Accordingly, school-based literacies serve to socialize students into particular versions of who they should be and how they should see the world in a process that is called education. Within this context, success in the classroom amounts to becoming literate in, or learning to control, the discourses of specific classrooms and particular disciplines, a process that, as David Bartholomae points out in "Inventing the University," is particularly difficult for students because of their relative lack of experience in academic contexts. In his words, he explains that students must "invent the university by assembling and mimicking its language while finding some compromise between idiosyncrasy, a personal history, on the one hand, and the requirements of convention, the history of a discipline, on the other hand" (590). In spite of the ways that his article offers insight into institutional realities, his explanation—in my view—has two significant shortcomings. The first is

From: Peter Elbow
To: Christopher Schroeder
Subject: Re: ReInventing

I hear a main story about the dissatisfaction of students with the rewards of literacy—bankrupt. But I hear a more "felt" story about how you found the rewards bankrupt [yourself]: as a student, as a job candidate, as a teacher (from student feedback). In a sense these stories are perfectly consonant.

And yet, somehow, your own story feels ... like a problem in how it functions. It feels kind of snuck in or quiet and somehow for me in a troubling relationship to the whole, as though you are scared to be outfront or direct about it. ... It functions somehow slightly covertly. (Notice how this was not true of Villanueva's own story.) I want to say that you don't have the courage of your pissed-offness. You somehow tell your story in a "cool," controlled, "intellectual" way[:] it's data, it's interesting.

But in the covertness of your feelings—feelings which we nevertheless feel lurking— it somehow comes off a little whining. Of course I acknowledge that you are in a hard position here. But unless you were going to entirely suppress your story (and pretend you are writing as a disembodied, unsituated God), you are stuck with that loaded story. If you moved in the direction I suggest, it could be felt as "more whining" or that it is overly sanguine about the agency that students have. From my experiences on both sides of the desk, students are rarely accorded the space in which to negotiate this compromise between individual experiences of histories and social conventions of disciplines. The second problem is that Bartholomae's explanation suggests that education is a monologic, one-way process in which the students are the ones who must accommodate disciplines and institutions, rather than a dialogic, two-way process in which students, teachers, institutions, and disciplines are challenged to change and are transformed by the acts of literacy that transpire in classrooms. If we reread and rewrite learning and education as a collaborative, dialogic process that centers upon transformation and change, then we, as teachers, must reinvent the university, classroom by classroom, as we challenge disciplines and institutions to respond to the literacies and cultures that students bring with them into the classroom. In collaboration with students, teachers, and others, *Reinventing the University* is an attempt to rewrite the conditions that are being called a contemporary crisis in literacy. This book examines the practices of conventional academic literaci(es) in an effort to foreground the cultures and values that they endorse and to offer an alternative approach to literacy that legitimizes alternative versions of cultural capital.

As I explained earlier, the conditions that have given rise to what

"more self-centered"—but it would be more direct and not have that tucked-in, hiding feeling for me. Victor took that risk and it worked. It would be a risky move if you did what I suggest, but it would be more unusual and interesting. Your voice throughout is kind of "cooler" than what I feel the real sub-rosa voice is. And since your book is about (or starts from) a hypothesis or foundation of pissed-offness or alienation, why not embody it instead of just talking about it? I feel it's already there but hiding.

From: Christopher Schroeder
To: Peter Elbow
Subject: Re: your mail

Yet what is a "real sub-rosa voice" if not another construction, a reading and writing of a self and a situation that may or may not align itself, more or less, with experiences and with interpretations?
There are many stories behind this story, told in multiple voices. Some of them truly *are* cool, academic, disciplinary. But yes, some of them are more personal. For instance, I used what became part of this book as my dissertation, and I think it's clear in the book that what I was trying to do—reread and rewrite classrooms through rereading and rewriting literacy—didn't go over well with my committee. Though my dissertation director trusted what I was trying to do, other

candidate George W. Bush and others have called a crisis in literacy are more indicative of problems with the ways that specific versions of writing and reading have been institutionalized within English departments and, by extension, of the function that English departments have played in American colleges and universities. Through denying the social contexts that make them meaningful, conventional academic literacies rely upon a cultural capital that is often foreign to and illegitimate for students. As Jimmie, a traditional student majoring in ceramics, explained to me on the second day of a composition course, "I wouldn't talk the talk even if I could." In the language of this *talk*, the alienation identified by Jimmie and countless others with whom I have worked has emerged from the ways that conventional academic literacies deny the legitimacy of the primary and popular literacies of students in favor of unified and totalized literaci(es) of the academy.[45] In striving to efface difference, conventional academic literaci(es) in classrooms ultimately deny students' subjectivities, or versions of who they are, and versions of the world that are constructed through their primary and popular literacies. In a similar way, the denial of difference at the institutional and disciplinary levels serves to obfuscate conflicts within disciplinary-specific epistemologies, let alone between and among disciplines, in favor of purportedly tran-

members read against my efforts, and several drafts later, I capitulated to conventional discourses and graduated. In a similar way, I have encountered resistance from colleagues, department heads, and deans as to the legitimacy of contingent literacies and the narratives of education invoked by them.

Clearly, Peter, these stories and others are part of the context from which this book is constructed, and I would never try to pretend that they aren't. The issue, however, and I get around to this in the book, is once again a question of legitimacy—an issue which you yourself acknowledge elsewhere, though to the best of my knowledge, you haven't foregrounded the ways that your own cultures converge with and diverge from the cultures of the academy.

Besides, narratives still have credibility problems in the academy, as we all know. To try to resolve this conflict, I have acknowledged the narratives in the prologue and epilogue. Their absence in the main chapters, at least from the surface, reflects my concern that my critique could be lost in the issue of legitimacy if/when readers discover the writer behind it.

The difference between the stories in Keith's *Voices of the Self* or Victor's *Bootstraps*, or even Mike's *Lives on the Boundary* or Xin Liu Gale's *Teachers, Discourses, and Authority* or, from the other side of the scendent meanings and universal truths, meanings and truths that, in turn, reinforce the states of universalized academic literaci(es).

At this early stage, allow me to issue a disclaimer: there will be no solutions forthcoming, no alternatives that provide a roadmap for others to follow, for to do so would be to revert to the mandates of conventional academic literacies that demand context-free uniformity and universality and, as such, would work against the contingency and specificity of constructed literacies. (And, perhaps more important to me than to others, to do so would misrepresent my understanding of intellectual work by aspiring to closure.) Rather, you can expect, in the forthcoming pages, to encounter my (re)reading of the current crises in American colleges and universities, particularly in light of the ways that these crises are generated and reinforced by literacy practices, and my efforts, along with those of students and colleagues, to respond to this understanding of the crises in education through classroom practices and theoretical speculation. In short, you shall find my efforts to construct literacies of the American academy and within the colleges and universities I have worked.

It may be obvious that the *constructed* of constructed literacies comes from *Women's Ways of Knowing*, which transformed my experience as a graduate student. As my friend Joe Camhi has been quick

department, Jane Tompkins's "Me and My Shadow," and the narratives here is that, by virtue of their cultural positions—their ethnicities, classes, genders, or other cultural variables—their stories are authorized by contemporary discursive and disciplinary formations in ways that yours and mine are not, and may never be. In today's academy, they are constructed as outsider-insiders; their experiences are granted authority that by virtue of our cultural contexts, ours have not been accorded.

I mean, what can I—a white, middle class, young male—say about my experience with literacies and classrooms that by all accounts should situate me as an insider, as one who (ought to) reaps the benefits of the very discourses and institutions that I want to brazenly and insouciantly critique?

Maybe Tompkins has it wrong. Maybe that "public-private dichotomy," which she translates as "the public-private hierarchy," is not merely "a founding condition of female oppression," as she argues it is, not "a standard of rationality that militates [only] against women as culturally legitimate sources of knowledge" (1080, 1081). Maybe it's a founding condition of oppression for people in general, students and teachers alike, whether they're female or male, black or white, rich or poor, or both or somewhere in between to point out repeatedly over the years, there are many flaws with the scientific legitimacy of the study that Belenky, Clinchy, Goldberger, and Tarule report, and others have criticized it for its competition-collaboration, man-woman, and cognitive-social binaries.[46] Nevertheless, the distinctions that the authors make among received,

or even beyond, positions that are not permitted by conventional literacies and institutions.

But try saying that from inside the academy as a white boy.

If I had more legitimacy, I might have written a different book.

subjective, procedural, and constructed knowing provided me with a language to discuss my experiences as a writer and a reader. Though I have become suspicious of linear narratives, I found that I could use Belenky et. al's *received knowing* to talk about my experiences with writing and reading in college classrooms, and I could understand my lifelong efforts as a writer and a reader outside the academy differently with their *subjective knowing*. I could identify a period of time during my master's degree where I began to shift from received knowing to procedural knowing (knowing that exchanges a mixture of received and subjective knowledges, with the concomitant problems of authority, for a knowing based upon reasoning and reflecting and that recognizes the differences of authority that distinguish between separate and connected knowing) At some point, *constructed knowing* (knowing that reconciles the authorial differences between separate and connected knowing) became a metaphor for my understanding of what it means to be a writer, reader, intellectual, and teacher. And the more I began to explore these issues, the more I discovered the cultural implications that were involved in understanding what it means to write, read, think, learn, teach, etc. For example, received writing and reading—or what, using a different discourse, we might call current-traditional rhetorics—amount to something very different from subjective writing—or what using that same different discourse, we might call expressivist rhetorics—and implicit in each were competing understandings of who readers and writers should be and what intellectual work, as well as learning and teaching, was. And I began to exploit these differences in my own work and gradually began to encourage students to do the same.

At some point, I began calling the convergences constructed literacies. Though I saw them as essentially dialogic literacies, I preferred the term *constructed*, insofar as it foregrounds the contingency and specificity of these literacies. The more I began to experiment as both a writer, reader, and a teacher, the more I began to construct an explanation for constructed literacies: the literacies that emerge from the conflicts of competing cultural practices. To this end, I have found the notion of the contact zone, or political spaces in which cultures come into conflict, to be another useful metaphor for talking about constructed literacies.[47] In practice within classrooms, constructed literacies shift the focus from the decontextualized practices of conventional academic literaci(es) to the context-specific practices of literacies that represent competing cultures. My belief is that, in classrooms, constructed literacies not only can dissolve the conditions that have generated what is being billed as the contemporary crisis in literacy and meaning but that they can also provide a legitimacy for what many have seen to be the impotence of postmodern classroom practices. Within the contact zones of classrooms, constructed literacies can escape what has been called the postmodern paralysis by supplementing the distinctly postmodern "contending with words," or literacy-crisis management (Harkin and Schilb 5), with a legitimacy and an agency that foregrounds the ways that writers and readers can reread(write) the wor(l)d. In so doing, constructed literacies can authorize the discursive practices of students' primary and popular literacies within classrooms and encourage them to integrate these with the practices of conventional academic literacies into powerful constructed literacies that generate new knowledges and competing forms of cultural capital.

The first two chapters of *ReInventing the University* provide historical and social contexts for the practices of constructing literacies. In the first chapter, I briefly recount the educational practices of American colleges and universities within the historical contexts of English studies and of literacy, before I turn to an analysis of the practices of best-selling textbooks in literature and composition as a way of understanding the cultural capital sanctioned by conventional academic literacies.[48] In naturalizing universalized discursive practices, I will argue, textbooks in literature and composition exacerbate the contemporary crises in education by invoking a version of literacy that effaces difference in favor of uniformity and universality. In chapter two, I turn from the practices of textbooks to the practices of ostensibly radical pedagogies, in order to consider the ways that they, too, participate in the contemporary crises of education in America. In traditional classrooms, students are disciplined into conventional literacies through emphasis on the mastery of traditional canons and academic analysis, at the expense of popular texts and practices, and through discourses that tend to ignore life experiences, histories, and cultures in favor of those experiences, histories, and cultures that are recognized as legitimate by the academy. In a not dissimilar way, the practices of what are considered nontraditional classrooms can also contribute to the conventional crises in literacy and meaning. In this chapter, I take up the classroom practices of James Berlin's postmodern critical pedagogy and the practices of Ira Shor's student-centered pedagogy in order to discover the version of literacy these practices legitimize and the ways that these literacies contribute to the current crises of literacy and meaning. In brief, I will argue that Berlin's practices seem to replace the totalized literaci(es) of the American academy with a similarly context-free Marxist literacy, and Shor's practices privilege students' primary and popular discourses in ways that deny the political realities of academic discourses, even as they ultimately authorize the conventional discourses of the academy.

With these chapters as critique, the remainder of *Reinventing the University* serves as my performance. In chapter three, I turn to the practices of my own classrooms and the version of literacy that these practices endorse, as well as the ways that they fall short of legitimizing students and their discourses. In chapter four, I consider some of the ways that the literacies my students and I have constructed (as well as have failed to construct) have challenged us to reinvent the academy, specifically by exploring how, in constructing literacies of classrooms, we have established alternative subject positions for students and teachers and alternative understandings of learning, teaching, and education. Throughout these chapters, I rely extensively upon students in constructing literacies of classrooms and in offering alternatives to current educational narratives, alternatives that emerge from practices and that are authorized by them.[49] In creating spaces in which writers and readers function as cultural producers, constructed literacies invoke postmodernity, in both aesthetic and social forms,[50] as a provisional foundation for legitimacy, and they provide students and teachers, within communities of dissensus, with the requisite legitimacy to reinvent the university.

Finally, the interludes that appear between chapters create a matrix of exigencies and constraints and, in so doing, chronicle the various responses to the legitimacy of these practices and literacies. Though I began this investigation years ago as an undergraduate in an advanced writing course, I decided, at some point near the end of graduate school, to use a part of it as my dissertation as a way of trying to bridge professional and personal concerns. In the first interlude, the director of my dissertation narrates the struggles that part of this text endured, in much earlier incarnations, to acquire a legitimacy within the unique setting of the academic dissertation. In the second interlude are various communiqués from former department chairs, in response to efforts of mine to authorize for them what I do in classrooms. In the third, students, who, in their training as writing center tutors, had been assigned to observe and critique one of my first-year composition courses, reflect upon their perspectives and perceptions of my classroom practices. In the fourth, two students who appeared in successive composition classrooms reflect upon their experiences over the previous year. In the last interlude, two practicing professionals (Peter

Elbow and Victor Villanueva) offer their responses to the practice of constructing literacies.

If, as I'm suggesting in this prologue, the literacy crisis is less a crisis of skills
and abilities and more a crisis of authority and legitimacy, then the arguments
that follow in the chapters are fairly straightforward. However, I don't make
these arguments as conventionally academic utterances. In addition to all the
differences mentioned earlier, still another difference about *ReInventing* is that it
attempts to make this case *differently*. In general terms, the differences are two.
The first is the arrangement/structure of the book. Unlike the hierarchical structure of conventional academic texts, the structure of this book is narrative. I
tend to agree with Lee Ann Carroll when she argues, generally, for the narrative
basis of meaning and knowledge, when she argues, specifically, that "the stories
we tell are the stories that are culturally available to us to tell," stories in which
"the conventions and the details" have already been "written and read by the
culture" and which are "constrained by the context" in which they are told "with
much left out or suppressed" (920-23). In an effort to acknowledge the narrative
basis of *ReInventing*, I have used a narrative, discursive organization. In the first
chapter, I have tried to offer the conflict, as in a conflict between the cultures of
the academy and the cultures that students bring into the academy and of their
worlds beyond the academy. In the second chapter, I have injected a complication in the form of the (unintentional) ways that the crises of literacy and education are exacerbated by purportedly radical pedagogies. In the third chapter, I
generate a crisis, in that, unlike what one might expect from conventional academic scholarship, the classrooms that students and I have inhabited have *not*
been able to adequately resolve the literacy and educational crises in classrooms.
Finally, I offer an anti-resolution in the fourth chapter, an effort to speculate
how, in spite of my failures in the classroom, my revisions of the crises in literacy
and education might play out at departmental and institutional levels.

The second difference has to do with the role that personal narratives play in
ReInventing. I also agree with Carroll when she argues that the "non-narrative
forms," such as conventional academic writing, are "closely related to suppressed personal narratives" (927). In fact, I would go beyond Carroll to argue
that (suppressed) personal narratives are central to intellectual work. Thus, I'm
offering the interludes here, along with the personal narratives that appear in
each chapter, as auto-ethnographies, balancing and contextualizing the more
conventional scholalship that is also here. As Mary Soliday has suggested, there
is a tradition of literacy narratives within composition and rhetoric, a tradition
of "autobiographical and self-reflective writing" as a way of understanding
"sociolinguistic assimilation" into the academy (263). What makes the literacy
narratives in *ReInventing* different from other literacy narratives is that these do

not presuppose a coherent essentialist self, as literacy narratives often do. In the pieces of literacy narratives I offer, I find myself working both to escape the culture of the academy even as I recognize its value. Furthermore, *ReInventing* invokes multiple literacy narratives, or at least pieces of multiple literacy narratives—professionals who have struggled with me in articulating this narrative; department chairs who have had to supervise me in my efforts to do intellectual work out of this narrative; students who, as outsiders and not from my classrooms, have had to understand these narratives; students from my classrooms who, as experiencing these narratives, have been unsure as to how productive they are for them; and finally, practicing professionals who have responded to this narrative from within their own contexts and with pieces of their own narratives—in the interlude chapters and throughout the second half of the book.

In addition, I would add that part and parcel of intellectual work is learning to read and write the world and to tell narratives that revision the world, and this may be the difference between Carroll and me. Where we might part ways is in the manner in which these narratives can be rewritten and reread when we bring different cultural contexts to bear on them, when we retell these narratives within different contexts. What I have tried to do is to tell the literacy crisis from within a different cultural context—one of an insider who has struggled to get outside, one who has seen the intellectual, emotional, and spiritual bankruptcy of the conventional academic game, as it is currently played, and who wants new, different ways of doing intellectual work, as a way of making the academic game more satisfying and rewarding. As a response to what has been called the contemporary crisis in literacy and education, *ReInventing the University* argues that constructed literacies provide an alternative to the conventional literacies of American colleges and universities. Situated within historical and social practices, constructed literacies foreground the politics of literacies, as well as the relationships between literacies and cultures; they authorize students and teachers to resist sanctioned knowledges, proffered subject positions, and endorsed versions of the world, in favor of alternatives that integrate competing discursive practices with the practices of the academy. In doing so, constructed literacies can serve, I believe, as a useful voice in the ongoing dialogues over the nature of education, as well as of what it means to be literate, in America.

INTERLUDE
Early Efforts to Read/Write Constructed Literacies:
Journal of a Dissertation Director

AUGUST 3, 1998

We are finally on our way. The prospectus is signed and the work can begin. Despite the conversations about and revisions of that preliminary document, however, I can't say that I really know where this dissertation is going. That can probably be said for all dissertations, but this one in particular seems so global that I worry about its focus. It seems to reach out in too many directions, wanting to remake our understanding of language, the academy, pedagogy, social systems, and beyond. One might as well want to heal the sick, raise the dead, and free the imprisoned. Noble sentiments, but not very likely.

I'll put my apprehensions in writing, in hopes of avoiding some rough waters ahead.

SEPTEMBER 20, 1998

The first chapter has arrived, which is actually the third chapter, or maybe the fourth. In fact, he isn't even calling these pieces chapters. As if I weren't confused enough already, now we're staring *in medias res* with a "unit" that isn't a chapter. At least it came in right on time.

Still, there is more pressure here than I would like, due to the late start, which was not the fault of the writer but of a system that requires approvals and signatures and the like. Now the number of weeks until the deadline for the defense and the number of needed chapters are not in the best ratio. I wish there were more time to play with the shape this dissertation is going to take and what its centering principle will be. As it is, the writer can't afford to go wrong. It will need to be headed in the right direction from the outset. Its concerns are still broad and inclusive, making it hard to find a sharp focus on the main idea. Like Derrida's chain of signifieds, the meaning just keeps rolling on and on, *ad infinitum.*

We've set a tentative April date for the defense in hopes that a deadline will spur all interested parties to be ready by then. It will also give us some time for last minute revisions before commencement in May. Is that too ambitious? It will be tight, I know. But possible.

NOVEMBER 3, 1998

The initial "pieces" (they still aren't chapters) that are coming in are interesting. I recognize many of the ideas we talked about during the course work: theories from Berlin, Ong, Burke. There is Toulmin, of course, not a surprise since he was the subject of the article published in JAC. Did we do Bakhtin that semester? For some reason I don't think we got to him, though I can't remember why. Well it's good to know that all that theorizing is not inert, just lying in a memory bank gathering dust. It's being put to good use, and, as far as I can tell so far, new use.

Actually, the reading in the independent study course from a couple of summers ago was probably more influential. (Good support for the argument that students learn more when they can choose their own materials, follow their own interests.) I recognize traces of bell hooks (who spoke less strongly to me), Shor, and others. Was Freire in there? Surely so. How quickly it all blurs. Anyway, the usual suspects are all showing up, sometimes in such quickly successive reference that I feel as if I'm reading an annotated bibliography. The breadth of reading is truly astounding. Now if we can just get it all sorted out into something coherent and (dare I say it?) linear.

NOVEMBER 17, 1998

I don't think *linear* was the word after all. I've mentioned *linear, sequential, less-global, less inclusive,* and several other terms, but this dissertation wants to grow. The problem has several dimensions: (1) the manuscript's desire to embrace all knowledge; (2) the circular organization favored by the author; (3) a temptation to mention every known postmodernist; (4) polysyllabic diction that, were it to be read aloud, would test the skills of Demosthenes. I marvel at what's going on here, but in the end I know it won't do at all. It's imaginative, creative, and learned, but it isn't traditional, and that's going to be a problem I'm afraid.

And now we have Interlude Chapters, short pieces drawn from teaching experiences centered around critical literacies. They are personal in nature, take a wide-variety of forms—e.g., e-mail correspondence and the like, and do not always present a positive view of the pedagogy being used. They include different voices: department head, instructor, students. At this point I am rather uncomfortable with them. I'm not sure they are making the point that the writer wants them to make. For instance, do complaints from unwilling students make a compelling case for exploring critical literacies? I'm not at all sure that they do.

Then, too, I have to wonder if personal narratives are appropriate in a dissertation? In my day "one" was not allowed to use the first person personal pronoun, much less tell a story about "self." Of course, academic discourse is less restricted now, but all of the old rules have not been rescinded. The last bastion of formality is probably the dissertation.

My main concern, though, is whether these interruptions, which I assume they are designed to be, add to or distract from the discussion. Do they enhance and enrich? Or do they divert and befuddle the reader's focus?

DECEMBER 8, 1998

My plan for the holiday break: read what's here, then take a vacation from critical literacies. On the other hand, that April deadline is coming up fast and I'm the only reader that has seen the manuscript thus far. Maybe I'll postpone that vacation.

JANUARY 14, 1999

this isn't how i expected to start the new year, writing with one hand. three days ago i broke my left wrist and am now in a cast that runs from finger tips to upper arm. that leaves me with five typing fingers. capital letters are out of the question. i can still read, but the responses are coming slowly. just trying to hold a book or manage loose pages with one hand is a problem i've never thought about before, much less tried to deal with. i'm getting to be really fast on the keyboard with the right hand. not very accurate. but fast.

JANUARY 25, 1999

i had the dissertation with me on a trip this past week, and at one point felt positively surreal sitting with cast and sling in the atlanta airport (with all its surging crowds and subterranean labyrinths) trying to make my way through all the "read(writ)ings of the wor(l)d" that "problematize" but sometime "legitimate" the "marginalized" or "privileged" people and things.

that's when it came to me that this text is definitely going to hit some road blocks. it wasn't just delta airlines or the nearly perpendicular escalators in the terminal or the immobilized arm that were making it hard to follow this discussion. i suddenly allowed myself to admit that the holistic approach is creating a manuscript that the academy is sure to reject. it doesn't follow the rules, and the academy likes rules, or at least until one is a full-fledged member.

must do something about this. the thinking is too good to lose.

FEBRUARY 11, 1999

ok. i have assurances that the next revision, or next chapter, or whatever we're calling them now, will adhere to accepted guidelines and diction for dissertations as established by convention (and lots of committees). i'm afraid i'm a disappointment here. in fact, i'm rather disappointed in myself for asking that this dissertation, which is trying to formulate new insights into constructed literacies and attempting to devise a pedagogy that would honor them, retreat to the safe position of traditional academic discourse. this writer has already proved he can do that. now he is trying to let presentation create meaning, marry idea and form. why shouldn't a postmodern dissertation assume a postmodern style? i admit that i find reading it to be demanding. sometimes it makes the thinking hard to follow. sometimes i wonder if anything is really new here at all, or if it's old knowledge said in a circular way that makes it sound new. the style problematizes the act of understanding, perhaps i should say. but is that a reason to discourage it? in one sense it legitimates the theorizing. now he has me doing it!

still haven't given any of the text to the other readers in this attempt to arrive at a version that conforms a little more to what is expected. maybe i should.

FEBRUARY 23, 1999

april is looking less and less likely for the defense. the job search is taking more time than expected. it's great that he has so many interviews, but every one of them takes time from the dissertation, and without it there's no point in the interviews. a double bind. catch-22. maybe a summer defense is more realistic. that would still serve for job purposes, and graduation could take place in december, later than hoped, but it wouldn't really be a problem.

it's still only february, and that makes april sound a long way off, but it's only a matter of weeks.

MARCH 9, 1999

Look! Capital letters! I have two hands. One looks like it belongs to an octogenarian, but the doctor assures me that physical therapy will take care of that. Now I get to spend hours in a different set of offices letting people hurt me. I'll take the dissertation with me for distraction. Discursive Transgressions in Contemporary Classrooms and a neo-Nazi forcing me to bend my arm in ways it is reluctant to go. What a combination.

MARCH 17, 1999

No go. Each revised or new portion starts off in an understandable, acceptable academic way, but by the second or third page is back to "read(writ)ings of the wor(l)d" and circling. It hasn't come down for a landing yet. The diligence with which all this is being pursued has to be admired. How many versions have we gone through so far? If I tire with reading them, I can only imagine what writing and re-writing them must be like.

I've been re-reading some of Richard Rorty, as it seems to me that he writes about very difficult material in a natural, comprehensible manner. Maybe there is something to be learned here. Perhaps a text that takes up postmodern theories doesn't have to be the verbal equivalent of Kandinsky. Maybe it could be a little more like Edward Hopper. Ira Shor manages to compose lucid texts, too. His human voice is recognizable in his prose. I'll recommend Rorty and Shor as possible models fit for emulation.

April is definitely out for the defense.

APRIL 6, 1999

Last week it seemed to be time to release some of this manuscript to the other readers. I don't know if they're as dazzled as I am by the knowledge base all this is coming out of, but I do know they're pretty mystified. As I said before, holistic dissertations don't come along every day.

The focus is clearer and the discussions tighter, but there are still many, many references to other texts, references that do not always seem closely tied to the point under development. In fact, one of the other readers came to me to ask what is new in this dissertation. What new idea is at its core? It refers to the thinking of so many theorists that it seems to be a rehearsal of what is already known rather than a presentation of what is innovative. I think I answered the question adequately, but I must admit the "thesis" gets buried pretty deeply sometimes.

I'm getting more and more anxious as time is passing, and the other readers have miles to go before they sleep. As for me, I've read this manuscript in so many incarnations that I can almost recite it from memory.

APRIL 13, 1999

A landmark date, the one selected for the defense, which isn't happening. I wish it were. On the other hand, the manuscript is getting clearer with input from the other readers. I see no reason why an early summer defense shouldn't be possible. I now understand more clearly than ever why a committee is involved. A single reader finally gets pulled into the text so deeply that, like the writer, she can no longer see clearly what needs to be done. I'm glad I have two other good critical minds to help me out.

My physical therapist asked me today what I was reading while picking up weights (or not) with my wizened fingers. I tried to tell him. He just shook his head.

MAY 5, 1999

Whoops. The unexpected has happened. The baby has come six weeks early. This is an unanticipated complication that affects everything: dissertation, graduation, job search. With the attendant emotional stress of leaving the newborn in neo-natal intensive care, I don't see how any energies will be available for working on the dissertation.

We'll see. The first concern is the well-being of the baby, a girl.

MAY 10, 1999

Well, the deadline for defending in time for May commencement has passed. It was going to be a push all along, but with the baby's interruption it just wasn't to be. Maybe that's best. It gives everybody more time to work together on this really rather brilliant opus.

We've had a request for a personal meeting. I think that's a good idea. If we could all sit around a table and discuss not only the idea of constructed literacies and the pedagogics that serve them, but also the form of the manuscript itself, we might make some real progress.

The idea of surveying textbooks is a real addition to this discussion. It concretizes it somewhat, connects it with classrooms and teachers and students. It sounds like a huge job to me, but I've been assured that it is do-able. Hope so.

JUNE 8, 1999

Amazing. Yet another version. I cannot imagine the effort that has gone into this dissertation. It shows. The chapters are now chapters. The Interludes (I think!) have been dropped. There is coherence among the chapters, as they now explore the topic in a sequential way. There is still a bit much jargon, though the author says not so. Is jargon in the ear of the listener?

Anyway, this is beginning to look like other dissertations. Is that a good thing?

JULY 9, 1999

The defense:

"Why were you writing this way? I know you can write conventional academic discourse."

"It was an experiment. I wanted to produce my own critical literacy. It seemed only right to do so given the material I was discussing."

"Does that past tense mean you're willing to go straight?"

"I want to finish."

"I understand. I'm sorry."

And so the academy exacts its payment, the candidate answers questions professionally and knowledgeably, secures the requisite signatures, graduates, and takes a job. But of course the story doesn't end there. There is the book. Freed of academic requirements, and possessing the legitimizing certificate, the Ph.D., the author can put the dissertation through yet one more revision with only editors and publishers to negotiate with about form and diction, audience and voice.

One cannot help but wonder: has anything really been de-centered?

1 THE CULTURAL CAPITAL
OF THE ACADEMY

Thus, thinking about the position of students can remind us that
neither nostalgia nor education can settle accounts with culture in a
non-Idealist sense. Culture here is both tradition and betrayal; we are
handed over to culture even as it is handed to us. Modernism tries to
forget this predicament in two ways: by the *conservativism* that says
we can live the tradition (it is not too late) and by the *progressive modernism* that says we can make an entirely fresh start, forget the
tradition and move on to build a bright new world (it is not too early,
we can teach ourselves). In each case, conservatives and progressives
talk about culture as if it ought to be, or is, synonymous with society.
Conservatives say that culture ought to provide the model for society,
that we should live in a world of high culture or of organic villages. In
short, they believe that culture should determine society. Progressives
tend to say that culture *is* society, or else it is merely ideological
illusion, that the self-definition of the human community should
define the model of our being-together.

Students know both that they are not yet part of culture and that
culture is already over, that it has preceded them. Neither nostalgia
nor education can solve the students' malaise. They cannot simply
mourn a lost culture (conservatism) nor can they forget the tradition
and move on to build a bright new world (progressive modernism).

Bill Readings
The University in Ruins

Good analytical writing, as these faculty members were describing it,
involves a multitude of values, skills, habits, and assumptions about
audience needs: it means setting down a clear, step-by-step,
transparently logical progression of ideas; it means critically
examining a variety of ideas and opinions and creating an original
interpretation that shows, very explicitly and directly, the writer's
point of view. It means using reference materials to add evidence and
authority to the writer's own argument, weaving together material
from a variety of sources into a pattern that "makes sense" to the
reader. It means attributing ideas to individual authors with
meticulous care. It means speaking with a voice of authority, making
judgments and recommendations and coming to specific, "reasoned"
conclusions. It means valuing literal meanings and precise definitions
and explicit statements of cause and effect. It means writing sparsely

and directly, without embellishments or digressions, beginning each paragraph or section with a general, analytical statement and following it with pertinent examples. In short, it is at once a writing style, a method of investigation, and a world view that has been part of western cultural heritage for hundreds of years and that is learned through a process of both formal and informal socialization that begins in early childhood, especially by those who come from "educated families," go to "good schools," and aspire to positions of influence and power in the dominant culture. But I did not understand all this at the time. It came only gradually to me, as students began to talk to me about their own socialization processes, their cultural assumptions and values, their communication styles, both oral and written, and their difficulties understanding why they didn't seem to catch on to this thing called "analytical writing" as easily as they or their professors had expected.

Helen Fox
Listening to the World

As I explained, my reading of what has been called by many—including critics, theorists, and George W. Bush—a crisis in literacy is that it is less indicative of some deficiency in literacy skills and more revealing of crises of meaning and legitimacy within schools and society. This reading is consistent with and builds upon the perspectives offered by others. For example, Paul Morris and Stephen Tchudi argue that conventional versions of literacy have failed schools and society and the alternatives that have been fashioned fail to respond to contemporary literacy needs. Maureen Hourigan asserts that any assessments of the literacy conditions in American colleges and universities must move beyond what she calls competitive colleges and universities, such as the ones in which Bartholomae, Bizzell, Rose, and others work, and must consider a complicated matrix of factors—gender, class, and community—rather than one or another of these features in isolation, in order to provide a more complete picture. In conjunction with these and other rereadings of the conditions of literacy in American colleges and universities, I want to consider in this chapter the sites—the classrooms—in which students must work in order to obtain their certification. This will give a better sense of the academic cultural capital that, I believe, is failing an increasing number of students. I believe that it is the illegitimacy of academic culture(s), which is established and maintained by the literacy practices of the academy, that has given rise to what Bush et al. are calling the contemporary crisis in literacy.

Given the histories of American colleges and universities, the place to turn in order to access the culture of the academy is the English department, for, at least in the U. S., it is in the English department that literacies and education are fused together. At the same time, Richard Miller argues that examining the practices of classrooms and students will provide us with an insider's perspective of the discipline of English studies. In light of both the history of English departments and Miller's insight into an insider perspective, I have elected to use the best-selling textbooks in composition and literature as a way to understand the cultural capital of the academy that is endorsed through its sanctioned literaci(es).

Before turning to textbooks, I want to consider, briefly, the historical relationships among education, literacy, English studies, and society, in order to construct a context for the practices of the best-selling textbooks in literature and composition.[1] As I explained in the prologue, the sites of literacy instruction have changed from families to churches to schools in a process that transformed literacy from apprenticeships in highly complex social practices to institutionalized instruction in classrooms whose sole function is to teach writing and reading almost entirely separate from the social contexts that make these acts meaningful. In postsecondary contexts, this increasingly decontextualized understanding of literacy was situated within institutions that, as Bill Readings explains, saw it as their mission to be the source and repository of culture centered around a unity of knowledge as the sign of cultured people—a mission that authorized English departments as the primary site where students would receive training in this cultural identity (62 ff, 70 ff). The relationship between literacy and English studies, of course, is extremely complicated and thoroughly political, and I make no pretense of addressing it in its entirety in the next few pages, particularly when there are many insightful explorations of this relationship already. However, I would like to identify several key moments in this history in order to provide a context. Such a context is useful in understanding the cultural capital of the academy, which forms the basis for certification through the mastery of academic literacy.

In *Politics of Letters*, Richard Ohmann argues quite convincingly that, from the beginning, literacy has served as a form of social control (238). In order to understand the relationships between literacy and social control, many have turned to Raymond Williams, who, in *Marxism and Literature*, situates this relationship in the tensions between literacy and literature. Historically, the prevailing understanding of *literary* (as in *literary* works, or literature) did not appear before the eighteenth and nineteenth centuries (Williams 45 ff).[2] As the **specialization** of areas formerly called rhetoric and grammar, the notion of *literature* originally indicated reading in a general way, and, by extension, the printed word and specifically the book. At this time, *literature* served as a generalized social condition that expressed a minimal level of educational accomplishments and referred to any printed works, including books on philosophy and history, as well as essays and poetry. Tellingly, the associated adjective of *literature* was *literate*, and the notion of *literary*, as in the sense of reading ability and experience, did not acquire its current meaning until well into the eighteenth century (46). Gradually, the notion of *literature*-as-literacy gave way to the notion of *literature*-as-literary, as a result of a shift in social interest from learning toward taste, an increasing **specialization** of literature toward imaginative or creative works and the development of national traditions (47-48). In other words, what had originated as simply the ability to consume any printed text had become much more narrowly defined as the ability to consume *certain* texts—those considered to reflect a particular taste, a particular aesthetic, or a particular culture.

In American colleges and universities, the transformation of literature-as-literacy to literature-as-literary provided English departments with a basis for disciplinary practices and, ultimately, a disciplinary legitimacy. As representative of a universalized taste, imaginative works, and a national cultural identity, literacy-as-literary provided the emerging discipline of English studies with a cultural capital, which would serve as the basis for, in Wallace Douglas's words, "the training system that the American people had developed for sorting themselves out" (127). Originally at Harvard and quickly spreading to other institutions, American colleges and universities institutionalized a cultural literacy—comprised of a universalized taste, imaginative works, and a national cultural identity—that would certify students as eligible for admission to the educated middle class. Situated within English departments, the process of certification, as Susan Miller argues, originally occurred in both literature and composition courses (*Textual* 51 ff). Separately, literature courses were to provide "the moral superstructure" or "set of driving principles" (Douglas 128-29), and composition courses, particularly grammar and spelling, were to serve as sites where students demonstrated their proficiencies in this literacy, or a "cultured propriety" (Miller, Susan, *Textual* 52). Together, literature and composition were to be the means to a well-educated citizens and the source of a national culture (51).

Given this function of English departments, the social context surrounding the early American colleges and universities, particularly the belief in what James Berlin calls the philosophy of the individual free of social class or institutional interference (*Writing* 60), becomes especially important. In the evolving social conditions of American colleges and universities in the latter part of the nineteenth century, the function of the English department was designed to prevent these newly democratic institutions from becoming too accessible (Berlin, *Poetics* 22-24). Part of this evolution involved a shift in the educational mission of postsecondary institutions away from uniform liberal arts educations that served as training for ministers, lawyers, or politicians to educations that served to certify a growing middle class in increasingly specialized literacies—a transformation that Berlin connects to economic shifts in America from an entrepreneurial to a corporate capitalism (17 ff). In terms of the practices of literacy instruction, the liberal arts tradition fragmented under the strain of increasingly specialized U. S. colleges and universities at the end of the nineteenth century, into three distinct constructs, which Berlin designates as a literacy of scientific meritocracy, a literacy of liberal culture, and a literacy of social democracy—each of which contributed different aspects to the culture of the American middle class. The literacy of scientific meritocracy represented the rise of a professionally trained middle class; the literacy of liberal culture reflected a belief in an American culture based upon a common core of liberal ideas of the middle class; and the literacy of social democracy responded to the economic and social conditions of the middle class (28 ff). Despite their surface differences, the literacies of scientific meritocracy, liberal culture, and social democracy were unified in their endorsement of a middle class culture, a cultural capital that was reinforced through the arrival of modernism and romanticism, particularly in their shared belief in the ultimate power of unity.[3] Over the years, the institutionalization of these literacies was widely successful, for, as Lester Faigley describes, the literaci(es) of the academy, at the end of the twentieth century, are clearly the literacies of an established middle class (*Fragments* 54 ff).

As the ultimate arbiter of classroom practices, English teachers, who provide the instruction in the literaci(es) of the academy, occupy a significant position within American colleges and universities. Despite the challenges brought by the arrival of postmodernism in America, contemporary American colleges and universities continue to construct English teachers at the end of the twentieth century—much as they did at the end of the nineteenth century—as the protectors and defenders of this cultural capital. They continue to serve this function, as the best-selling textbooks in composition and literature demonstrate, by certifying students in the sanctioned literaci(es) of the academy.

As is widely recognized, culture is a historically contested meaning, particularly at the end of the twentieth century. As an alternative to the high culture of Matthew Arnold and the Enlightenment—culture as uniform experience that can be embodied in the practices of consuming (and producing) canonical texts—culture has been variously defined at the end of the twentieth century by Marxists, sociologists, and anthropologists as the complex responses of humans to their experiences, situated within the social and historical contexts in which they exist. This understanding denies the decontextualized and universalized

Enlightenment version of culture in favor of an understanding of culture as lived experience. As a result of the influence of poststructuralist-postmodernist theories of language, culture has come to include the ways in which language has *constructed* these lived experiences, rather than merely *reflecting* these experiences. Among other implications, this distinctly postmodern understanding of culture has challenged the autonomous individual self and the totalizing narratives of meaning and culture in ways that, for me, have emphasized the role of specific discursive practices in the construction of culture itself.

In order to understand culture, many have used the notion of cultural capital, a term (for which Pierre Bourdieu is perhaps best known) that brings together multiple dimensions of culture into an explanation of social relations. Bill Readings has translated Bourdieu's notion of cultural capital as the confluence of "symbolic capital and socioeconomic capital," a term or tool, Readings is quick to point out, that has played a significant role in cultural studies in North America (105 ff). Terry Eagleton has used Bourdieu's notion of symbolic violence and cultural capital to suggest that, in educational settings, the cultural capital of classrooms, or what Rob Jacklosky understands as the legitimacy that accompanies "monetary capital and societal power" (321), is often used to shame and silence those students who do not possess it (Eagleton, *Ideology* 158; qtd. in Jacklosky 321). Obviously, this shame and silence becomes a significant problem if, as I have been suggesting, the cultural capital of the academy represents an increasingly alienated culture for students, a culture that no longer serves American society.

Clearly, there is much debate over whether we can talk about culture in any way that legitimately resonates with American society, as the fervor of the debates over E. D. Hirsch's cultural literacy list indicates[4] (debates that, given the range of contradictory positions staked out by supporters and detractor, suggest that the issues over cultural literacy are not as clear cut as they might have once been described). These debates notwithstanding, it is possible, I believe, to recognize the ways that the culture of the academy, at least as it is inscribed through its sanctioned literacies, represents increasingly elitist communities and not students or society, particularly in the postmodern conditions of the twenty-first century. As the practices of the textbooks in literature and composition indicate, the sanctioned literaci(es) of the academy and academic cultural capital are foreign and alien for even the most mainstream of students, not to mention the growing numbers of multicultural students in American college classrooms.

In the remainder of this chapter, I will turn to the best-selling textbooks in composition and literature in order to understand the cultural capital of the academy, and, near the end of the chapter, I will also take up several textbooks that, while perhaps not possessing the same (economic) authority that the best-selling textbooks, by virtue of their popularity, have, nonetheless may have more theoretical currency among many of us in the profession.

THE PRACTICES OF TEXTBOOKS AND THE CULTURE OF THE ACADEMY

When I contacted an editor[5] at one of the most successful textbook publishing companies during the summer of 1998, he conferred with his colleagues and then wrote to me that, although sales figures are proprietary, they had nonetheless determined the list of textbooks that appear most often in literature and composition classrooms. For literature classrooms, the best-selling textbooks are all anthologies—*Perrine's Literature* (Arp/Seventh Edition); *Literature: An Introduction to Reading and Writing* (Roberts and Jacob/Fifth Edition), *Literature: An Introduction to Fiction, Poetry, and Drama* (Kennedy and Gioia/Seventh Edition) and *The Bedford Introduction to Literature* (Meyer/Fifth Edition). As for composition textbooks, the best-selling textbooks were different, depending upon the category: rhetorics—*The St. Martin's Guide to Writing* (Axelrod and Cooper/Fifth Edition), readers—*The Macmillan Reader* (Nadell, Langan, and McMeniman/Fifth Edition), and handbooks—*The Elements of Style* (Strunk and White/Third Edition), the *Harbrace College Handbook* (Horner, Webb, and Miller/Revised Thirteenth Edition), the *Simon and Schuster Handbook for Writers* (Troyka/Fifth Edition), and *The Writer's Reference* (Hacker/Fourth Edition). Within the tradition of textbook analysis, critics have recently begun to consider the cultural conditions of textbooks in composition,[6] yet there is little, if anything, that has been done to consider textbooks in literature.[7] What I intend to do is to examine the best-selling textbooks in literature and composition, within the historical contexts of English studies in American colleges and universities, in order to get a sense of what the sanctioned versions of literaci(es) within the academy are and what these literaci(es) suggest about the cultural capital of the academy. Obviously, these textbooks carry a currency within English departments, a currency that does not fluctuate often—when I checked with my source in the spring of 2000, he indicated that the list had not changed. Furthermore, most of these textbooks are fifth or later editions.

I will begin with literature textbooks, as literature classrooms have historically been the most likely site for socialization into the culture(s) of the academy,[8] and then, in light of the function of composition (according to administrators, faculty members in other departments, and even some composition specialists) as the newer site of socialization into academic culture,[9] I will turn to composition textbooks. Since, as Xin Liu Gale points out (187), textbooks are often written for new teachers and misrepresent current theories in the discipline, I will supplement the economic credibility of the best-selling textbooks by considering three composition textbooks that have a theoretical currency among specialists: a rhetoric—*The Call to Write* (Trimbur); a reader—*Negotiating Difference: Cultural Case Studies for Composition* (Bizzell and Herzberg); and a handbook—*A Writer's Reference* (Hacker), which, interestingly, also appears on the list of best-sellers. By considering textbooks with both economic and theoretical legitimacy, I want to establish a sense of the literaci(es) of the academy and the culture(s) that they legitimize, and are legitimized by. Finally, I want to issue a disclaimer for the upcoming analysis of literature and composition textbooks. While I am generally suspicious of reductive explanations that elide difference, I have been most struck by the uniformity and universality of the literacy practices legitimized by the best-selling textbooks. Though I intend to focus predominantly upon the uniformity and universality of literacy practices in them, I do not want to suggest that these textbooks lack difference. To be sure, *Literature: An Introduction to Reading and Writing* opens with a chapter on reading, responding to, and writing about literature while *Bedford Introduction to Literature* places this section near the end (though they all are organized ontologically, beginning with fiction and followed by poetry and then drama), and the *Simon and Schuster Handbook for Writers* places its section on grammar second while *The St. Martin's Guide for Writers* includes it as a supplementary section at the end (though all, except for *Elements*, invoke the rhetorical modes). Nevertheless, the divergences are far fewer than the convergences, which accounts for the focus of my analysis; as I argue in the prologue, it is these convergences, and particularly in the ways that they legislate against difference, that have given rise to the conditions that critics are calling a crisis in literacy.

THE BEST-SELLING LITERATURE TEXTBOOKS

As I explained in the prologue, I understand a literacy to amount to not only specific discursive practices (or ways of writing and reading) but also the naturalized versions of the discursive self (who to be) and of reality (how to see the world) inscribed by, with, and in these discursive practices. Though, interestingly, the practices of reading and, to a lesser degree, writing in schools are bound up within the historical relationship between literature and literacy, there is generally little space devoted in literature textbooks to explaining how the act of consuming literature or producing discourse about literature is different from other ways of reading or writing. On the contrary, the act of reading literature tends to be totalized into a universal act of reading. For example, *The Bedford Introduction to Literature* explains that reading amounts to first considering "how the work makes you feel and how it is put together," as "the author's words ... work their magic on you" and then rereading "more slowly and analytically as you try to establish relations between characters, actions, images, or whatever else seems important"—that is, universally important (2064). In a similarly universalized manner, *Literature: An Introduction to Reading and Writing* (*LRW*) characterizes the act of reading literature in general terms of "responding actively" (3), which, despite what it implies, depends, at least in part, on whether one is responding actively to what is called a primary text or to teacher's instructions, which, for students, often serve as primary texts.

In other words, not all instances of "responding actively" are legitimate. Students who, for example, elect to respond with silence or to respond nonverbally are not seen as responding differently but as not responding at all. Though most of the texts suggest that responding actively to poetry, for example, is somewhat different from responding actively to fiction, all of them universalize a formalistic, New Critical way of reading that, specifically, relies upon students' abilities to use a decontextualized vocabulary to generate meaning.[10] For example, *Literature: An Introduction to Fiction, Poetry, and Drama* (*LFPD*) opens each chapter with an explanation of specific terms and then alternates these explanations of terms with specific texts that, presumably, are especially appropriate illustrations of the aforementioned terms. In the section of the textbook, for example, devoted to fiction in *LFPD*, the titles of individual chapters provide clues as to the featured element in that chapter—such as "Point of View," "Character," "Setting," "Tone and Style," Theme," and "Symbol"—each of which uses selected text that identifies the featured element in one way or another. In the chapter that features point of view, students are considered to have read "A Rose for Emily," by William Faulkner, or "Cathedral," by Raymond Carver, if, regardless of anything else, they can articulate the point of view of each, as requested by the opening question at the end of each selection (37, 53). In the remaining chapters in this section on fiction, students discover, in no less a universalized manner, that "Evaluating a Story" and "Reading Long Stories and Novels" involve additional skills that go beyond merely identifying point of view or exploring character.

All of the best-selling textbooks naturalize this formalistic, New Critical way of reading as what it means to read, in fact devoting the bulk of the textbook to privileging this formalistic way of reading; yet all of them except for *Perrine's* include a section, separate from the rest of the text, about alternatives ways of reading. According to *Bedford Introduction to Literature*, this section serves as an "overview of critical strategies for reading," a section that "is neither exhaustive in the types of critical approaches covered nor complete in its presentations of the complexities in them" and, in spite of the predominant orientation of readings in the rest of the textbook, enables readers "to develop an appreciation of the intriguing possibilities that attend literary interpretation" (2023). Unlike the others, however *Bedford* integrates alternatives to formalist reading practices in other chapters. Yet even it engages in formalist readings of texts for the bulk of each section before using these alternatives on a single story. For example, *Bedford*'s fiction critical case study takes "several critical approaches to a well-known short story by William Faulkner" (480ff). Nevertheless, like all the others, it devotes the bulk of each section to formalist readings of texts, while *LRW* and *LFPD* engage in only formalist readings throughout their texts and while *Perrine's* does not even recognize them. Though the message is complicated and convoluted, it is, ultimately, clear: reading formalistically/New Critically is the natural(ized) way to read.

As for producing discourse, students are clearly instructed that, while they might be reading literature, they are to be writing *about* literature, which is different, obviously, from *writing* [ ] literature. Using terms familiar to those of us in composition and rhetoric, the prescribed methods for producing discourse *about* literature are, again, formalist ways of writing, or what we would classify as current-traditional practices. According to the version(s) of academic literacy proffered by literature textbooks, the sanctioned ways of writing fit within a traditional hierarchy that privileges the consumption of literary discourse. Consequently, the sanctioned practices for the production of discourse *about* literature are defined solely in relation to the privileged literary texts. Though *Perrine's* suggests, in more general terms, that writing in literature classrooms provides "additional practice in writing **clearly** and **persuasively**," it has two primary functions, both of which reinforce the privileged status of reading, and reading literary texts: to deepen students' **"understanding** of literary works by leading [them] to **read** and **think** about a few works more **searchingly** than [they] might otherwise do" and "to **enlighten** others," even if the only readers of the texts they produce are their instructors (1444). Obviously, a particular way of writing—writing that is academically clear and persuasive—is universalized within a prescribed rhetorical context that identifies an artificial audience and, given this audience, an impossible exigency—enlightening these artificial readers—that is misleading at best. Within this context, the acts of textual production are narrowly defined: "(a) papers that focus on a single literary work, (b) papers of comparison and contrast, (c) papers on a number of works by a single author, and (d) papers on a number of works having some feature other than authorship in common" (1446). In a similar way, the function of writing is equally narrow and equally prescribed—"to **convince**" these implied readers that their readings of primary texts which students have made are **"valid and important**" and "to **lead**" these readers "to **share**" these understandings (1451). Finally, the sanctioned ways of writing in literature classrooms rely exclusively upon standards that have been separated from their social contexts: while ways of writing about other subjects might depend upon "various rhetorical means," such as "eloquent diction, devices of suspense, analogies, personal anecdotes, and the like," all of which could conceivably appear in the texts that student readers are consuming, the prescribed way of writing *about* literature depends solely upon **"proof,"** which comes from the **"mastery** of reading and writing" and which is "primarily an exercise in strict definition" (1451-52).

Consistent with formalist literacies, the means of writing, according to literature textbooks, begins with a consideration of the constraints imposed by the teacher. *Bedford*'s instructions are fairly explicit:

> Before you start considering a topic, you should have a sense of how long the paper will be because the assigned length can help to determine the extent to which you should develop your topic. Ideally, the paper's length should be based on how much space you deem necessary to present your discussion clearly and convincingly, but if you have any doubts and no specific guidelines have been indicated, ask. (2067)

In a similar way, both *LRW* and *LFPD* describe a mechanistic way of writing that begins with the selection of topics, and all of the texts emphasize the importance of outlining before drafting (*LRW* 1816; *LFPD* 1853). Never deviating from these formalist methods, these sanctioned ways of writing direct student writers, after considering the externally-imposed constraints, to turn to their "notes and annotations of the text" in order to generate a topic, at which point they should generate a thesis, or "the central idea of the paper," which will enable them to begin textual production: "After you have chosen a manageable topic and developed a thesis, a central idea about it, you can begin to organize your paper. Your thesis, even if it is still somewhat tentative, should help you decide what information will need to be included and provide you with a sense of direction" (2068, 2074). Finally, in devoting considerable space to academic citations and documentation, as well as, often, the use of literary terminology, all of the textbooks reinforce a formalistic and decontextualized way of writing in which, for example, the degree of clarity or appropriateness of structure are presumed to be universally known.

Obviously, then, the ideal reader-writer is one who already knows, or can intuit, how much context must be articulated in order to ensure that an idea will be seen as clear, what structures will be recognized and considered legitimate, and what patterns will be misunderstood or not recognized at all. The world of these textbooks is one in which standards for contextual explication are clearly identifiable, and in which universally recognizable, and universally relevant, structures exist, *a priori* and separate from discursive producers and consumers. In short, these literacy practices are practices of uniformity that privilege essentialized selves and foundational worlds. For example, the ideal (i.e. formalist) reader is one who can identify the formal elements of texts and who can use the appropriate (i.e. academic) terms, such as those listed in bold or in the indices or back covers of textbooks, for discussing these elements—terms, the textbooks suggest, that are meaningful outside of specific contexts and discursive relations. As prescribed by the universalized practices of reading and writing, the (formalist) world is an empirical world with an underlying unity and coherence, and right readings of texts are those that reinscribe this empiricism, unity, and coherence in their interpretations. Furthermore, these features become the standards for literate performance: the degree to which such acts of reading reinscribe an empiricism, unity, and coherence is often used to distinguish between good and better readings. These texts admit the possibility of difference in the ways that they recognize alternative ways of reading, such as feminist or reader-response or, in the case of *Bedford*, cultural studies (though, interestingly, they are silent about alternative ways of writing), but the explicit message, in light of the fact that formalist ways of reading (and writing) comprise the bulk, if not all, of the textbook, is that formalist students, with their academic clarity and linear epistemologies, are the surest of earning the institutional certification that they need.

Perhaps a more obvious example of the interrelationship between literacy practices and reality can be seen in the ways that these practices give rise to a definition of literature. As I indicated, the enculturation of students into cultural values has been the primary function of literature classrooms in American colleges and universities, and, as the best-selling literature textbooks suggest, it is still an important function of literature classrooms. However, these explanations are articulated in decontextualized ways that deny the contingency of literacy practices and, in so doing, they hide the cultural values at stake. According to these textbooks, literature, is "a kind of art, usually written, that offers **pleasure** and **illumination**" (*LFPD* xxxviii), and it enables readers to **"grow**, both personally and intellectually" and "provides an **objective** base for **knowledge** and **understanding**" (*LRW* 1). *Bedford* defines the function of literature as nourishing readers' emotional lives and broadening their perspectives on the world; in addition, while reading literature is **"pleasurable**," the acts of "reading and understanding a work **sensitively** by **thinking, talking**, or **writing** about it increase the pleasure of the **experience** of it" (5). Implicit within these understandings of literature is the socializing function of literature. Toward this end, *Perrine's* goes so far as to distinguish between what it calls literature of escape, which is "written **purely** for **entertainment**," and literature of interpretation, which serves "to **broaden** and **deepen** and **sharpen** our **awareness** of life" (3).

Drawing upon this distinction, *Perrine's* goes on to construct two corresponding subject positions for readers: "At one extreme are readers who find their demands gratified by escape fiction. Even when they suppose that they are reading for interpretation, they expect what they read will return them always some pleasant or exciting image of the world or some flattering image of themselves" (4-5). These readers "often make fixed demands of every story," such as "a sympathetic hero or heroine," "a plot in which something exciting is always happening and in which there is a strong element of surprise," "a happy outcome that sends the reader away undisturbed and optimistic about the world," or "a theme—if the story has a theme—that confirms the reader's already-held opinions about the world" (5). These readers are "frustrated and disappointed unless those demands are satisfied" (5). In contrast, the subject position constructed for readers "who seek out interpretive literature" is one that is characterized by finding a **"deeper pleasure** in fiction that **deals** significantly with life than in fiction based on the formulations of escape" (6). While not "totally dismiss[ing] escape literature," these readers would recognize that "an exclusive diet of escape, especially of the cruder sorts, has two dangers: (a) it may leave us with merely **superficial** attitudes toward life; (b) it may actually **distort** our view of **reality** and give us **false** concepts and **false** expectations" (7). In producing discourse about literature, such readers can avoid **"unnecessarily intruding"** in their "critical statements, with a consequent loss of power and precision," and they "should adopt the stance of the **sensitive** person" who is certain of their perspectives even when they "may feel tentative or unsure" (1469). Clearly, these textbooks endorse culturally-specific discursive practices and, through them, value-laden versions of who student readers-writers should be and how they are to see the world, versions that end up privileging those who come from such cultural communities, or who can assimilate these values easily, and that subjugate those who do not.

THE BEST-SELLING COMPOSITION TEXTBOOKS

The relationship between literature and composition within English departments is a highly contested relationship. For example, Susan Miller challenges Stephen North, James Berlin, and others who would offer a narrative of continuity in describing the discipline of composition studies. Such an explanation ignores, she claims, composition students themselves, the scholarly emphases in the discipline of composition studies, the dominant images of composition teachers, and the relation of composition studies to administrative structures within the academy. In lieu of a narrative of continuity, she offers a version of composition studies "as an instructional and professional discontinuity" with the earlier formations of English departments in U.S. colleges and universities, a reading which, she suggests, offers a way to account for the experiences of students and teachers. Central to her alternative is the simultaneous condition of composition studies as separate from literary studies, insofar as it has a different identity and different discourse(s), and, at the same time, of composition studies as being situated within this difference by literary studies in the marginalized, yet powerful, role of the Other (81, 79 ff).

Though literature classrooms provide a cultural context for English departments and, as a result, are influential upon the literaci(es) that are constructed and endorsed in the academy, composition classrooms have assumed the primary role in certifying students in the literaci(es) of the academy. Unlike literature textbooks, composition textbooks have some presence in the scholarship of the discipline.[11] For example, Xin Liu Gale and Fredric G. Gale have edited a collection of essays, entitled *(Re)Visioning Composition Textbooks: Conflicts of Culture, Ideology, and Pedagogy*, that examines the relationships among textbooks, culture, and ideology, the interactions between textbooks and pedagogy, and the material and political conditions of textbook publication. Among other issues, the essays in this collection consider the biases of cultural readers, the narratives of progress in composition handbooks, the contradictions between textbooks' theories of argumentation and contemporary scholarship, and limitations in textbooks' treatment of critical thinking. In solidarity with following these authors, I want to analyze the textbooks of composition classrooms in order to understand the literaci(es) and the culture(s) of the academy by first considering the ways that these textbooks define writing, reading, and thinking—the discursive practices of the academy—and then turning to the cultural capital that is inscribed within these practices. In *Fragments of Rationality*, Lester Faigley argues that contemporary composition textbooks deny contradictions and conflict in an effort to achieve a uniformly and universally coherent rational subject (132 ff). Building upon Faigley's analysis, I want to argue that the contradictions and differences of academic literaci(es), such as those between expressivism and formalism that Faigley, Michael W. Kleine, et al. have pointed out, are naturalized within the notion of *the critical*—as in critical writing, critical reading, and critical thinking—which serves as both the center for academic literaci(es) and as the fundamental standard for literate performance within the academy.

In the ways that the acts of critical thinking are defined, the links among education, society, literacies, and academic culture are forged.[12] For example, the *Harbrace College Handbook* claims that the practices of critical thinking and critical reading enable writers and readers "to distinguish between ideas that are credible and those that are less so" (392). This distinction, it is implied, is based upon some universal standards, such as the difference between facts, which, according to the *Simon and Schuster Handbook for Writers,* "can be verified," and opinions, which are "statements of personal belief" (108, 101 ff), a distinction that is, to a large degree, contextual and rhetorical. In order "to participate actively," *Simon and Schuster* asserts, "in the ongoing exchanges of ideas and opinions that you encounter in college and beyond," (academic) writers and readers must "understand **critical thinking** as a concept (see 5a) and as an activity (see 5b), **critical reading** as a concept (see 5c) and as an activity (see 5d through 5f), **writing critically** (see 5g), and **reasoning critically** (see 5h through 5k)": "Critical thinking is an attitude as much as an activity. If you face life with curiosity and a desire to dig beneath the surface, you are a critical thinker. If you do not believe everything you read or hear, you are a critical thinker. If you find pleasure in contemplating the puzzle of conflicting ideologies, theories, personalities, and facts, you are a critical thinker" (101). In spite of the tacit acknowledgment of conflict, any potential for difference is elided in the ways that the practices of critical-ness are defined, as if critical thinking can dissolve these differences. At best, the conflicts and difference inherent in these rhetorical values are merely sublimated within a universalization of these practices.

Often, these practices are defined in universalized and unproblematic acts that have been separated from the contexts that make them meaningful. What is lost in such a universalization is the contingency of these practices upon social and historical contexts, which these practices deny in their efforts towards universal coherence.[13] Though it is true, as Zebroski points out, that context shapes texts and their meaning (233), and though it is true, in spite of the implicit denial of composition textbooks, that a context does exist, the best-selling textbooks in composition suggest that the legitimacy of these discursive practices transcends contexts, that the practices of (academic) literacy are relevant and meaningful in spite of, and perhaps regardless of, context. Thus, *Simon and Schuster* explains that the practice of critical thinking is a universal process:

> Critical thinking is a process that progresses from becoming **fully aware** of something to **reflecting** on it to **reacting** to it. You use this sequence often in your life, even if you have never called the process critical thinking. You engage in it when you meet someone new and decide whether you like the person, when you read a book and form an opinion of it, or when you learn a new job and then evaluate the job and your ability to do the work.

"Applied in academic settings," *Simon and Schuster* goes on, "the general process of critical thinking is described in Chart 30," which identifies such practices of critical thinking as analyzing, summarizing, interpreting, synthesizing, and assessing critically. Nowhere is it suggested that, for example, summarizing a short story for an introduction to literature course might actually be different from summarizing the results of an experiment in a biology course. On the contrary, the universal practice of "summarizing" requires that critical thinkers "[e]xtract and restate the material's main message or central point at the literal level (see 5d.1)" (102). As described by *Simon and Schuster*, critical thinking is a universal and uniform process that begins with analysis and concludes with a critical assessment. "That process," the textbook explains in the ultimate act of universalization, "holds not only for thinking critically but also for reading critically (see 5c and 5e) and writing critically (see 5g)" (102-03). Apparently, 5c, 5e, and 5g merely repeat 5b, "Engaging in critical thinking" (102).

This process of sublimating difference within universalized practices is evident in the ways that these best-selling textbooks define writing (academically), as resting upon a universal practice that can be applied in any setting. For instance, as *Harbrace* describes it, the act of writing amounts to engaging in a universal set of steps:

> Whenever you write an essay, you engage in a process of developing an appropriate topic (28b) for a certain audience. You often need to explore various possibilities to discover what you want to write (28c(1)), how to focus your subject (28c(2)), how to form a thesis (28d), and how to develop an appropriate plan of organization (28e). Your writing will benefit if you write more than one draft, rethinking and restructuring what you have written. If you try to engage in all of these activities simultaneously, you may become frustrated. (322)

In spite of these instructions for a universal process, *Harbrace* includes additional chapters for writing in other contexts, such as writing under pressure (383 ff), writing arguments (415 ff), writing research (432 ff), writing about literature (575 ff), or writing for businesses (615 ff), all of which seemingly amount to different practices. In a related way, *Simon and Schuster* acknowledges the difference inherent in writing as "an ongoing process of considering alternatives and making choices," and yet it defines this process in similarly universal terms—planning, shaping, drafting, revising, editing, and proofreading (19)—that, nonetheless, aspire to uniformity and universality.

Similarly, (academic) reading is a contradictory act that is ultimately subsumed within a universal practice. For example, *The Macmillan Reader* claims that reading (academically) involves "a three-stage approach" (2). In the first stage, readers, once they are "settled in a quiet place that encourages concentration," are instructed to obtain "an **overview** of the essay and its author" by considering the title, reading it once for pleasure, and then describing the text and their reactions to it (2-3). Next, readers are to **"deepen"** their **"sense"** of the text by reading it a second time in order to "identify the specific features that triggered" their "initial reaction" (3). Finally, readers are to read the text a third time in order "to make judgments about the essay's **effectiveness**" (4). At each stage in the process, readers are encouraged to read "carefully and thoughtfully" with "the same willingness" that the authors of the texts used to write them (5). (Certainly, *Macmillan* cannot be speaking to students who are strapped for time or interest.) According to *The Macmillan Reader,* this practice of reading (academically) will **"enhance** your **understanding** of the book's essays, as well as help you read other material with greater **ease** and **assurance"** (2). In other words, this universalized approach is legitimate not only for the texts specifically included within *The Macmillan Reader* (regardless of whether they appear in later sections devoted to narration, exemplification, or process-analysis) but also have relevance and legitimacy outside of the context of this specific textbook.

Reinforcing their denial of difference, the best-selling composition textbooks invoke the rhetorical modes in their definitions of textuality. To a greater or lesser degree, all of the best-selling textbooks except *The Elements of Style*[14] privilege the rhetorical modes. According to *The Macmillan Reader,* these are description, narration, a variety of expositions,[15] and argumentation-persuasion (vi-xv).[16] Actually Aristotelian *topoi,* the modes were universalized within nineteenth century rhetorical traditions as formal categories in an effort to connect classical rhetoric to the teaching of writing.[17] Variously described as "strategies for development," the "means to achieving specific rhetorical purposes," and patterns for "presenting evidence in an orderly, accessible way," these rhetorical modes are presented as having universal legitimacy as, in *Harbrace's* terms, "natural thinking processes" (*Harbrace* 342; *St. Martin's* 24; *Macmillan* 44; and *Harbrace* 342). If these modes are "natural thinking processes," then clearly the discursive practices of the academy privilege uniformity and universality at the expense of difference, and not only in argument, as Lizbeth A. Bryant suggests (129), but in (academic) writing in general.

In short, the sanctioned versions of academic literaci(es)—not only ways of writing, reading, and thinking but also, through these practices, versions of who to be and how to see the world—serve as the cultural capital of the academy (and, by extension, American society at large). If I were to characterize the subject positions inscribed within the discursive practices legitimized by composition textbooks, I would call it a present absence (or maybe an absent presence). According to *The Elements of Style,* successful writers actively strive to construct this present absence:

> Therefore, the first piece of advice is this: to achieve style, begin by affecting none—that is, place yourself in the background. A **careful** and **honest** writer does not need to worry about style. As **he** becomes proficient in the use of **the** language, **his** style will emerge, because **he himself** will emerge, and when this happens **he** will find it increasingly easy to break through the barriers that separate **him** from other **minds**, other hearts—which is, of course, the purpose of writing, as well as its principal reward. (70)

Interestingly, *Elements* goes on to acknowledge, in the very next sentence, the link between discourse and consciousness: "Fortunately, the act of composition, or creation, **disciplines** the mind; writing is one way to go about thinking, and the practice and habit of writing not only drain the **mind** but supply it, too" (70). Similarly, *St. Martin's* invokes a universalized subject position when, in describing practices for generating ideas, it defines them as "not mysterious or magical" but "tricks of the trade available to **everyone**," which "should appeal to your **common sense** and **experience** in solving problems. Developed by writers, psychologists, and linguists, they represent the ways writers, engineers, scientists, composers—in fact, **all of us**—creatively solve problems" (429).

Within the formalist literacies of the academy, the sanctioned discursive practices privilege a (universal) version of the world that is comprised of foundational knowledge and objective truth, characterized by coherence and uniformity, in which language represents and reports reality. Not surprisingly, all of the textbooks invoke standard American (written) English as the criterion for grammatical and mechanical correctness, a standard that has been contextualized and critiqued extensively.[18] Surprisingly, these textbooks seem to acknowledge at least the cultural biases in the versions of the world proffered by academic literaci(es). For example, *Harbrace* explains that **"American** readers are accustomed to finding a clearly stated

It was one of those hot summer afternoons where the humidity rose so high that even breathing was a chore. The miles of farmland around us were relatively flat, but the breeze rarely scraped the cottonwood leaves together, and the barns and buildings that congregated around our old farmhouse, which had no air conditioning, merely reinforced the close, oppressive heat. My mother announced that whether we wanted to or not, all seven of us were going shopping with her.

Trips to the library meant riding my bicycle alone beneath a hanging sun, across a truck road with acres of breathing corn stalks on either side, and then most of the way across town—past the junior high, past the Catholic Church, past my father's medical office and the police station and the court house—to thesis statement early in an essay. If you [i.e., ESL students] introduce your ideas more gradually—which is the custom in some cultures—you may **confuse** American readers. Stating your main idea early will help **Americans** understand what you write in **English**," and *Simon and Schuster* suggests, in a section devoted to English as a Second Language, that, in spite of all the challenges for ESL students, they actually have "much in common" with the author and with "many U.S. college students" (348; 718). The impressions of American readers notwithstanding, there are three obvious problems. First, cultural values have been essentialized into a false binary of American culture(s) and other culture(s)—assuming, for example, that being an American reader amounts to engaging in a hierarchical reading process that requires a thesis statement at the beginning of texts. Second, the standards that are authorized as having the ultimate legitimacy are those that emerge from this essentialized American culture, thereby situating all ESL students outside of (the) American culture. While students are encouraged to "honor [their] culture's writing traditions and structures," they should "try to adapt to and practice **the** academic writing style characteristic of the United States" (*Simon and Schuster* 719), regardless, I suppose, of whether these cultural differences come from communities that have acquired an indigenous status within the United States or that are considered foreign,

Liberty Street, only to be hassled by spinster librarians over checking out books from the adult shelves. So here was a chance to look for a book and escape from the heat at the same time. My mother gathered us into the blue Suburban, and with the artificial wind from windows blowing across us, we drove the twenty miles toward the big city and the closest shopping mall.

At the first store, I managed to find what I was looking for. In an orange discount bin, sitting near the checkout lanes in one of those engulfing discount stores, scattered among others on gardening and cooking, was a book about writing. It had a hard, mahogany colored cover, which pictured an expensive calligraphy pen and a distinguished hand scrawling on expensive parchment paper the words Effective Writing in large, white, cursive letters across the top. While my mother weaved in and out of aisles, I followed along behind the orange shopping cart and my trailing siblings, clutching the book tightly to my chest.

Back home, I ignored the sweat on my lip as I leaned against my bed in the back of the small, second floor bedroom that I shared with one of my brothers. As soon as I cracked the spine of the book, I found, printed on the inside cover, the secrets outlined in clear, sequential steps—writing a thesis statement, unity and because "the academic writing style" is the only one that has credibility within colleges and universities. Third, and perhaps more difficult to acknowledge, class and gender biases, including those that exist within what is considered mainstream American society, are consistently ignored. As the research in literacy has demonstrated, gender and class are variables, even within American society, that have *significant* influence upon meaning, education, and literacy.[19]

ACADEMIC LITERACI(ES) AND ACADEMIC CULTURE

If textbooks are indicators of institutional and disciplinary forma-

coherence, logical fallacies, all the tricks of the trade that, up to this point, no one had ever told me. Here were the answers that I needed to transform what I was scratching on paper into real writing. I uncapped my pen in order to mark the important parts.

Ten pages into the first chapter, I knew something was wrong. I closed the book and slid it under my bed. Though I continued to fill notebooks, it was some time before I resumed my efforts to discover what it means to write. For reasons I don't entirely understand, I kept the book for many years.

tions, or, at least institutional and disciplinary desires,[20] then they can provide a perspective on the literacies and the cultures of the academy. Though literature classrooms may not occupy the same position in the process of certification in American colleges and universities, their influence upon this process can be seen both historically and (by virtue of their prominence within English departments) culturally, and thus they can provide a context in which to understand academic literacies. For example, students are to recognize the difference between reading for escape, which, according to *Perrine's*, can lead to a distorted view of the world, and reading for interpretation, which can broaden readers' awarenesses of life (3). Within these classrooms, reading is to mean reading formally or identifying formal features such as character or end-rhyme; and even as alternative (though nonetheless academic) ways of reading, such as feminist or reader-response, are receiving minimal recognition, the message about the most legitimate way of reading, as well as the version of the world that supports this practice, is explicitly clear. In these classrooms, the practice of writing (academically) is subordinated to the experience of reading literary texts, which, according to *Bedford*, are sources of "enjoyment, delight, and satisfaction," not unlike other art forms (2). Such a decontextualized understanding of literature can be seen in the following explanation from *Literature: An Introduction to Reading and Writing*:

Literature helps us **grow,** both personally and intellectually. It provides an **objective** base for **knowledge** and **understanding.** It **links** us with the cultural, philosophic, and religious **world** of which we are a **part.** It enables us to **recognize** human dreams and struggles in **different** places and times we otherwise would never **know** existed. It helps us **develop mature sensibility** and **compassion** for the condition of all living things—human, animal, and vegetable. (1)

Within English departments, composition classrooms have exchanged the literary dimensions of the specialized works, the essentialized taste, and universalized culture for the critical. Critical (academic) writing-reading-thinking is to be the means to discerning, in *Harbrace*'s words, "between ideas that are credible and those that are less so," identifying "which ideas make more sense than others," and determining "the extent to which those ideas are reliable and useful" (392), practices that rely upon ostensibly universal values that are, in fact, thoroughly contingent. Any and all difference is to be sublimated within universalized practices of writing, reading, and thinking, which, despite current composition theories, consistently invokes the rhetorical modes in a variety of roles. As a result, writers and readers are still to assume subject positions that invoke the faculty psychology of the eighteenth and nineteenth centuries that defines these modes—or, in *Harbrace*'s terms, "[s]trategies for development," as **"natural** thinking processes" (342)— that have, *Macmillan* implies, universal legitimacy. Furthermore, writers and readers are to navigate their worlds through the use of (academic) reasoning, which *Simon and Schuster* explains as **"natural** thought patterns that **people** use every day to think through ideas and make decisions" (129), an explanation that sounds surprisingly like the justification given to the (culturally contingent) rhetorical modes.

In short, the literaci(es) of the academy is/are comprised of universalized discursive practices, which give rise to essentialized subject positions and foundational versions of the world based upon the primacy of reason and the search for truth. As Ron Scollon and Suzanne B. K. Scollon have argued,[21] these literacies privilege elaborate syntactical and sequential relations, large amounts of new information, and truth values, as opposed to rhetorical and social conditions. As such, they endorse versions of writers and readers as rational minds communicating with other rational minds and an objective, transcendent world in which the complete accessibility to reality corresponds to its complete expressibility in texts (49 ff). Since the implications of these versions of literacy and culture have been thoroughly documented, I will offer short summaries of some of them:

- A denial of the political processes of standardization, the indexical fixing of texts, and the relationships among literacies, education, and (the myth of) individual-social mobility (Collins);

- A belief in established fictionalized stabilities of the self (Faigley, *Fragments*);
- Literature classrooms that have lost touch with everyday readers (Winterowd) and composition classrooms that simultaneously sympathize with marginalized communities and accept (academic) discourses that exclude them (Clifford and Schilb);
- A transformation of social advantages into educational ones (Bourdieu) and a naturalization of class-based cultures as natural indicators of skills and abilities or aptitude (Donald);
- A denial of the cultural biases of standard American English and a depoliticization of the dissonance between the discourses of students and of the academy (Lu);
- An increased powerlessness of writers (Ohmann, "Use");
- A privileged status for particular students (Gee) and certain experiences (Bizzell, "Acadmic" 147); and
- An epistemological alienation (Chiseri-Strater).

If students resist academic literaci(es), the educational and social costs are, obviously, great and becoming greater. If, however, students agree to be assimilated by academic literaci(es), the costs, some might say, are also significant (not equal but different). For student whose histories are not those of the American middle class, there are obvious problems, as Helen Fox has documented. And increasingly for students who, like myself, come out of a white, European-American middle class, the cultural capital of conventional academic literaci(es), I would argue, is suffering from a crisis of legitimacy, a condition that has been mistakenly read as a crisis in literacy.

According to the best-selling textbooks in literature and composition, academic literaci(es) is a literacy of high stakes in which both resisting or assimilating comes at a significant cost to students. So what about the composition textbooks that have a theoretical currency within the discipline? Though not representing the same economic credibility as the best-sellers, are they any less costly to students? Well, the answer is yes and no. In many ways, the literacy construct of *A Writer's Reference* is similar to those of the best-selling composition textbooks. Similar to *Simon and Schuster*, *A Writer's Reference* opens with a section on composing, as opposed to grammar and mechanics, suggesting that the practice of (academic) writing is more than using standard language forms. Still, while somewhat less prescriptive in its explanation of writing, it ultimately offers a practice of (academic) writing that is different only in degree from the others. For example, while it uses the word *tentative* when describing the focus and arrangement of initial drafts, and it distinguishes between global revision and sentence-level revisions, it still privileges absolute definitions of unity (24) and coherence (31), when these and other "static abstractions" actually rely upon the subjective responses of readers.[22] And although it offers a qualified explanation of the rhetorical modes as "nothing particularly magical" but "some of the ways in which **we** think" (26), this qualification does little, I suspect, to dissuade students of the privileged status of the modes. Similar to both *Harbrace* and *Simon and Schuster, A Writer's Reference* devotes separate sections to writing (academic) arguments and researching (academically), as if to suggest that arguments and research are not always everywhere in (academic) writing or that first-year composition can prepare students for arguing and researching in different disciplines.[23] Yet, somewhat unlike the others, it restricts its explanation of the critical to a section on evaluating sources within the unit of research writing (68), which sends curiously contradictory messages about what it means to occupy the position of critical.

Perhaps the greatest advantage of *A Writer's Reference* is its explicit recognition of cultural differences and literaci(es). It usually acknowledges these within small rectangular boxes inserted within the text that contain small type and a green and black picture of the world with green letters "ESL." Three-fourths of the way down the first page, the first of these boxes appears: "What counts as good writing varies from culture to culture and even among groups within cultures. In some situations, you will need to become familiar with the writing styles—such as direct or indirect, personal or impersonal, plain or embellished—that are valued by the culture or discourse community for which you are writing" (3). Perhaps more importantly, *A Writer's Reference* links the cultural differences of discursive practices to versions of the world when, thirteen pages later, it explains, "[i]f you come from a culture that prefers an indirect approach to writing, you may feel that asserting a thesis early in an essay sounds unrefined or even rude. In the United States, however, a direct approach is usually appreciated; when you state your point as directly as possible, you show that you value your reader's time" (16). However, any advantage that is gained from the recognitions of these cultural differences is mitigated by the text itself, which ultimately aspires, as do the others, to a universalization and uniformity. Though *A Writer's Reference* acknowledges the differences among "groups within cultures," it denies the legitimacy of these recognitions, in the first example, by failing to acknowledge that, even within groups, or communities, within academic culture, there are differences in literacies.[24] In its efforts to universalize a direct discursive style in the second, *A Writer's Reference* essentializes the United States, even as some might argue, with reasonable grounds, that such a proclamation about (academic) style is simply wrong.

If *A Writer's Reference* is more similar to, than different from, the best-selling composition handbooks, then *Negotiating Difference* and *The Call to Write* are noticeably different (though no less different, I hasten to add, in their mixed experiences for students). Almost immediately, it is evident that *Negotiating Difference* and the *Macmillan Reader* have little, if anything, in common.[25] While the *Macmillan Reader* implicitly aspires to uniformity and universality, *Negotiating Difference* explicitly foregrounds difference and diversity. In the preface to instructors, *Negotiating Difference* clearly adumbrates its theoretical presuppositions:

> Since the moment the first inhabitants met the first immigrants from Europe, since the first African slaves were brought here in chains, America has been a multicultural land. People from virtually every nation in the world have worked and struggled here. Part of their struggle has been to communicate across cultural boundaries, and not only to communicate but to argue for rights, to capture cultural territory, to change the way America was imagined so that it would include those who are newer or less powerful or spoken about but not listened to—in short to negotiate the differences of culture, race, gender, class, and ideology.

In light of the historical conditions of multiculturalism in the United States, "students must understand the historical contexts in which cultural conflicts have taken place" if they are "[t]o learn to communicate in the overlapping discourse communities of such a society" (v). Later in the same section, it explains that "*Negotiating Difference* invites readers to study contact zones—places where cultures clash, where power between groups is unequal, where positions of power are unstable," by asking them "to analyze original materials so that they can understand historical circumstances, positions taken and refuted, audiences addressed, and rhetorical strategies employed" (vii). It seems fair to suggest that, for *Negotiating Difference*, being critical amounts to situating one's self "in the systems and institutions that are the sites of debate," not, it explains, "through the simple assertion of a position" but through negotiation, which "requires an understanding of other arguments and positions," which "are grounded in material circumstances and ideological premises" (vii, viii).

To this end, *Negotiating Difference* offers six cultural case studies "that explore past conflicts in American culture," from "English colonization of New England to the Vietnam War," which are represented by "texts that constitute the actual rhetorical sites of conflict" (vi). At the end of each text are two sets of questions—Reading Critically questions, which "ask students to identify key arguments and rhetorical strategies" and Writing Analytically questions, which "call for analysis, evaluation, comparison, and even imitation of the texts" (viii). Finally, each unit concludes with "a Research Kit that provides a large number of suggestions for research projects," which are also divided into two sections—Ideas from the Unit Readings, which "contain suggestions for projects that will expand students' knowledge of the issues raised by the readings" and Branching Out, which "contains suggestions for topics on issues analogous to those in the unit but pertaining to other social groups as well as topics that fill in the historical context of the period" (viii-ix).

As an example, the cultural case study entitled "Policy and Protest over the Vietnam War" is comprised of three sections—1965: Year of Escalation and Protest, The War at Home, and Veterans Remember—each of which contains a range of texts, such as Ho Chi Minh's "Declaration of Independence of the Democratic Republic of Vietnam;" poems by Barbara Beidler and Huy Can ("Policy"); Martin Luther King Jr.'s "Declaration of Independence from the War in Vietnam;" John F. Kerry's testimony to the U.S. Senate Foreign Relations Committee ("War"); Tim O'Brien's "On the Rainy River;" and an excerpt from Ron Kovic's *Born on the Fourth of July*. Additionally, the introduction provides a historical and social context for the readings, and the Research Kit encourages students to investigate Lieutenant William Calley and the My Lai incident or women's experiences in Vietnam ("Ideas") and to connect the antiwar movement with the women's movement or war resistance before the Vietnam conflict ("Branching").

Clearly, *Negotiating Difference* has many advantages over the best-selling textbooks for considering the cultural dimensions of literacies, such as the recognition of the cultural diversity throughout the history of the United States and the presence of cultural differences in literacies (presumably) of the "overlapping discourse communities of such a society" (v). Furthermore, its suggestion is that dialogic negotiation that recognizes material experiences and ideological presuppositions, rather than monologic argumentation that aspires to be context-free, offers a potentially productive alternative discursive practice. (Notably, the sections that follow each selection—Reading Critically and Writing Analytically—generally suggest surprisingly conventional discursive practices, such as (academic) comparison or analysis, that seem to undermine the professed recognition of cultural, and hence discursive, differences).[26] Nevertheless, the disadvantages of *Negotiating Difference*, within the contexts of the conditions that have been called the contemporary crisis literacy, seem to be two—both problems of legitimacy. The first is that, to a greater or lesser degree, the literacies of *Negotiating Difference* seem to have been appropriated by the academy itself, insofar as none of the (cultural) case studies has to look any farther than the academic institution itself for authority or credibility. In other words, all of the contact zones, which serve as the center of these units, have an institutional legitimacy, or alternatively, none of them challenges the conventional boundaries of institutions and disciplines. Perhaps more problematic (though not unrelated), the second is the source of legitimation. Similar to those of the best-selling textbooks, the (cultural) literacies invoked by

Negotiating Difference are external literacies that are imported into classrooms and imposed upon students. In other words, these (cultural) case studies, as well as the ways they configure what counts as literacy within these contact zones, have been authorized by people and in places other than students and teachers of particular classrooms.[27] Both of these problems, in addition to the ways that the apparatus privileges conventional discursive practices, reduce the chances that the versions of literacy that emerge from the practices of *Negotiating Difference* will respond to the conditions that have been called a crisis in literacy. However, neither of these disadvantages necessarily guarantees that the cost to students will be as high as those of the best-selling textbooks and conventional (academic) literacies. If situated within contexts that have been identified and legitimized by students, in dialogue with teachers and institutions, the practices of *Negotiating Difference*, particularly in light of Bizzell's recent work on hybrid discourses, can go a long way towards resolving the conditions that critics have called a crisis in literacy.

In a related, though somewhat different, way, *The Call to Write* offers a mixed situation for students. As with *Negotiating Difference* and the best-selling composition reader, *The Call to Write* and the best-selling rhetoric—*The St. Martin's Guide*—have discernible and significant differences. Perhaps the most significant difference is the way that *The Call to Write* foregrounds context and function. In the introduction, *The Call to Write* begins in this way:

> People write in response to situations that call on them to put their thoughts and feelings into words. The call to write may come from a teacher who assigns a paper, or from within yourself when you have ideas and experiences you want to write down. In any case, as you will see throughout this book, people who write typically experience some sense of need that can be met by writing. And accordingly what a person writes will be shaped by the situation that gave rise to the need. (2)

Later, it explains that the recognition of context is central to the way it defines discursive success: "As you can see, writing takes place in many different settings and for many purposes. By thinking about these various occasions, you can deepen your understanding of your own and other people's writing and develop a set of strategies that will help you become a more effective writer" (2). After considering "how writers identify the call to write" and determining "whether and how to respond to it," *The Call to Write* turns, in Part One, to "four contexts in which writing occurs—everyday life, the workplace, the public sphere, and school" before focusing "on how writers read in order to develop their own writing projects" and considering "what makes writing persuasive and how you can build a responsible and persuasive argument" (2). Part Two focuses exclusively on "how writers' choice of genre takes into account the occasion that calls for writing, the writer's purposes, and the relationship the writer seeks to establish with readers" by exploring what it calls "eight of the most familiar genres"— letters, memoirs, public documents, profiles, reports, commentaries, proposals, and reviews (115). In Parts Three, Four, Five, and Six, *The Call to Write* focuses collaborating on projects, conducting research, presenting texts through pre-scribed forms, and editing final drafts, and, in doing so, it comes the closest to resembling more conventional texts.

Much like *Negotiating Difference*, *The Call to Write* has many advantages of the best-selling composition textbooks for centering upon literacies and legiti-macy. One of the most significant is the way in which writing is situated within social and, to a somewhat lesser degree, historical contexts of everyday life, the workplace, the public sphere, and school (2), which, obviously, has the poten-tial to connect classroom practices with the world beyond it. This contextual-ization has implications that reverberate throughout the text, such as in its explanation of facts as "basically statements that no one calls into question" that have been authorized as such through disciplinary-specific methods (51). Another advantage is the way that it offers alternatives to conventional ways of (academic) writing. For example, *The Call to Write*, much like *Negotiating Difference*, includes a section (which, in fact, it calls "Negotiating Differences") that exchanges conventional "pro or con" approaches to arguments for strate-gies, such as using dialogue or recognizing ambiguity and contradiction, that "enable writers to remain committed to their own goals and values but at the same time to avoid some of the limitations of simply arguing for or against, pro and con, in an adversarial relation to others" (104). Still another advantage is the way that it distinguishes between the ways of reading that it presents as "typical of those used by working writers, when the purpose of reading is to find out what others have said about a topic or research an issue the writer plans to write about," and other ways of reading, such as "reading a novel for enjoyment, consulting a user's manual to program a VCR, [or] checking the newspaper for today's weather report" (36).

However, the disadvantages of *The Call to Write* prevent it from resolving the conditions that have been called the current crisis in literacy. First, it resembles other best-selling textbooks in that, when it does present academic literaci(es), it does so in conventional, that is, universalized, terms. Though it seems to differentiates between the literaci(es) of the academy and literacies of the world beyond it, it undermines this distinction by universalizing practices, such as substantive reasoning, that, it implies, both transcend contexts and, themselves, are rarely contextualized.[28] For example, it offers a laundry list of "the parts that go into making an argument"—claims, evidence, enabling assumptions, backing, differing views, and qualifiers—without explaining the implications of what it means to have chosen this "model of argument developed by the philosopher Stephen Toulmin" (90). Surprisingly, its failure to acknowledge how enabling assumptions, or what it calls "the connection in an argument between the evidence and the writer's claim," always and everywhere involve cultural values and presuppositions seems to deny the very importance of context that it foregrounds elsewhere in the text.

Perhaps worse, *The Call to Write* ignores the political realities of literaci(es) within the academy, which is the second way that it fails to resolve the conditions that have been called the contemporary crisis in literacy, and in so doing, it relegates the literacy practices of the academy to the margins. For example, chapter one explores writing in everyday life, writing in the workplace, and writing in the public sphere before turning, near the end of the chapter, to writing in school (8 ff). To cite another example, within Part Two—which, the preface suggessts, will be "for most teachers the core of the book"—only one of the eight "guided writing assignments based upon the eight common genres" is the analytical essay, which falls, along with creating a class charter or other public documents, under the genre of public document. Though it does present argumentation in what would primarily be considered academic terms, and though it devotes space to academic documentation and other features of academic literaci(es) later, conventional literacy practices are marginalized within discussions that center upon letters of appeal, memoirs/time capsules, proposals, casebooks, and other genres. Further, not unlike the ways that conventional textbooks present the rhetorical modes, *The Call to Write* presents these other genres in relatively conventional and unproblematic terms, terms that, incidentally, ignore opportunities to consider the intertextuality of merging and/or embedding competing genres. Furthermore, it completely ignores the gender, class, and ethnic biases inherent in all of these competing literacies. Though the most appropriate function for first-year composition may be contested among certain practioners of composition studies, there is little question in the minds of administrators, faculty members in other departments, and even some composition specialists themselves[29] of the actual function of first-year composition. By immersing academic literaci(es) within a clamor of multiple competing literacies, *The Call to Write* denies the political realities of composition classrooms in academic institutions and, within this context, neglects students' literacy needs.

SOME IMPLICATIONS

What I hope to have suggested is that, within historical and social contexts, the practices of the best-selling textbooks in literature and composition situate the literaci(es) of the academy. By this I mean not only mastery of the acadamy's discursive practices but also the abilities to use these practices in such a way to construct sanctioned versions of the student-self and to participate in the academic version of the world, as the academy's cultural capital, in a process that relies upon denying political dimensions of classrooms. Given that literacies are meaningful only within the discourses that legitimize them, academic literaci(es) are meaningful only within the discourse(s) of the academy, which is always and everywhere political.[30] Within the historical and social contexts of American colleges and universities, academic discourses are academic ways of writing, reading, and thinking, as well as existing, valuing, and believing. As is with all discourses, the discourse(s) of the academy are inherently ideological, or enmeshed in particular social relations, and resist analysis from within the academy, and its discourses. Furthermore, the versions of who is to be inscribed within academic discourse(s) are not only defined internally but also in relation to opposing discourses, such as the discourses of pop culture (e.g., the reader of interpretive, as opposed to escape, literature). In focusing upon specific objects (e.g., vocabulary terms or rhetorical modes) and in sanctioning certain concepts (e.g., unity and coherence), perspectives (e.g., meaning as hierarchal), and values (e.g., linear reasoning), the discourses of textbooks, and, by extension, of the academy, marginalize alternative versions of who to be and how to see the world. Furthermore, the discourses of the academy are also intimately involved in the distribution of power within the academy and, at least to the degree that academic degrees have a social credibility, American society. Though some have suggested that academic discourses are a secondary product of academies themselves,[31] I would argue that, within historical and social contexts, these discourses are part and parcel of these institutions. As such, they discipline those of us in the academy by naturalizing and legitimizing necessary cultural and cognitive associations, or certain ways of making sense of the world.[32] In classrooms, these discourses are cast as centripetal discourses, predicated upon a unitary discourse that reflects the purported unity of academic endeavors, that strive to efface all traces of difference.[33] Theoretically, Bakhtin and his translators have demonstrated the illusion of centripetal discourses (e.g. "Discourse"), and in practice, academic discourses display far less uniformity and universality than is commonly believed, as Barbara Johnstone carefully documents (59 ff). However, such ostensible uniformity and universality is crucial to conventional academic literaci(es) because it serves to deny the provisional nature of academic culture.

The insights that Helen Fox describes in the epigraph to this chapter parallel many of the same experiences that I had as I tried to understand what often was and was not happening in my own efforts to appropriate, rather than be appropriated by, academic literaci(es) and what was and, more often, was not happening in classrooms in which I struggled to facilitate students' acquisition and learning of these same literacies. In a similar way, before I stumbled across *Listening*, I began listening to and talking with students, and—much as Fox did—I gradually began to recognize not only that academic discourses inscribed particular cultural values but also that students struggled to recognize these cultural values in their efforts to appropriate, or to be appropriated by, academic institutions. Unlike Fox, who worked primarily with internationals, I started to recognize that even many of what are regarded as mainstream college students—at community colleges, liberal arts schools, and research universities—struggled to assimilate the styles, methods, and world views that are part and parcel of academic literaci(es) and academic discourses. The more I began to explore students' struggles to assimilate the cultural values that were animated and inscribed within academic literaci(es), the more I began to recognize, as Joseph Janagelo did with respect to rhetorical handbooks, the ways the academic literaci(es) posit a "decidedly rational, and deliberatively reductive vision of" literacy, one that implied that "by evincing logic, reason, and industry," academic writers and readers can "vanquish the profound dissonance" that emerges between their discourses and the discourse(s) of the academy (94). For example, what counts as critical—as in critical thinking, critical writing, and critical reading—is, as Fox points out, culture-specific (125). More so than she does in *Listening*, I want to suggest that, even within what are considered mainstream American communities, there are cultural—class, gender, and ethnic—differences, differences that render the universalized literaci(es) of the academy illegitimate, irrelevant, and in-credible to and for students.

In reflecting on the textbooks I've explained here, I suppose that discursive universalization and cultural uniformity, even outside of the historical and social contexts of English departments and American education, is not wholly unexpected, particularly in light of the conditions of production and distribution of literature and composition textbooks in America. Three of the best-sellers—*Literature: An Introduction to Reading and Writing*, *The Simon and Schuster Handbook*, and *The Macmillan Reader*—represent a single conglomerate,[34] and two others—*Perrine's Literature* and *Harbrace College Handbook*—represent another.[35] In other words, one-half of the best-selling literature and composition textbooks in America come from only two corporations. If I include the texts with more theoretical currency to the list of best-sellers, the situation becomes even more incestuous: in addition to the two already mentioned, Bedford/ St. Martin's Press is represented four times (i.e. *The Bedford Introduction to Literature*, *The St. Martin's Guide*, *A Writer's Reference*, and *Negotiating Difference*), and Addison Wesley Longman is represented twice (i.e. *Literature:*

An Introduction to Fiction, Poetry, and Drama and *The Call to Write*). Assuming that my calculations are accurate, eleven of the twelve textbooks I have considered—almost ninety-two percent—are produced and distributed by only four different businesses, each of which has at least one textbook in both literature and composition. Suddenly, the conditions that have been called a contemporary crisis in literacy look very different.

To be fair, textbooks cannot be singled out as sole contributors to what I am calling the crisis in literacy and education in America. For example, contemporary scholarship on literacy has tended to foreground prestigious institutions in ways that essentialize the experiences of students at what Maureen Hourigan calls the "academies of the privileged" (24 ff), such as the University of Pittsburgh (David Bartholomae), Holy Cross (Patricia Bizzell), the University of Michigan (Helen Fox), and UCLA (Mike Rose). Hourigan goes on to point out that, additionally, the investigations into students' literacies often privilege one element—class, gender, or ethnicity—over another and that often more than one of these dimensions comes into play when students are struggling to acquire and learn academic literacies.

Obviously, the crisis in legitimacy over the meaning and literacy in American colleges and universities extends well beyond the textbook and scholarship industries, beyond even the institutional problems that many others have identified. It extends all the way to pedagogical problems,[36] for, as Bill Readings also explains in the epigraph to this chapter, neither a longing for a (past) cultural heritage nor denying this heritage will resolve the cultural dilemmas in which students find themselves. Consequently, it is to the pedagogies—Berlin's and Shor's—that I now turn.

INTERLUDE
Read(Writ)ing Classrooms With Department Chairs

From: Chris
To: Jean
Subject: pedagogy
Jean,

In thinking about the problems I've encountered with writers and readers in the classroom, like confusion and vagueness, I wonder if many of these *miscommunications* stem from the fact that I'm beginning with a different understanding of knowledge, learning, and meaning than many of them are accustomed to. At the beginning of each semester and regardless of whether it is a literature or a composition course, I feel this tension between outlining my immediate understandings of knowledge, meaning, discourse, and world, in which case the course becomes an introduction to postmodern rhetoric, and simply beginning with the ostensive material of the semester in the hopes that they (i.e. the students) will elicit my understandings of knowledge, meaning, discourse, and the world along the way . . . .

To this day, I've never found a good way to mediate this tension. Given what seems to me to be the radically different understandings of the nature of discourse, knowledge, meaning, and reality that, for me, are generated by postmodern insights (see, even language itself trips me up—"insights" elicits a foundational/essentialist epistemology, which is not at all what I'm trying to suggest.), I feel a certain sense of responsibility to explain, at the very least, that what goes under the heading of *learning* in my classrooms may not resemble what they've come to see learning to be. (So how much are teachers responsible to give students the learning they think they need (i.e. conform to their expectations), and how much should we remain consistent to what we believe to be true about learning, even when our understandings might be incredibly alien to them?)

Invariably on the first day, I ask all of my students to fold their hands and then to refold them in such a way that changes the position of their fingers.

"How does that feel?" I ask, and I always get the same answers: strange, awkward, uncomfortable, etc.

"But are your hands still folded?" I ask, and they always tell me that they are.

I go on to explain that this exercise is a *metaphor* for what will happen in the classroom over the course of the next sixteen weeks: that what might feel awkward, uncomfortable, strange is actually learning, only learning done in different ways.

Unfortunately, this explanation seems to dissipate even before the next class. It seems like the more I try to explain where I'm coming from, in an attempt to attenuate the inevitable confusion, the more complaints I receive that I'm teaching things they're not interested (i.e. shouldn't be expected, given the description of the course, to consider; can't see the relation to the purported content of the course; etc.) in learning. Over the years (I'm merely finishing my sixth year, but I've encountered this situation too many times to ignore it), I get the feedback, either during the course but, more often, on evaluations afterwards, that the students think my courses are filled with too much theory. The other consistent complaint is that I'm talking over their heads(, which, I'm wondering, may not be over their heads but about issues that seem too complicated, such as discursive formations, because they've never been asked to think about knowledge, language, or the world in these ways). What they're calling "too much theory" or discourse that is "over [their] heads," I suspect, is my attempt to explain how my understandings of knowledge, meaning, discourse, and the world may be substantially different from what they are bringing to the class or my effort to talk about fundamental issues that they don't have enough prior experiences, or requisite language, to discuss! If I don't explain these differences or talk about these issues, I'm concerned that they will be overwhelmed and frustrated by what is happening in the classroom(, which they confirm in their comments), but if I do take the time to explain these alternative understandings, I receive all kinds of complaints about how there is too much theory or too complicated language(, which they also corroborate with their feedback).

The second reason, I think, to explain the confusion and uncertainty that students in my classrooms encounter emerges from one of the key components in this pedagogical approach, which I and others call a problem-posing pedagogy. Consistent with postmodern understandings of meaning, a problem-posing pedagogy provides students with problems and holds that learning occurs in both how they solve them (the process) and the solutions they generate (the product). Perhaps the biggest difference between traditional pedagogies and problem-posing pedagogies is the fact that p-p pedagogies don't posit a single, coherent answer. Rather, they believe that *answers* are context-specific and are products of the participants, their languages and the ways they use it to negotiate contexts, and their experiences of the world (in other words, more indicative of the discursive formations of particular classrooms, specific disciplines, and individual teachers rather than reflective of transcendent answers). One of the difficulties that this pedagogy creates, then, is that it cannot provide students with the *right* answer because notions like *right* and *correct* represent particular contexts and specific situations, ones that may not be consistent with the contexts and situations that students create for themselves. (This pedagogy is not entirely relativistic, rather protean (others, like Vitanza, use the term *rhizome*), one that takes its shape substantially from the parameters and boundaries that students establish in their *reading* of the posed problem.) Consequently, I turn writers and readers back to themselves and to their understandings and descriptions of contexts and problems in order to discover their own answers to their questions (Of course I don't leave them to flounder; I will assist them in eliciting these answers when they appear to be having problems.). What often happens, however, is that the student starts acting out angrily, like one did this summer, and/or refuses to engage in the process of learning. (I must admit that I feel somewhat betrayed by this particular student: throughout the semester, she came to me with her problems, many of which were unique to her particular circumstances (e.g. her anxiety about poetry, her general panic about the world), and, I believe that I was more than helpful. (She even went so far as to request to do extra credit in order to facilitate her application to a prestigious university on a 3:2 plan!) throughout the entire experience with her, I was patient and cooperative, offering her suggestions, watching her act out her anger without taking offense, and providing opportunities for her to supplement her grade. The fact of the matter remains, though: for whatever reasons, this reader, and other good students like her, didn't feel comfortable enough to bring those problems to me, a condition that undermines all that I'm trying to accomplish in the classroom.)

I think that there are two main explanations for the complaints from writers and readers in my classrooms about confusion and uncertainty: the fact that I'm beginning from places different from them and the fact that my pedagogical approaches are context-specific approaches. My options, I think, are three: to abandon what I believe about discourse, knowledge, meaning, and the world in order to provide students with what they expect; to persist in teaching composition and literature from where I am in my understandings of discourse, knowledge, meaning, and the world and hope that they'll *get it* somewhere along the way (even if it isn't before the end of the semester); or to negotiate and collaborate with students in beginning with where they are and explaining where I'm coming from. Abandoning what I believe isn't a viable option (feels too much like intellectual dishonesty), and ignoring the problems won't work either (learning doesn't seem to be occurring). All along, I've tried this third option, attempting to negotiate and to explain, but it doesn't seem to be working as well as I would like . . . . The problem is not, I don't think, that I cannot communicate these things in ways that the writers and readers with whom I work can understand. (I may, however, need to take more time to explain them or explain them in alternative ways.) Rather, my reading of the problem is that the bigger obstacle is that students are unwilling to even consider these issues(, which would account for, among other aspects, the startling silences (absence of questions) in spite of pervasive confusion), in which case, no amount of explanation is going to help. For me (at least today), the tension seems to emerge from the conflict of modernist understandings of discourse, knowledge, meaning, and world and revisions of postmodernism. I wonder if students have been conditioned to these modernist perspectives and if what I'm asking them to consider requires them to rethink issues that are easier to leave untouched. One student this semester has already written: "I have thought about language more in the past three weeks than I probably have in my whole high school career. Maybe this is good, but maybe I am looking too much into language and not just letting it flow."

Given what I've called a conflict between modernist and postmodernist understandings of discourse, knowledge, meaning, and the world, how are teachers of language to negotiate these differences?

From: Jean
To: Chris
Subject: pedagogy
Chris,

I'm afraid my response will be rather rambling as I try to reflect on all the issues in your correspondence that interest me. When you say that "postmodern understandings of what knowledge is necessitate some changes in pedagogical approaches," I'd (1.) like to hear a bit more specifically what those changes look like, and (2.) whether they are to take place on all levels of education, K-college? Moreover, if we say that they are, what do we do in making a switch with people who have been educated more traditionally? Actually, I think this is the question you are struggling to answer right now—right?

What you explain as start-up problems seem very clear to me—how to prepare students to expect something different without turning the course into a theory course at the outset. While I am a proponent, in general, of telling students what to expect when they are about to encounter the unfamiliar, here I think one needs to blend familiar with unfamiliar, creating exercises, perhaps, that resemble what students are used to doing, and then talking about them in new ways. I'm not sure, in relation to this issue, what you mean when you talk about "distilling," and "learning to play the game." I think we all want to "teach students to fish," but writing and reading are so infinitely more complex than fishing, that the metaphor limits one's thinking. Throughout our lives we learn language skills, and in some ways composition instruction has to fit into that pattern of learning. Some one who has never heard of fishing can learn the rudiments in a day, (although my husband has been reading fishing magazines and learning new techniques for years,) but someone who has never used language has lots of skills to develop before he or she can hope to advance a position.

I have felt the exact response that you describe when you ask if we are responsible for giving students what they want and expect. When students on evaluation forms start telling me how to teach them, I get cranky. I think we have the right to teach in ways we think will facilitate learning.

I would venture to suggest that your hand-folding exercise dissipates before the class is over because our students do not think metaphorically or at least not with ease. I know you want to give them every bit of credit for their expertise with language and for their banks of cultural capital, and I respect that assessment, but experience has convinced me that they have no confidence in these resources and that a lack of awareness is just as bad as a lack of capital. I recognize that your efforts are directed at facilitating their awareness of these resources, but I think such goals cannot be achieved through the explanation of a theoretical position. I think that in addition to the negotiation and collaboration that you mention later on, skills have to be a part of courses like comp. and lit. I've seen you teach them so I know you agree. The skills areas may provide that dose of the familiar that you are looking for since students are familiar with skills development.

As I read and reread your discussion of problem-posing pedagogy, I'm not sure I find it any different from anything I've ever believed or ever done. Does any teacher of literature and writing ever say there is a single, coherent answer? Isn't it inherent in our discipline that we are content with ambiguity and multiplicity. Still, as a teacher of literature I like to lead my students, with at least some texts, to a single coherent interpretation so they know what one looks like—always, of course, with repeated emphasis on the idea of *a* reading rather than *the* reading. I taught business writing for many years and even in that most formulaic of courses, I steadfastly resisted the formula, suggesting that each communication act was a particular problem to be addressed, and yet we had to know some things about letter writing to understand the singularity of the particular problem and the range of considerations for reaching a solution. And I have always, in fact, used some issues from physics to explain some issues in both 19th and 20th century literature.

At the moment I'm not prepared to answer your questions about the impact of postmodernism on my own pedagogy—although I'd like to try. I think I could have done better with the question 20 years ago before I'd seen quite so many students with quite so many different needs. I've been in the classroom for too long even to find the question very compelling, and I need help to get involved with your enthusiasm. I think I need such involvement, however, so I challenge you to bring me along! I've been through waves of theoretical approaches to teaching writing, and I'm convinced that anything works for some students and nothing works for others. There are others in the middle who can be reached if we do the "right" things. My own experience is that the teacher's character may have more to do with success in these instances than anything else. A teacher who cares and who goes the distance with a student can do more than any theoretical position. I wish you could see [colleague] in action with students and I wish you could see some of the great results he achieves with Advanced Comp. students, with a pedagogy that you might find problematic.

There is much more that I should say, but I'm out of time—for now. Just a few random observations for further discussion.

(1) When I took your classes last year, I really liked the way you have students in groups working on the same topic. I thought this seemed a very effective way to create dialogue which might lead to a rather rich approach to a topic. I plan to try it. But when I sat down with a group of students, who told me they didn't know what to do, and I heard that their topic was abortion, my heart sank. They could not use the process on this old topic, and they were destined I felt to produce a construct from the old, old world of composition. In fact, no legitimate dialogue took place. Students held forth and used my questionings to pin down my position.

(2) How does evaluation work with your pedagogy? I have not checked, but rumor has it that you are a very easy grader who gives almost all A's (?)

(3) Point of information: I believe that campus statistics show that the majority of [our institution's] students are first generation college students. I fear you may be over-estimating them. Our average ACT is about 22—not very impressive.

I look forward to continuing this discussion. Have a good weekend.

Jean

From: Chris
To: Constantine
Subject: Re: conversation on authority and classroom presence
Constantine,

Okay, here goes. (I'm working out this question as I write, so you might have to read a bit before you understand what I'm asking.)

Your initial response after visiting my classroom was surprise at the degree to which the students were engaging in critical thinking, and then, after some reflection, you were talking about a classroom presence that was missing (but that you could see in the videotape I sent last year. In both of your responses lies the issue that I'm trying to understand: authority and dialogue. In . . . ReInventing . . . , I [talk] about dialogues, which are the kind I'm advocated, and Socratic dialogues/ordinary discussions. In *Science, Order, and Creativity*, David Bohm and David Peat describe the difference between what I'm calling postmodern dialogues and other forms of communication:

> a key difference between a dialogue and an ordinary discussion is that, within the latter people usually hold relatively fixed positions and argue in favor of their views as they try to convince others to change. At best this may produce agreement or compromise, but it does not give rise to anything creative. (241)

The question I'm wrestling with right now has to do with these postmodern dialogues and authority . . . . I'm stuck, however, in trying to work out the relationship between postmodern dialogues and authority.

I would say that the students from class that day were so engaged in the act of critical thinking, and thinking for themselves, because, at least in part, I was restricting my authority to a facilitator and a participant. If I were more authoritatively involved in the discussions, I wonder whether they would have been as engaged or whether they would have waited for me to tell them The Answers, rather than their own answers. In other words, I would say that what you observed was what I'm calling postmodern dialogues. As for socratic dialogues and ordinary discussions, I can readily see the role that authority plays. But, if postmodern dialogues are valuable, then the role of authority becomes much more murky. What's your sense?

From: Constantine
To: Chris
Subject: Re: conversation on authority and classroom presence
Chris:
Thanks for your thoughtful remarks and distinctions between the traditional, Socratic, and the postmodern type of dialogue. Such things are truly the great concerns of a teacher, especially in the postmodern era.

The first I want to say is that it is a delusion to think the Socratic dialogue as uncompromising authority. Those that spread this particular point of view have a limited idea of what the Socratic dialogue is.

For one thing, I believe the Socratic dialogue is open-ended (as well as the grandest intellectual theater in western civilization), and not always leading to a Socratic victory. Socrates has his opinions, but Socrates does not always win—in fact most dialogues seem to go on, permitting the reader to surmise, or imagine, that antithetical positions will go being so, with no established positions in the end; in fact the idea "dialogue" means that: two views being debated, not one. Evidence of the openendedness of Platonic dialogue is to be found in early Socrates dialogues, such as "Euthedemus," "Laches," and "Lysis," though most critics concentrate on "Gorgias" and "Protagoras," which bear the names of the famous sophists.

In the first three, Socrates is engaged—with much humor—in the debate whether education is given by the teacher to the student, or by the student to the teacher, and whether the teacher can make anyone "wiser." Euthedemus, the name of the sophist in question, claims that the teacher's position is far from clear. In fact, he and another sophist on his side, examine the same student from two opposing points of view, and the student admits that what he thinks he knows one moment he does not know the next. It's great fun to read this one, and one can have students read it in a class.

It is worth reviewing these dialogues to see that the crux of the idea lies in the reciprocity; many Platonic scholars have noticed this, and, in fact, they argue that the Socratic interrogator is not an authority—which Socrates himself never admits—but one who stirs up thought—the "gadfly" being the most famous metaphor. Or "the unexamined life is not worth living," and such things. Postmodern rhetoricians have simply forgotten that, and view Plato from his metaphysics, from the top down (ontology, etc.) I believe semioticians and postmodernists have seen Plato as the basis of "logocentrism," and therefore the arch-enemy of rhetoric, when Plato was indeed the first to employ rhetoric in the open-ended form. He did hate the sophist, but for their relativism; his own method is itself largely sophistic.

This for the time being; I will write further on this, as time permits, as I have not been able to get to your question of authority in the classroom. I'll drop a hint: I believe authority in the classroom derives from the ability of the instructor to be balancing the dynamic tension between contradictory positions: on the one hand, he not only permits but encourages students to think for themselves, and to express critical views, on the other he maintains a "center" not of opinions, but of presence; students know he knows, and know (as Socrates does) that he can admit his ignorance—but Socrates never so never sounds ignorant. How one maintains that balance is a teacher's innermost secret. Henry James advised a young novelist who asked him how to write to get into the fray: "Fend for yourself."

A young Greek athlete bragged that in Rhodes he had leapt a great distance. "Now," a companion said, "here is Rhodes, and here is the leap." (In Greek this sounds better.)

By the way, my brother, Gerasimos, is a Platonic scholar at Irvine, having written much on Socrates; I will ask him for some materials and authentication.

C

From: Constantine
To: Chris
Subject: Re: conversation on authority and classroom presence
Chris:
A few more things regarding presence in the classroom came to mind. I will give an anecdote.

Yesterday, a former student came to office to ask for a recommendation. I had not seen her on campus recently, and she informed me that she is interning.

She was quite excited with her new situation, standing in front of a class and conducting a class (in high school). I noticed her demeanor had changed, and told her. She told me she had to make an enormous transition from a student to a teacher. Now she dresses up, and her students regard her as authority. She cannot slip; she has to know everything (she told me all that); her students now regard her as old-fashioned, straight-laced, and a little bit of an outsider, intruding on their lives (she told all this). She was amazed at how much work she had to do to get prepared. Now she understands ME! the former teacher. Now she is on the outside. She sees the young kids as rebels (their age), but up to this moment she had regarded herself a rebel.

She is quite happy, though, and thankful she is given the opportunity to pass on knowledge she received from us.

I don't know what this all means—is this the deconstruction of the teacher, or of the student? She seemed intense, as always, exhilarated, and thankful. The transition does not bother her; she only hopes she is up to the task.

Well, is not this the transformation of an extremely shy figure (this girl almost fainted in my class once, having to read a paper before a group), a non-authoritarian figure, to one who had gained authority? How does this happen—overnight I might add?

Let me have your reactions to this. I think this episode might be related to your question, since this transformation seems to have happened of itself—as soon as one is transferred from one cubicle to another. Therefore, a teacher is not born—a teacher is made?

Is, therefore, the authority one has to gain (one does gain) unavoidable?

C

From: Chris

To: Constantine

Subject: Re: conversation on authority and classroom presence

. . . I'm intrigued by this discontinuity between Plato's discursive practices and Plato's philosophy. In fact, you've articulated something that I've always felt but never formulated about Socrates and Plato (though other contradictions, such as Plato's fear of writing, were easier to identify). There are places in the dialogues where Socrates does seem to be operating in a dialogic manner (although I can't seem to ignore the ways that he serves as Plato's technique, and I have a hard time thinking that Plato was engaging in expressivist writing when he wrote the dialogues).

I think you're right when you say that postmodern rhetoricians attribute logocentrism to Plato, and to do so, we must ignore the ways that Socrates does contradict the laws of noncontradiction, excluded middle, and third. Nevertheless, I cannot reconcile these dialogic threads of Socrates with the absolutism of his author, and this distinction is the one that I make between Plato and the Sophists (and between monologic and dialogic discourse). For Gorgias, Protagoras, and other sophists, timing and appropriateness were part of determining relevance and meaning (knowledge even) whereas Plato's search for the ideal seems to deny the context-specific conditions of sophistic epistemology and of dialogue.

Basil Bernstein and his distinction between elaborate and restricted codes come to mind. If I have the difference right, elaborate codes, as you probably know, are those in which the text carries virtually of the information needed to make sense of it in its syntax, sequential relations, et al., and restricted codes are those in which the context is necessary in order to make sense of the situation. To me, dialogues are restricted codes, insofar that participants, time of day, what has come before, and numerous other features factor into the meaning of the *text*, if you will.

As I understand them, restricted codes seem to contradict conventional academic discourse and traditional classroom discourse, and yet elaborate codes cannot be dialogic, I don't think, because of their need to codify the context in the text itself. For restricted codes, authority is contextual, I think, and for elaborate codes, authority is textual.

As for your former student, I can't help but wonder whether her transformation could be described as a process by which she acquired or learned this elaborate code of academic discourse. As I argue in this book and elsewhere, become proficient in a discourse amounts to more than simply learning to speak it, write it, or read it but also to use it to construct both the appropriate faces and sanctioned versions of the world of the community for which the discourse speaks. (That sentence doesn't seem very clear—was it?)

Ah, the (de)construction of the teacher-student, what a paradox! At what point is the authority generated? What do you think?

Chris

From: Constantine

To: Chris

Subject: Re: conversation on authority and classroom presence

Chris:

I was just referring to the difference of the early dialogues, where the process is clearly open-ended, and the later dialogues, in which Socrates is used as a tool—or better yet—mouthpiece for Plato's philosophy. Plato, as a thinker, is honest enough to grant that a dialogue never really ends; it stops. Now, a reading of the Euthedemous (which I plan to re-read) will confirm that. The dialogue can favor the rhetorician as much as it does his opponent. I know Socrates has gotten on everyone's nerves—after all he was executed—but ultimately, given his premises, he would probably re-examine himself if he lived today. Plato, unfortunately, is read through a series of footnotes (what Whitehead said of him), rather than for what he actually says. I have asked my brother for some help—none has come yet, because he is closer to the recent scholarship on this point. Besides, Socrates never admits that he knows anything—that in itself is a contradiction, for Plato stuffs him up with lots of lumber as things go along.

Sorry—have to write a test!

C

From: Chris

To: Constantine

Subject: Re: conversation on authority and classroom presence

I'm rushing out to catch my plane to Denver, but I couldn't resist responding to our conversation about authority and classrooms.

I can see what you're saying about dialogues being open-ended for Socrates, at least in some of them. But where, then, does authority come from in an open-ended dialogue? From one's history? Credentials? Or constructed in the moment? Or somewhere in between?

I look forward to continuing this conversation when I return. Have a great weekend.

Chris

From: Constantine

To: Chris

Subject: Re: conversation on authority and classroom presence

Good question, Chris! Where does authority come from in the open-ended dialogue?

The way I have always seen this—and I admire Plato basically because he gave us the dialogue, not so much for his metaphysics—is that the authority here collapses in favor of the truth; the dialogue is a form used in pursuit of truth. Now, truth for Socrates was the ideal, something that the dialogue would reveal. But as authority is no longer in the Socratic truth, but in the pursuit of truth, the dialogue merely serves as the tool for that pursuit. The dialogue will take you wherever IT goes—not necessarily where you WANT to go. If the truth only matters—whether one can ever reach it or not—then the truth is the authority. If truth is not reached—and some early Platonic dialogues the final conclusion remains open—then there is no truth, and, thence, no authority. What would then happen?

Nothing but further pursuit. One can imagine an endless pursuit, thence an endless dialogue.

The teacher can form himself in this mold: he is the conduit of the pursuit of truth—regardless of whether he and his class and his dialogue will ever attain it.

Still, the teacher has to give exams; but that is a different question—a different authority; an artificial one imposed by the administration—and the need for a salary.

If I were to teach in an ideal/Platonic state, I would not give exams or grades, would not receive any salary, and would only have conversations with my students. I would not claim any authority, but if anybody liked to follow me or find me interesting, that's OK with me. In fact, that's what Socrates did. (but of course I'm not Socrates.)

From: Chris

To: Constantine

Subject: Re: conversation on authority and classroom presence

I like the way that you've invoked the dialogue as a model for classroom practices though I'm somewhat suspicious about the notion of truth (Truth? truth? it always seems so context-specific and contingent, but i suppose i can recognize a provisional truth, i guess.) How do you see it? How might the notion of a provisional truth affect (or not affect) dialogues?

I like the way that you've raised the question about the political realities of the institutions in which teachers must work. There are ways, I think, of reconciling the politics of institutional authority with the authority of dialogue, ways of lessening the ways that institutional authorities corrupt the dialogic process. (I'm assuming that we agree that institutional authorities corrupt dialogic discourse by implementing an externally-imposed authority upon it—is this a fair assumption?) For example, we can involve students in the process of evaluation in a way that transforms evaluation from a monologic response to a dialogic text that raises questions about standards and legitimacy. Would you agree? If so, were would be places where we could reconcile institutional authorities with the authorities of the dialogue?

From: Constantine
To: Chris
Subject: Re: conversation on authority and classroom presence
Chris:
As for truth, let's settle with provisional. Who knows what it is? It only seems to me that unless truth, of some kind, is the aim, dialogue will be meaningless. Derrida suggests that dialogue can go on ad infinitum, even without truth—just "affirmation," as he calls it.

I agree about institutional authority, but I don't know what to do about it. It is too entrenched, and in its way useful; students do need GPAs to graduate and find jobs. The authority of the classroom can be different, depending upon the art of the professor. In this case, we have talked too much of authority, why not presence? Presence in the classroom; again, how this is established depends upon methods. I like the lecture, basically; in the film class, I have deconstructed myself, for I am absent; whatever I say, students don't see me, because I am in the back, in the dark, and they only hear my voice. They told me in the evaluations this is very effective, since "I walk them" through the movie. Still, the movie is more of a presence than I am. It's almost weird, and it bothers me at time, because I don't enjoy this as much as I do a vibrant lecture—which, unfortunately, comes only once in a while.

This is a game one plays; and it is a creative and long-lasting one. It takes many years to perfect, but one is never safe. I can see Drew Dillon, a master in the classroom, sweating before he goes to his first class every fall. I never feel safe, and a class can collapse suddenly for any reason, including bad weather and heat in the classroom. Once, while teaching at the circle in Chicago, it was 15 degrees below zero outside, and not much warmer inside. I could not life a spirit; if one cannot do that, the center cannot hold.

Have to go back to classroom preparation.
Constantine

must negotiate a position within academic cultures through an effort of will from which they can "speak our language" or "carry off the bluff" until such time as they have developed proficiencies in these literacies.

However, he seems to idealize the college student and the social institution of the university, which leads to two significant problems. First, he appears to be overly sanguine about students' agency, as if they can generate such a compromise between relatively uniform personal and disciplinary histories with ease. Second, he seems to ignore the political realities of academic institutions, which, on their own, are relatively inflexible and impervious to students' efforts. From the perspective I described in the prologue, I want to argue that Bartholomae's compromise is perhaps better defined as a paternalistic "take it or leave it," in which the students (and teachers, I would add) must accept the terms established by the institutions. Or they can resist, often at significant personal and intellectual cost if they're tenacious enough to remain in the institution (as Elizabeth Chiseri-Strater, Helen Fox, and others have demonstrated) or a social and, ultimately, economic cost if they opt out altogether—which, according to ACT, Inc., more and more are doing. Bartholomae's compromise, and perhaps even Bizzell's,[5] situates the authority and legitimacy entirely within institutional cultures. In order to establish a credibility, students must acquiesce, or give the appearance of acquiescing, to these cultural values, or, if they intend to resist, they must do so within institutionally prescribed ways—what Bartholomae calls taking "possession" of the discourse by locating "themselves within it aggressively, self-consciously" or doing intellectual work "within and against conventional systems" (607). Thus, the forms of resistance are determined before those students who dare to resist even do so.

Now, I do not want to deny the insights that Bartholomae has into the realities that students encounter in classrooms. In fact, he has done much to help me, and others, I'm sure, understand students' experiences—both what I was up against when I was a student and what the students with whom I work today encounter—in their efforts to earn their degrees. What I would like to do, however, is to reconsider the issues of authority and legitimacy with respect to academic cultures. If the crises in literacy and education are, in fact, crises of meaning and legitimacy, then looking for ways to help students invent the university, particularly through the compromises that Bartholomae has suggested, cannot dissolve these conditions. In beginning and ending in academic institutions, Bartholomae leaves the sole basis for authority and legitimacy in academic cultures, which are alien to students already. What I want to suggest is that, in order to resolve these crises in meaning and legitimacy, academic literacies and academic institutions must be *re*invented in ways that recognize the legitimacy of both the cultures of the academy and the cultures that students bring with them into classrooms. However, this is much easier said than done, as Bizzell explains near the end of her article "Arguing About Literacy":

> I do not know that anyone has yet articulated a truly collaborative pedagogy of academic literacy, one that successfully integrates the professor's traditional canonical knowledge and the students' noncanonical cultural resources. Certainly I cannot do so. It is extremely difficult to abrogate in the classroom, by a collective act of will, the social arrangements that separate professors and students outside the classroom. Integration has not been achieved if the students are simply allowed to express affective responses to canonical knowledge as conveyed by the professor, or if the professor simply abdicates the role of guide to the tradition and encourages the students to define a course agenda from their own interests. (251)

Ignoring, for now, Bizzell's implicit denial of the legitimacy of teachers' *noncanonical* practices, often referred to as lore,[6] and of the legitimacy of students' *canonical* practices, however fragmented, which they bring with them into classrooms, the political difficulties that she acknowledges must be negotiated in order to generate a collaborative literacy. And this can lead to a dialogic legitimacy, one that emerges from both academic cultures and students' cultures, that can resolve the conditions that critics have called crises in literacy and education, not to mention the concomitant issues of authority that, even within her explanations of her own classrooms, has drawn critical attention.[7]

In classrooms in American schools, the effort that comes the closest to generating such a dialogic legitimacy is what critics and teachers have called critical literacies. From Maxine Greene to Patricia Bizzell and Henry Giroux to Donaldo Macedo and countless others, there are many who argue, both in theory and in practice, for the potential of critical literacies to transform English studies and education in American colleges and universities. Though many neo-Marxists, such as Louis Althusser, Göran Therborn, and Michel Foucault have influenced the tradition of critical literacies and radical pedagogies in American colleges and universities,[8] the authoritative source for critical literacies has been Paulo Freire, and, in particular, his early works, which bring together marxist theories of culture with Freire's own personal, political, and religious experiences into a social humanism and marxist materialism. In *Education for Critical Consciousness, The Pedagogy of the Oppressed*, and other early works, Freire argues that reality is constructed through concrete social relations, which can be subject to critical analysis through literacy practices. For Freire, oppression is the condition of accepting naturalized and legitimized class relations as natural and legitimate, a condition in which, according to Freire, some people have constructed the world for others.[9] Using Freire's own terms, the "ontological vocation" of humans is to become subjects who act upon and transform their world in ways that lead to fuller and more satisfying experiences, both collaboratively and individually.[10] According to Freire, people can come to understand the historical and social nature of reality, as situated within social relations, through the acquisition of what he calls a critical consciousness, which emerges from an analysis of experience, an awareness of contradictions between the world as described and the world as experienced, and action that rereads and rewrites the world through literacy acts.[11] When combined with authentic dialogues, critical consciousness can lead to a praxis that transforms the world, a praxis that, Freire maintains, is a necessary element of critical consciousness and, obviously, social transformation. In educational situations, the praxes of Freire's critical literacy, or what he calls a critical pedagogy, involves students and teachers in a dialogue that originates in the specific material and social conditions in which they find themselves, a dialogue that, unlike Socratic dialogues, denies universal and transcendent knowledge and meaning in favor of a constructed intersubjective reality.[12] Also called a problem-posing pedagogy, these praxes involve historical and social contexts through the use of generative themes in order to problematize reality and to dissolve the traditional subject positions of students and teachers, which Freire sees as being antithetical to critical literacies. Along with reconfigured relationships between students and teachers, the praxes of critical literacies lead students and teachers to collective action that alters social conditions.

Though, in his early work, Freire limited his analyses primarily to class, his later work acknowledges additional cultural variables, such as gender, and later theorists and teachers have resituated his original observations within postmodern contexts. In U. S. educational contexts, these postmodern rereadings and rewritings of Freire have, in general, taken three different forms. The first is that of postmodern critical rhetorics, which has largely focused on using rhetorical approaches to understand the intersections of class and society. For example, Raymie McKerrow has defined postmodern critical rhetorics as a synthesis of Freirean critiques of domination and power into a theory and praxis of critical rhetoric, freed from the dominations of Platonic theory, that rely upon contingency, epistemological doxa, and critique as performance.[13] Other manifestations of postmodern critical rhetorics have called for using rhetorical studies as a way of recognizing the rhetorical designs of an epoch and critiquing postmodern culture, and for bringing together rhetorical practical wisdom with audiences.[14] The second is that of postmodern critical literacies, which focus predominantly upon the politics of schooling in American society. For example, Colin Lankshear and Peter McLaren have edited a collection of essays entitled *Critical Literacy: Politics, Praxis, and the Postmodern*, in which numerous theorists and teachers advocate postmodern critical literacies as an approach to studying writing and reading practices, as a way of preparing students with the skills to critically assess dominant and subordinate traditions and to disrupt universalized versions of reason and linear notions of history, as a means of interpreting the social present for the purpose of transforming cultural life through investigating the communication strategies that construct and position subjectivities, and others.[15] The third is that of critical multicultural literacies, which, though not wholly distinct from the second, deliberately extends the context beyond class to identify other cultural variables, such as gender and ethnicity. For instance, Danny Weil in *Towards a Critical Multicultural Literacy*, defines a critical multicultural education as one that invokes an educational equity, a culture-specific reasoning, and an understanding of the logic of oppression (131 ff).

In spite of the increasing popularity of critical literacies in American education and their reinscriptions within rhetorical, postmodern, and multicultural contexts in American colleges and universities, the ways that critical literacies have been practiced in classrooms often fail to resolve the conflicts between competing cultures that have generated the conditions that critics have been calling crises in literacy and education. While I do not pretend to speak definitively on these failings, I can see at least two related reasons for this failure. First, the proponents of critical literacies in American colleges and universities have generally avoided analyzing the practices of each other—which, given the politics of critical literacies, is unexpected though often seems to be the case in early generations of scholarship. In some ways, it seems as if Freire's explicit and implicit assertion that, while the theories transfer, the practices of critical literacies must emerge from specific contexts has granted an authority to those who have been associated with Freire specifically and with his practices generally.[16] The second reason, and one that is more clearly linked to the conditions that critics have called a crisis in literacy and education in America, has to do with the issues of legitimacy in classrooms characterized by teachers as critical. In short, these classrooms tend to grant legitimacy either to institutional cultures, or to the cultures of students lives, and they often ignore the ways that the praxes of critical literacy invoke a collaborative legitimacy that emerges from the dialogic interactions of these cultures. Often, these classrooms tend to impose an ultimate legitimacy upon the practices of the institution though, perhaps more alarming, such a legitimacy is often couched within an appearance of privileging students' cultures at the expense of institutional cultures.

In each of these shortcomings, the problem is the way that these classrooms maintain the distinction between literacies-from-above and literacies-from-below, which often take the dualism of school-based literacies and popular literacies.[17] In "Literacy, Technology, and Monopoly Capital," Richard Ohmann uses the terms *literacy-from-above* and *literacy-from-below* to describe the literacy practices that occurred within communities in England during the late eighteenth and early nineteenth centuries and the practices that were appropriated by state institutions, such as school, in both England and America.[18] These terms, I believe, can be used to understand the relationship inscribed between school-based literacies and popular literacies, a hierarchy in which school-based literacies, as literacies-from-above, have legitimacy and other versions of literacy, as literacies-from-below, do not, regardless of the cases to be made for (e.g., the intellectual sophistication and linguistic aesthetics of) these alternative literacies. For instance, Geneva Smitherman makes a powerful case for African-American English in *Talkin and Testifyin,* and Patricia Bizzell makes a similar case in "Hybrid Discourses," and yet the classrooms that recognize the legitimacy of using Africa-American English or Bizzell's hybrid discourses for intellectual work are, I would argue, few and far between. In maintaining this distinction, these classrooms fall prey to the danger that Freire outlines in the epigraph to this chapter, for a distinction between literacies-from-above and literacies-from-below often gives rise to an objectivism and subjectivism. In these situations, classrooms grant a legitimacy either to literacies-from-above or to literacies-from-below, or, even more confusing for students, some, as I shall demonstrate, appear to authorize students' literacies, as literacies-from-below, while ultimately privileging conventional academic literacies, as literacies-from-above, making it all the more difficult for students to appropriate, or to allow themselves to be appropriated by, the literacies of the academy.

In this chapter, I shall turn our attention to the classrooms of James Berlin and Ira Shor, whom I have chosen for two reasons. First, both of them have been influential in the theories and practices of postmodern critical literacies and English studies, and second, each of them represents an opposite end of the objectivism-subjectivism dualism that, almost by necessity, denies a collaborative legitimacy. Within the critiques that I have been making of literacy, meaning, and education in America so far, as well as my critique, in this chapter, of critical literacies in college classrooms, one way to read Berlin's and Shor's

I cannot remember when I first learned to write and read, though I do have distinct memories of trying to teach myself. Shortly after I was two, my parents moved us from St. Louis, where my brother and I had been born, to a small rural community in southern Illinois, where my father set up his medical practice and where the Catholic church would play a significant role in my life for the next fifteen years. I remember sitting on the concrete stairs outside my father's medical office, mimicking the scrawls I had just seen him scratch across his classroom practices is to see them in the terms that Freire uses in the epigraph to this chapter. Particularly when the world of students, at least within the classroom, is limited to academic institutions, the terms that Freire uses enable me to offer a reading of Berlin's and Shor's classrooms that indicates the ways that they, too, are complicit with academic institutions and participate in the conditions that have given rise to what critics have called a crisis in literacy. Using Freire's terms, I would want to argue that the *objectivism* of Berlin's classrooms lies in his insistence upon neomarxist methods for reading and writing the world that leave students without the will or means to assume responsibility for their own literacies. By contrast, the *subjectivism* of Shor's classrooms is in the ways that he focuses primarily upon transforming students' consciousnesses while leaving the material structures of classrooms and academic institutions intact and unchanged. In the case of the former, the goal is to master a particular way of reading and writing, which reenacts a classroom narrative not unlike the banking mode of education—an exchange of cultural values being the only difference between Berlin's literacies and conventional academic literacies. In the case of the latter, the focus of classroom attention is upon students' worlds and students' lives beyond the classroom, and—potentially, at the expense of their lives within the classroom—is achieved in

patients' charts, and I recall the recognition during one morning mass of discovering the discursive organization behind lines and stanzas of church songs.

For the most part, writing and reading were things I did at home, because my peers were different, and things I did at school. In my mind, reading and writing were obvious responses when the adults grew weary of conversations or when I had finished the week's homework on Monday because, for as long as I can remember, I have been obsessed by language and discourse. As a child, my nickname was WJBM—the call letters of the local talk radio station. My mother claims that the year before I started school, I approached a future teacher to explain that my father was an obstetrician and gynecologist and that I would explain those words if she wanted. During elementary school, I would read the dictionary for hours, fascinated by things I'd learn later to call polysemy and etymology. Early in my first year at the Catholic grade school that I would attend for eight years, one of the nuns' took me to the pubic library after school and persuaded the angry librarians to allow me to check out whatever books I wanted. Teachers began to send me to the school's library during class, so often, in fact, that most of my memories from grade school are of climbing chairs to retrieve a book from the shelf and then reading, for hours on end, ways that leave them without the literacies to survive their psychology classes and their economics courses, let alone to transform the institutionalized ethnic, gender, and class biases of academia. Moreover, again, I will suggest that Shor's classroom practices are particularly difficult for students to negotiate because of the ways that they embed an ultimate legitimacy in the literacy practices of the academy while appearing to recognize the legitimacy of students' literacies.

And while I may be tipping my hand too early, let me explain that, in subsequent chapters, I want to examine classroom practices that aspire to a collaborative legitimacy by bringing together both the objectivism of sanctioned discursive practices (including, yet not limited to conventional academic ways of writing and reading) with the subjectivism of students' and teachers' experiences, both inside and beyond the classroom, and aspire as well to a version of literaci(es) that enables students to reread and rewrite classrooms and the academy through the ways that they negotiate contingent ways of reading and writing in specific contexts. First, a word about the postmodern critical literacies of Berlin and Shor.

THE CLASSROOM PRACTICES AND LITERACIES OF JAMES BERLIN

Though James Berlin consistently challenges the practices of conventional English departments, he is perhaps most explicit about his

until I wandered back to the classroom. By fourth or fifth grade, I had read myself through most of the books in that small, Catholic school library, at least the books I wanted to read, such as Poe's *The Fall of the House of Usher* or biographies of Benjamin Franklin or Allan Pinkerton. I even tried reading some of the ones that were uninteresting, such as *Punt, Pass, and Kick,* but I quickly abandoned these in favor of rereading the ones I previously read.

From that day in first grade, I became an outsider even within my own homogeneous—white, middle class, rural, catholic— community. Increasingly aware of this outsider status, I began to insist that I was being sent to the library because I was being punished for talking too much in class, and I started arguing with older students that A's actually meant awful and F's fantastic. By the time that one teacher began bringing books, such as Orwell's 1984 or Dickens's *A Tale of Two Cities,* for me, I had perfected elaborate resistances, which I would detail to my peers, until I succumbed to my curiosity a night or two before my response to the book was due.

High school was worse though by this time I had learned to sit silently through honors courses as I completed grammar drills and read ahead in the textbook while the teacher lectured on the genealogy of Zeus and alternatives in *Rhetorics, Poetics, and Cultures*, and since, as he explains in his acknowledgements, *Poetics* elaborates and expands upon texts and ideas that previously appeared in a number of other venues, I will rely predominantly upon it in my efforts to describe his classrooms and the literacies they endorse (ix). Specifically, the part of *Poetics* that I want to focus upon is his description of two hypothetical courses, based upon experiences which he and teaching assistants had over the previous four years,[19] that serves as his material performance of his disciplinary and institutional challenges. His introduction to these courses is important, particularly in the ways that he theorizes about them: "Both are designed to involve students in an equal share of writing and reading, with student responses at the center of classroom activity. The two courses insist on a balanced inclusion of poetical and rhetorical texts. In short, they are intended to challenge the old disciplinary binaries that privilege consumption over production and the aesthetic over the rhetorical" (*Poetics* 115). His prototype for an alternative literature course, which he calls "The Discourse of the Revolution," is organized around "a consideration of signifying practices and their relation to subject formation within the contexts of power at . . . important moments in political and textual history, focusing on texts and their contexts in England during the time of the two

Hera. All the while, I maintained that distinction between the writing and reading outside of school and the writing and reading in school.

In my first year of high school, I qualified for the summer Gifted Program with the second highest score in the school, and refusing scores directing me towards math and science, I persuaded school officials to allow me into the English program, where I publicized my desire to learn to write. After a session or two of the thesis statement and unity and coherence, I explained to the teacher that I wanted real writing, not school writing. So the next day, upon returning from a walk in the neighborhood around the school, she asked us to describe what we had seen, and on reading my description, she assured me that I would never become a writer.

That fall, I was assigned to Charles Tom VonAlmen's sophomore honors English class. The rumors about him—that he had been a green beret in the war, that he had stuffed a student in a locker, that he was the meanest teacher in the district—scared me more than the summer teacher's declaration. On the first day of class, VonAlmen cursed at me because I was too frightened to ask my question again, and yet before the semester was over, he would become my best friend. Partway into the semester, he approached me during class revolutions at the end of the eighteenth century—roughly between 1775 and 1800"(131-32). The course serves as a site where students examine both rhetorical and poetic discourse in "interacting generic, ideological, and socioeconomic environments" in order to enable them "to consider the ways in which the signifying practices in texts were working to form subjects, to create particular kinds of consciousness along the lines of gender, class, race, age, sexual orientation, and related categories" (135). In this classroom, students would read rhetorical texts in ways that elicit "the recommended subject position" and poetic texts in order to understand "the intense conflict over poetic forms that appeared at this time and the relation of these differences to economics and politics" (137, 139). In a related way, Berlin's prototype for an alternative composition course, which he calls "Codes and Critiques," centers, at least in theory, around "reading and writing the daily experiences of culture, with culture considered in its broadest formulation" through a variety of texts, including advertising, television, and film: "The course consists of six units: advertising, work, play, education, gender, and individuality. Each unit begins by examining a variety of texts that feature competing representations of and orientations toward the topic of the unit" (116). With the central concern as "the relations of current signifying

because he heard that I was training for the St. Louis Marathon, and he had just started running. Besides our affair with language, our interest in running became the basis for our friendship until his death just before I finished the Ph.D. Over the next several years of high school, he and I would talking about books as we ran across miles and miles of empty country roads, and on the weekends, I would sit in his living room with his wife and kids as he talked about a piece of my writing I had shown him.

In many ways, college wasn't much different. To be sure, there were certain classes that engaged me, such as my introductory history course where the professor asked us to read Neil Postman's *Amusing Ourselves to Death*, or my introductory composition course where Jeff Skoblow, who would become my mentor for the Dean's College, spoke about writing in ways I could recognize. However, most of my classes were more of the same—sitting through lectures, memorizing lists, taking multiple choice exams, etc. My literature and composition classes were so dissatisfying that I changed my major seven or eight times, yet I always returned to English hoping, like a battered spouse, that this time, things would be different. Unfortunately, the Shakespeare comedies classes and the American literature surveys were more about tests and grades and less about practices to the structuring of subjectivities," this course begins with students' experiences and encourages them to negotiate and to resist these codes towards "more democratic and personally humane economic, social, and political arrangements," which is the only way for students to become "genuinely competent writers and readers" (116). In exploring these units, students are to "discuss the culturally coded character of all parts of composing—from genre to patterns of organization to sentence structure" in an attempt to understand how inconsistencies are not problems of reference but rather "interferences of a social and political nature," and the ultimate goal of "Codes and Critiques" is to prepare students for "critical citizenship in a democracy" (130-31).

From these classroom practices, it is possible to understand the version of literacy that dominates Berlin's classrooms. In theory, the literacy of Berlin's classroom identifies the practices of reading and writing as "inescapably political act[s], the working out of contested cultural codes affecting every feature of experience" that rely upon "teachers in an effort to problematize students' experiences, requiring them to challenge the ideological codes students bring to college by placing their signifying practices against alternatives" (131). In fact, he is quite explicit in his theorizing about the functions of discursive practices in his classrooms:

satisfying reading and writing. During my last semester, I signed up for an advanced writing course, where I first began writing about the problems I encountered in classrooms, the same problems that would become the basis for this book.

Unconvinced that graduate school would be any different and yet unsure of what else to do next, I took the GRE examination one bright January morning and emerged to gloomy winter afternoon feeling stupider than I had ever felt before. Five weeks later, I discovered that I had earned a nearly perfect score in math, an almost perfect score in logic, *and a mediocre score in verbal abilities*. Convinced that the problem was mine, I explored philosophy, education, and other graduate programs and, in fact, sat through my first graduate course in a different department, before returning to the English department, where in pursuing a M.A. with a specialization in writing, I once again hoped for the reading and writing that were satisfying and fulfilling. The writing classes were interesting, and the classes in women's literature, class literature, and gothic literature were less stultifying. At the same time, I entered the classroom as a teacher at the veteran age of twenty-two at the St. Louis Community College teaching two sections of at-risk writers.

In the spring, I arranged to do an independent study on

In enacting the reading and writing process, students learn that all experience is situated within signifying practices and that learning to understand personal and social experience involves acts of discourse production and interpretation, the two acting reciprocally in reading and writing codes. Students discover that interpretation involves production as well as reproduction and is as constructive as composing itself. (130)

From this theoretical vantage, the practices of reading and writing in Berlin's classrooms are acts in which "different conceptions of economic, social, and political conditions are contested with consequences for the formation of the subjects of history, the consciousness of the historical agent," which necessarily rely upon context in order to generate meaning (132).

Comparing the practices of Berlin's two classrooms, the acts of reading and writing appear somewhat different. In his literature classroom, the act of reading involves a conventionally prescribed method from secondary to primary sources, a method that, in the end, maintains the rhetorical-poetic distinction that he seeks to dissolve. For example, students begin their reading of rhetorical texts with a "consideration of concrete economic, social, and political events of the period," such as Michel Beaud's *A History of Capitalism* or Linda Colley's *Britons: Forging the Nation*, and then turn to "changes in publication practices and the reading public, in Ian Watt's "The Reading Public and the Rise of the Novel" or

T. S. Eliot and Wallace Stevens when I discovered the Gateway Writing Project, the local site of the National Writing Project. Immediately, I dropped the independent study and applied for Gateway's summer invitational institute, which was scheduled to meet for six weeks during July and August at Harris Stowe State College. During these six weeks, Michael Lowenstein, Jane Zeni, and others at Gateway provided me with a model of education (teachers teaching teachers), a methodology (reflective practice and action research), and, perhaps most importantly, a discourse which would enable me to talk about my experiences as a student and, increasingly, as a teacher, thereby extending what had, up to that point, been a personal search into a social context—the discourse of critical literacy.

That summer, Michael concurred that the legitimacy of a Ph.D. in English would afford me the authority to continue my efforts to understand the disparity between literacies in the world and literacies in the classroom and to construct classrooms in which I could bring the satisfying experiences of writing and reading from my life outside of the academy. Because of my previous experiences with

Bridge Hill's *Women, Work, and Sexual Politics in Eighteenth-Century England* (132-34). Only after completing their readings of the context can students turn to reading primary texts, such as George Campbell's *The Philosophy of Rhetoric* or Hannah More's *Strictures on the Modern System of Female Education*, a process which is prescriptively begins with determining "the recommended subject position" by eliciting "who is allowed to speak and who is allowed to listen and act on the message of the speaker," then considering "rules for evidence" in ways that raise "questions of epistemology and ideology" by uncovering "the available means of persuasion, principles that distinguish true from untrue knowledge, indicating what counts as real and what is ephemeral, what is good, and what is possible," and finally ascertaining "the manner in which language is conceived in each rhetoric, considering its relation to knowledge and its role in bringing about agreement and disagreement" (132-34, 137-

the GRE, I refused to retake the general test, and could see no merit in taking the literature sub-test, so I found myself limited in the graduate programs to which I could apply. Eventually, I found a small program that would enable me to concentrate in the areas that fascinated me since childhood even as I could also do minors in linguistics and American literature. As it turned out, working with Ann Dobie and others in this program offered a productive blend of independence and direction, and in addition to continuing my association with the National Writing Project, I also began to explore the politics of literacies inside, across, and outside the academy, along with critical pedagogies, the cultures of institutions, and postmodern theory. Surely I would be able to understand my experiences and to generate the satisfying writing and reading, at first for myself and, more and more, for the students with whom I continued to work.

138). As for reading poetic texts, students follow a similar pattern for secondary texts except for the fact that the texts are identified as works of poetic theory and criticism, such as Samuel Johnson's *Rasselas* or "Preface from Shakespeare," appropriate sections from Hugh Blair's *Lectures on Rhetoric and Belles Lettres*, and William Wordsworth's "Preface to *Lyrical Ballads*"(140). Again, students can, only after completing their readings of a theoretical context, turn to "poetry itself," beginning with canonical texts, such as Johnson's *The Vanity of Human Wishes* or George Crabbe's *The Village* and then, considering noncanonical texts, such as Anna Leatitia Barbauld's "Washing Day" and "To the Poor" or Phyllis Wheatley's *Poems on Various Subjects Religious and Moral* (141-42).

In a similar way, Berlin is surprisingly prescriptive as to what it means to read in his composition classroom. In his explanation, for example, of how students are to read a newspaper article from *The Wall Street Journal* entitled "The Days of a Cowboy Are Marked by Danger, Drudgery, and Low Pay" from a unit on work, he instructs them, first, to begin by considering the context through "exploring the characteristics of the readership of the newspaper and the historical events surrounding the essay's production" in order to identify "key signifiers" (117). Next, readers are told to "place these terms within the narrative structural forms suggested by the text, the culturally coded stories about patterns of behavior appropriate for people within certain situations," such as race, class, and gender (118). Finally, they are directed to "situate these narrative patterns within larger narrative structures that have to do with economic, political, and cultural formations," such as examining "capitalist economic narratives as demonstrated in the essay and their consequences for class, gender, and race relations and roles both in the workplace and elsewhere," such as the distribution of work in beef production (118–19). In the same unit on work, Berlin instructs students to read "selected episodes" from situational comedies in order "to learn to analyze television codes as well as to gather evidence for their essays on the cultural organization of work and its place in forming subjectivity in their lives" (120). In reading this way, students "learn to see these domestic comedies not as simple presentations of reality but as re-presentations—that is coded constructions—of an imagined reality" (120).

Given his ostensive agenda, it is surprising that Berlin is much less explicit and voluminous about the practices of writing in his classrooms.[20] At one point, he writes that students **"should** keep journals, prepare position papers for the class, and even imitate and parody the materials of the late eighteenth century in an attempt to understand the methods of signification called upon and their relationship to economic, social, political, and cultural constructions" (136). Besides this list, Berlin suggests that "students' final project might thus be to critique these simple binaries [in neoclassical and romantic poetry], testing the adequacy of them when measured against their own estimates" (144). Nevertheless, he is much more elaborate about the practices of writing and thinking in his composition classroom though he is no less prescriptive in both form and functions. For example, he asserts that students, in response to their readings of situational comedies, should begin by producing "descriptions of the physical settings of the homes and the characteristic dress of the characters depicted in the two programs" in order "to recognize that the sets and costumes are created by the producers of the shows" and "not simply video copies of actual homes and people . . ." (120). Such descriptions, he claims, lead students naturally into dialogues about the depicted class differences and the relation of these differences to "work, income, and ideology," which, in turn, become discussions and analyses of "subject formation, television, and cultural codes" (120-21, 122-23). Finally, students are instructed to consider "the medium's effects in shaping subjectivity among views" and to discuss "the manner in which they negotiate and resist cultural codes championed in the programs that they watch" in order "to come to terms with the apparatuses of culture as they create consciousness" (123-24). The net result of this and other prescribed processes are fairly traditional texts, such as descriptions or analytical essays— though, to be fair, he does encourage parodies, and reports that he has "experimented with students producing their own short videotaped productions" (120, 129, 136, and 128).

Given these discursive practices, the sanctioned subject positions of the literacy in Berlin's classrooms are somewhat different from those positions endorsed by conventional academic literacies. Theoretically, Berlin asserts that, in his classrooms, discursive practices are explicitly connected to "larger historical conditions and the formation of historical agents" in the process of "consciousness formation within concrete historical conditions" (*Poetics* 105; "Literacy" 261). As such, the subjectivity of readers and writers represent "the point of convergence of conflicted discourses" and is "itself the product of discourse rather than the initiator of it," and not, he seems to suggest, what students do with these discourses ("Literacy" 261). In practice, the sanctioned subject positions are ones from which students can interpret and critique alternative discursive practices and see the value of political struggle and democratic education (*Poetics* 112). For example, students must assume positions from which they can compare "representations of the two revolutions" in order to understand "the varied formulations that different generic, ideological, and socioeconomic frames encourage," as is the case in his literature course, or from which they can analyze newspaper articles from *The Wall Street Journal* within their "generic, ideological, and socioeconomic environment[s]" (145, 117). To assume these positions, students must be willing to resist the "cultural codes, the competing discourses that influence their position as subjects of experience," including, presumably, those they have experienced in more traditional classrooms (116). For another example, students must assume vantages from which they can identify textual binaries, cultural conflicts, sanctioned subject positions, textualized rules for evidence and meaning, and the function of language in knowledge and communication (117, 132, 137, and 138). Through developing awarenesses that language and textuality are "the terrain on which different conceptions of economic, social, and political conditions are contested," students can develop "different conceptions of economic, social, and political conditions" in ways that give rise to new subject positions of readers and writers for **"critical** citizenship in a democracy" (131).

In a related way, the discursive practices of Berlin's classrooms give rise to versions of the world that challenge those sanctioned by conventional academic literacies. Berlin theorizes that his alternative classrooms define literacy as the act of empowering students and others to name the world as it is experienced, in order to act and to assume control even as literacy "enables the individual to understand that the conditions of experience are made by human agents and thus can be remade by human agents" (101). In his classrooms, meaning and knowledge, he asserts, are the results of experiences situated within discursive practices, and reality—which is defined by economic, social, and political terms—is negotiated through discourse and language (130, 131). Similar to shifts in the subject positions of students, the sanctioned positions for teachers and the versions of learning and education shift, theoretically, in Berlin's classrooms to one from which teachers encourage "complex reading and writing strategies and practices" in order to facilitate an understanding of English studies as "the signifying practices of text production—academic discourse, political discourse, poetic discourse, scientific discourse, media discourse—as well as the signifying practices of text reception," both of which must be considered in historical and ideological contexts in ways that foreground the politics of literacy (111). In a similar, and theoretical, way, canonical epistemologies, as well as the canon itself, are a product of discursive practices and the functions of literacy and education are primarily to prepare students "for public discourse in a democratic political community" and secondarily to prepare them "for personal and private pleasure" and for "communication in their careers" (110).

However, the practices of Berlin's classrooms suggest a different story, one that comes much closer to resembling conventional classrooms insofar as traditional academic literacies and Berlin's political literacy are both literacies-from-above. At least in the ways that he describes his classroom practices in *Rhetorics, Poetics, and Cultures,* his agenda, and an academically legitimate agenda at that, is imposed upon students through his classroom practices, as well as the version of literacy that they naturalize, that center upon rhetorical and poetic discourse in "interacting generic, ideological, and socioeconomic environments," an agenda for learning and literacy that is imported into classrooms and imposed upon students rather than being an agenda that is collaboratively negotiated with students. (As other critics have pointed out, Berlin privileges his own cultural capital, an academic cultural capital, at the expense of others.[21]) Though, in theory, he does do something of a postmodern reading of critical literacy, his classroom practices subordinate this postmodern critical literacy to his neo-marxist cultural agenda in a way that denies the context-specific conditions of critical literacies in favor of the context-free, or universalized, culturally neo-marxist literacy. Though he professes to recognize the authority of students' experiences, he situates them, at best, as qualified participants who merely supply their experiences and react, for example, to teachers, who select the six units of study and the texts to be analyzed in composition classrooms and who determine which versions of "the history of the time" are most useful and which primary and secondary texts to consume in literature classrooms (116-17, 132, 136). Surprisingly, Berlin acknowledges the significance of authority: "As I indicated earlier, authority should be shared **as much as possible**. While the teacher sets up the syllabus, maps out a diverse body of readings, and offers methods for responding to them, students should have a choice in activities, assume leadership roles in instruction, and participate in an ongoing dialogue on the issues explored" (135). In designating teachers alone as the source of syllabi, readings, and literacy practices, Berlin endorses paternalistic practices in classrooms. In spite of any professed desire to authorize students, these classrooms constrain students, for instance, to presenting their groups' interpretations of texts recommended to them, seeking conflicts in social narratives identified for them, and completing assignments given to them (135-36), none of which invests them with legitimacy.

As is always the case, his classroom practices, as discursive acts, give rise to subject positions for students and teachers. In his descriptions of his classroom practices, Berlin actually acknowledges the ways that his classroom practices give rise to qualified positions for students characterized by an explicit essentialism that reflects his neo-marxist agenda:

> We start with the personal experience of students, with emphasis on the position of this experience within its formative context. Our main concern is the relation of current signifying practices to the structuring of subjectivities—of race, class, sexual orientation, age, ethnic, and gender formations, for example—in our students and ourselves. The effort is to make students aware of cultural codes, the competing discourses that influence their position as subjects of experience. Our larger purpose is to encourage students to negotiate and resist these codes—these hegemonic discourses—to bring about more democratic and personally humane economic, social, and political arrangements. From our perspective, only in this way can students become genuinely competent writers and readers. (116)

What makes it more confusing is the way that he professes to be examining the relation of "signifying practices to the structuring of subjectivities," all the while providing essentialized subject positions for students, the positions of cultural studies, through his classroom practices. In a similar way, not only does Berlin deny difference in the subject positions of the co-teachers in his "mentor groups at Purdue" whose "shared experiences over the past four years" gave rise to these practices, but he also sanctions essentialized subject positions for student readers and writers, through his own (hegemonic) discourse, that prescribe against difference. Not surprisingly, these practices and subject positions produce universalized versions of meaning and learning and education that are imposed upon classrooms and students. For example, engaging in the naturalized ways of reading imposed upon his composition classrooms "leads, in turn to the a consideration of the ways conflicts in cultural codes are typically resolved in television programs," which, in the case of *Family Ties*, "the program tended to present the upper-middle-class professional nuclear family as in itself the answer to all of life's problems—an extension, one student noted, of the Reagan administration's contention about the place of the family in resolving economic and social problems" (123). Though I believe that one student whom Berlin cites did, in fact, connect *Family Ties* to the Reagan administration, I wonder whether the readings of other students, whose voices are conspicuously missing, were permitted to read *Family Ties* differently. If we are to take Berlin at his own word ("From our perspective, only in this way can students become genuinely competent writers and readers."), I think we can safely assume that they were not.

As such, Berlin's practices produce a classroom literacy in which students have education done to them, from above—versions of literacy and education that are discredited in Freire's most cited work on critical literacies[22]—rather than classrooms in which students' literacies have any credibility or authority. In this way, Berlin enacts an objectivism that seeks to transform the objective world without a corresponding shift in students' subjectivities. In Berlin's classrooms, students exchange the uniformity of conventional academic literacies for the uniformity of culturally neo-marxist literacies. Though Berlin, in theory, connects students' awarenesses of the relationships between discourses and experiences to "more democratic and personally humane economic, social, and political arrangements," the ways that he insists upon naturalized ways of reading and writing, conventional roles for students and teachers, and traditionally hierarchical versions of meaning and education ensure that students continue to do student-ing in the authorized ways. Again, there is a seeming inconsistency between Berlin's practice of theory and his practice of teaching. In theorizing about the ways of reading rhetorical texts in his literature classroom, Berlin writes that

> [i]n examining the sections of these rhetorics selected by the teacher—or, as often happens, by a student group working collaboratively—class members should

interrogate the texts in a particular way. This does not mean, I should caution, that one only method of reading should be tolerated in the class. No one expects students to abandon their customary methods of interpreting texts. Indeed, old and new hermeneutic strategies should interact in the students' reaction to the text, and this interaction should become a part of the ongoing class discussion as well as written assignments. (137)

First, Berlin's ostensive collaboration is not quite a shared authority but a qualified authority that ultimately fails to challenge the authority of the teacher.[23] Earlier, he explains that, since "[a]ll texts cannot be read in their entirety," small groups are assigned, or perhaps allowed to select among "the diverse body of readings" that the teacher "maps out" (135). Second, what seems to be a contradiction between instructing students to "interrogate the texts in a particular way" and tolerating multiple methods of reading is resolved in Berlin's ensuing explanation: "Students **should first** determine the recommended subject position of the interlocutor portrayed in the rhetoric along with the corresponding subject position indicated for the audience," and "[s]tudents **should also** examine the rules for evidence these rhetorics display, a concern that deals with questions of epistemology and ideology" (137). In a similar way, Berlin's explanation of reading situational comedies in his composition course invokes a determined way of producing texts, beginning with students "writing descriptions of the physical settings in the homes and the characteristic dress of the characters depicted in the two programs" and concluding with them discussing "the manner in which they negotiate and resist the cultural codes championed in the programs they watch" (120-23). Furthermore, he fails to consider whether the students who appear in his classrooms actually value discursive practices that interrogate cultural codes or whether they are forced to accommodate them in order to pass the courses, almost implying that these particular ways of reading and writing are relevant and credible to all students. Moreover, Berlin is silent about his classroom practices in response to readers and writers who, for one reason or another, refuse to engage in the discursive practices that he suggests the "must" or "should" do.

By prescribing the results of these and other discursive practices and by neglecting to consider their relevance for specific students and particular semesters, Berlin has virtually ensured that all of the students in his classrooms remain relegated to conventional roles in traditional classrooms—the same ones that many students with whom I have worked have encountered throughout most of their educational histories. Similar to the idealized reader sanctioned through the practices of the best-selling textbooks, the ideal reader in

Berlin's classrooms is essentialized with only the basis for this essentialization different. For example, a reader who cannot, or will not, distinguish between the function and authority of Colley's *Britons: Forging the Nation* and More's *Strictures on the Modern System of Female Education* or who cannot, or will not, recognize "narrative patterns" or who cannot, or will not, situate them "within larger narrative structures that have to do with economic, political, and cultural formations," or who cannot, or will not, even recognize such formations as authoritative or relevant, will not be able to read successfully, at least in the ways that Berlin defines reading in his classroom assignments (134, 137, and 118). In a similar way, Berlin's classrooms invoke a foundational world that gives rise to universalized understanding of education and of English studies, with the only difference being that Berlin privileges a neo-marxist foundationalism instead of the enlightenment foundationalism. For example, Berlin's foundationalism can be seen in his explanation of the context for his literature classroom:

> Convictions about the existent, the good, and the possible are premises based on conceptions of the **economic**—the **production, distribution, exchange,** and **consumption** of **wealth**—and of political power—the distribution of authority in decision making. During the late eighteenth century, for example, disagreements in England about the colonies usually involved the place of the New World in the **economic** pursuits that England was encouraging for its own **profit**. Yet the arguments that disputants offered frequently underplayed the **economic** interests of an emergent **merchant** class and the compromise it had reached with the old **aristocratic** class in favor of religious or patriarchal concerns—the moral responsibilities of the governed to their government or the natural duties of a child to a parent. The emergence of a new ruling group in **economics** and politics was thus at the heart of the dispute, but the ideological terms of the issue often assumed the language of the old order. Arguments about taste in literature likewise usually involved **class conflicts** created by the **economic** ascendancy of the **capitalist class**. (107)

Though he uses conditionals, such as usually and frequently, he clearly privileges a neo-marxist narrative, which he offers as an undisputed basis for meaning, knowledge, and understanding not only of eighteenth century England but also of his literature classrooms. Not only does this neo-marxist narrative form the basis for meaning in Berlin's literature classrooms, but it also serves as the foundation for his version of the discipline:

> English courses **must** become self-consciously committed to the study of divergent reading and writing practices. Whatever literary and rhetorical texts are chosen, all **must** be considered in relation to their conditions of **production, distribution,**

> **exchange**, and **reception**. Students **should** examine both the variety of audiences for these texts and the variety of ways that texts were received in their own time as well as the corresponding audiences and reception strategies across time. (105).

In failing to acknowledge that conflict is the defining characteristic of education and academia (as Gerald Graff argues in *Beyond the Culture Wars*) Berlin denies the provisional condition of his narrative and offers it as a foundation from which the eighteenth century in England, his literature classrooms, and the discipline of English studies can be understood. Finally, it is telling, I think, that Berlin is able to recognize the political dimensions of authority and decision making in the eighteenth century, but he does not acknowledge the same dimensions of his classrooms, a condition that while perhaps leading to minor changes in the focus of English classrooms, ultimately leaves students' subject positions, as well as their experiences in and of meaning and education, unchanged.

In spite of the ways that his classroom practices impose a literacy-from-above and enact versions of meaning and education that ignore the presence of students, there is much that I value about Berlin's classroom practices—the ways that it foregrounds the interplay of discursive practices and reality, the use of historical and social contexts in which to understand texts and meaning, or the importance of education that produces social change (117-19, 131-35, and 102 ff). However, their shortcomings ultimately raise important questions about legitimacy and literacies that his classrooms cannot resolve. Though, personally and professionally, I value the ways of reading and writing that Berlin endorses in his classrooms, I am uncertain whether teachers should insist that students read and write in these ways. And I am even less comfortable with the idea of assessing and evaluating on these terms students who do not find these literacies relevant to their experiences and their lives. By insisting upon the literacies that Berlin has sanctioned, teachers potentially deny the autonomy and legitimacy of students' own literacy agendas. For example, his emphasis upon a particular methodology leaves students without the will or the means to assume responsibility for their own literacies, and his classroom practices do not enable students to reread and rewrite his own classroom, let alone academic institutions. At the same time, these practices deny the contingency of the classroom upon teachers and students, and they give rise to a version of literacy that, at least in its essentialism and foundationalism, maintains the conditions that critics have called a crisis in literacy and meaning. I would argue that the literacies that Berlin endorses would be relevant only in classrooms in which, prior to instruction, all of the students indicated a desire to develop neo-marxist, or, at the minimum, resistant, ways of reading, writing, and thinking. As a result, I question how much his classroom practices empower students, as he claims they do, for in the end, they amount to naming the world for students in particular ways.

THE CLASSROOM PRACTICES OF IRA SHOR

At this point, I want to shift the focus from Berlin's classroom practices to the classroom practices of Ira Shor in order to consider a somewhat different problem with the ways that postmodern critical literacies are produced in the classrooms of American colleges and universities. If Berlin's problem is an objectivist literacy-from-above, then Shor's problem lies in the ways that, in his practices, he neglects the politics of the dominant literacies by privileging literacies-from-below, all the while tacitly dismissing these literacies—a contradiction that not only fails to resolve the conditions that have been called a crisis in literacy and education in American but also neglects students' literacy needs and disempowers them further. Since Shor spends most of his time describing classroom practices generally and much less time on the practices of literature and composition classes specifically, I will follow his lead and describe his theorizing about his classroom practices in general (about which he is most explicit in *Empowering Education*) and then I will turn to his descriptions of literature and composition classrooms specifically.

In theorizing his classroom practices as "student-centered" yet "not permissive or self-centered," Shor explains that the practices are "negotiated, requiring leadership by the teacher and mutual teacher-student authority" that "does not teach students to seek self-centered gain while ignoring public welfare" (*Empowering* 15-16). In his classrooms, students "develop skills and knowledge as well as high expectations for themselves, their education, and their future" (16). Though teachers lead and direct the curriculum, they do so "democratically with the participation of the students, balancing the need for structure with the need for openness" (16). Theoretically, teachers contribute "lesson plans, learning methods, personal experience, and academic knowledge to the class," and yet, at the same time, they negotiate "the curriculum" with students and begin with the "language, themes, and understandings" of students (16). Within his explicit "agenda of values," these classrooms, he theorizes, are participatory, affective, problem-posing, situated, multicultural, dialogic, desocializing, democratic, researching, interdisciplinary, and activist (17 ff). Later, Shor outlines a general framework of model for classrooms practices:

Pose a problem→Write on it→Literacy development→Peer group discussion/ selection→Class dialogue→Pose a new problem→Write on it→Literacy development→Peer group discussion→Class dialogue→Integrate reading material→Writing/dialogue on the

readings→Interim evaluation/adjustment of the process→Dialogic lecture→Student
response to lecture→Discussion solutions/actionsIf possible, take action and reflect on
it→Pose new problem→End-term evaluation. (252-53)

Though he suggests that "[t]he dialogic process is self-evolving, not standardized," he explains that these "phases," in his own words, "help me focus on dialogic practices" (237). Nevertheless, he acknowledges that the model "should
not be followed as a prescription or taken as guarantee of success" because
"[t]eaching requires the creative reinvention of even good suggestions so that
methods reflect the local situations" (253).

Elsewhere in *Empowering Education*, Shor describes how his theories about
a "dialogic process" would be reflected in classroom practices of literature and
composition classrooms. In a hypothetical literature classroom in New York,
Shor explains that he might begin by asking students to write and discuss their
responses to the question "Is street violence a problem in your lives?," after
which he would instruct them to transcribe their "family members' opinions
on the issues" for class discussion, thereby extending "the inquiry into everyday life and make the theme a family experience, not merely a classroom-
bound exercise" (81). Next, he explains that he would ask students "to jot
down their ideas, expand their notes, and choose the order for the points they
wanted to make in their essay" before using peer critiques designed to discuss
good writing and the problem of violence. Then, he describes how he would
"stimulate their imagination in rethinking this social problem" by asking them
"to produce fiction," such as a story in which "someone tries to stop violence in
[their] neighborhood," which, after revising in response to feedback they had
received from their families, he would publish in "booklets for the school and
neighborhood" (82). Only after "seeking the audiences to read the students'
stories to encourage their self-image as writers" would he turn to the literary
texts by comparing "how violence has appeared in different texts through the
ages—the official literature published in books"—including nonfiction narratives and sociological essays, as well as fiction—"compared to their unofficial
self-created texts" (82). Turning to history, this literature class next "could
move backward in time, to examine other moments of violence, like the slave
revolt of Spartacus or accounts of Wat Tyler and the Middle Ages or *Romeo
and Juliet* or *Henry IV* or the Puritan Army debates of the 1640s or chronicles
of Columbus pillaging the Native American societies that he found or narratives of slave life and rebellion in the Old South" or numerous others (82).
Regardless of which direction it took, Shor explains, he would instruct students to compare the reactions of their families to one piece of "literature" that
the students read aloud. Finally, he would ask students to respond to another

set of questions, such as "what changes are needed to reduce violence? What should the mayor do to make your neighborhood safe? What should the police do? What should neighbors themselves do?," which, with the students' permissions, he "might send . . . to the mayor, the police chief, to local papers, and to community organizations for their reply" (82).[24]

As for typical composition classrooms, Shor describes a first-year writing course at a "mostly white college in New York City," in which he began by asking students to write in response to a series of questions: "What is good writing?," "How do you become a good writer?," "What questions do you have about good writing?," and "What are the hardest and easiest things for you as a writer?" (37). After rereading their responses individually, students read their responses to a partner, focusing upon similarities and differences in their answers, and then they read their responses to the entire class, after which Shor and the students discussed each question (38). The students' replies, along with his own, formed the basis for following classes, which, after exhausting this initial focus, centered upon other social issues: "I asked them to write down the social issues most important to them and to bring in news articles about them, as their self-selected themes and reading material. I photocopied some of their readings for class discussion and compiled a list of their themes in ballot form. They voted on which we should take up in class" (38-39). Finally, Shor "re-presented their most popular themes," such as personal growth, in what he describes as "a long process of writing, reading, discussion, and critical inquiry" (39).

If the sanctioned version of literacy in Berlin's classrooms is noticeably different from conventional academic literaci(es), then the version of literacy that Shor's classroom practices, at least at first glance, seems more so. These practices, Shor theorizes, take part in what he calls "a dialogic pedagogy," which is "initiated by a critical teacher but is democratically open to student intervention," a pedagogy that strives to balance "the teacher's authority and the students' input" in a way that includes students' "right to question the content and the process of dialogue, and even to reject them" (85-86). Drawing on Freire, Shor asserts that not only does dialogue connect people "through discourse" and "moments of reflection to moments of action," but it also offers an implicit challenge to the practices and content of traditional classrooms:

> Dialogue is a democratic, directed, and critical discourse different from teacher-student exchanges in traditional classrooms. For one thing, it becomes a meeting ground to reconcile students and teachers separated by the unilateral authority of the teacher in traditional education. Secondly, dialogue is a mutually created discourse which questions existing canons of knowledge and challenges power relations in the classroom and in society. (86, 87)

Unlike Berlin, Shor seems to make no distinction between poetic and rhetorical discursive practices in the way he theorizes literature and composition classrooms. In these, reading and writing are established as mutually informing practices that, at least to some degree, invoke each other. For example, Shor offers a number of approaches to *Henry V* in a Shakespeare class that invoke this dialogic relationship among various discursive practices: enacting the opening scene and relating it to students' experiences; responding to the theme of power throughout the play; debating Hal's right to the throne within the context of Salic Law and Hal's family tree; using the play to launch a discussion about the relative status of national laws, such as slavery or the unions; comparing the play to other social injustices in American society; rewriting scenes and speeches in order to experiment with alternatives; and others (152-56). In regard to the composition classroom described earlier, Shor writes that

> [i]nstruction in writing began with this participatory approach. It continued in a student-centered way as I used their questions about good writing as starting points for more exercises—"How do you begin writing an essay?" for instance. Instead of delivering a lecture about good writing or assigning exercises in grammar or providing a model essay for students to imitate, I presented good writing as the first problem to write on and discuss, drawing out their words and perspectives as initial texts for discussion and more writing. This class began from their own starting points, which I re-presented to them as further problemsfor writing and debate. (38)

As dialogic and mutually informing, these discursive practices theoretically supplement traditional academic practices of reading and writing, insofar as they legitimize traditionally dismissed practices, such as producing ethnographies in literature classrooms or reading newspaper articles in composition classrooms.

According to Shor's theoretical explanations, the version of literacy sanctioned by his classroom practices offer a range of subject positions for students. Unlike Berlin, Shor acknowledges the legitimacy of positions of resistance, both to traditional classroom practices and to his own classroom practices. For example, he describes the ways that students were able to resist his learning contracts or attendance politics (*When* 92 ff). To this end, Shor's practices even authorize various resistant positions, such as the "scholasticons", or positions assumed by the "handful" of students who "want to sit" near the teacher and who "identify with school discipline while expressing their own novel forms of resistance," and the "siberians", or the positions assumed by those students who fill "the distant corners first, representing their subordinate and alienated position, which drives them to seek the remote seats of any classroom they inhabit," these self-constructed "intellectual exiles as far from the front of the room as they can be" (13, 12). Through the practices of his classrooms, he theorizes, students recognize "that socialization and curriculum are political processes of inclusion and exclusion," and they are thereby authorized to reread and rewrite their positions as students and their classrooms and educations (*Empowering* 119). Furthermore, he authorizes these positions with a greater legitimacy when he situates the causes for students' resistance within larger historical and social contexts, such as uneven levels of development, vocationalism, prior schooling, acceleration and amplification of mass culture, exposure to regressive ideologies, short amount of time in class and on campus in institutional settings, disadvantaged languages, discourses, and literacies, demanding family lives, and poor health and nutrition, and, additionally, in the ways that he assigns responsibilities for overcoming these positions to both students and teachers (210, 217 ff).[25]

As expected, Shor theorizes a link among his classroom practices, these subject positions, and challenges to traditional versions of teachers and classrooms. According to Shor, the practices of his classroom, which "focus on power relations in the classroom, in the institution, in the formation of standard canons of knowledge, and in society at large," examine "the social and cultural context of education, asking how student subjectivity and economic conditions affect the learning process," which situate "[s]tudent culture as well as inequality and democracy" as "central issues to problem-posing educators when they make syllabi and examine the climate for learning" (*Empowering* 31). Drawing extensively upon Freire, Shor theorizes that his classroom practices posit "human beings, knowledge, and society as unfinished products in history, where various forces are still contending" and where students participate "in the contention over knowledge and the shape of society" that, at least theoretically, situate students directly in the construction of knowledges and classrooms:

> This does not mean that students have nothing to learn from biology or mathematics or engineering as they now exist. Neither does it mean that students **reinvent** subject matter each time they study it or that the academic expertise of the teacher has no role in the classroom. Formal bodies of knowledge, standard usage, and the teacher's academic background all belong in critical classrooms. As long as existing knowledge is not presented as facts and doctrines to be absorbed without question, as long as existing bodies of knowledge are critiqued and balanced from a multicultural perspective, and as long as the students' own themes and idioms are valued along with standard usage, existing canons are part of critical education. (35)

What is transformed is the relationships that students and teachers have to learning and authority: teachers and students, as "allies for learning and for democracy in school and society," are no longer "adversaries divided by unilateral authority and fixed canons" (35). Instead, they "redefine their relationships to each other, to education, and to expertise," and they "re-perceive knowledge and power" by challenging "[f]ormal bodies of knowledge, standard usage, and the teacher's academic background" through generative, topical, and academic themes (35, 55 ff). According to Shor, generative themes, which "make up the primary subject matter," emerge from "student culture and express problematic conditions in daily life that are useful for generating critical discourse" (55). At the same time, topical themes are "social question[s] of key importance locally, nationally, or globally" that are not "generated directly from the students' conversation[s]" but are products of teachers' intervention that "ask students to step into territory ignored or covered uncritically by the standard curriculum and the mass media" and "to push against the limits of knowledge in everyday life" (55, 58). In addition, academic themes are comprised of "material brought to the discussion by the teacher, not generated from student speech" that originate "in formal bodies of knowledge studied by specialists in a field," which neither come from "student culture" nor from "a political issue or topic society" but from "structured knowledge in a teacher's field" (55, 73-74). According to Shor, both topical and academic themes offer ways to problematize "formal and advanced learning" in ways that generative themes cannot, insofar as topical themes expose "the social world of events mystified by the mass media and by the official syllabus" and that academic themes provide access to "the remote world of specialized knowledge" (83).

According to Shor's explanation, the versions of literacy sanctioned by his classroom practices enable students to investigate "social experience[s] in education" and offer students "new values, relationships, discourse, knowledge, and versions of authority." These, in turn, enable them to resist their "socialization into the myths, values, and relations of the dominant culture," such as "the official content of the textbook or the canon," through "a dialogic discourse in a mutual inquiry," an "invented discourse" that he theorizes as "the *third* idiom, because it is different from the two conflicting ones brought to class by students and teachers: nonacademic everyday speech and academic teacher-talk" (117-18, 255, original emphasis). Given the degree to which the third idiom theoretically represents the literacies of Shor's classrooms, I want to provide a lengthy explanation in Shor's own words:

> The dialogic third idiom is simultaneously concrete and conceptual, academic and conversational, critical and accessible. As dialogue begins, the students' language of everyday life is familiar and concrete but not critical or scholarly; the teacher's language is academic but not colloquial or concretely related to students' experience. The dialogic process overcomes their noncommunication. It transforms both idioms into a new discourse, the third idiom, which relates academic language to concrete experience and colloquial discourse to critical thought.

Everyday language assumes a critical quality while teacherly language assumes concreteness.

This invented third idiom philosophizes experience while experientializing philosophy. As a discourse evolved in a democratic process, it rejects the unilateral transfer of culture from the teacher to the student. A mutual transformation of academic and community cultures is necessary because teacher-talk and everyday talk are both products of an unequal society. The knowledge and language that exist in daily life and in the academy cannot by themselves produce social and intellectual empowerment. The culture of schooling and the culture of everyday life in nonelite communities need something from each other to transcend their own limits. The current academic canons of language and subject matter need to be transformed in a multicultural way with and for students, to reflect their language and conditions. (255-56)

In other words, the dialogic interaction between the literacies that students bring with them to the classroom and the literacies of the academy transforms students' and teachers' discourses in such a way that, in the tradition of Hegelian synthesis, produces a new discourse, a discourse that, in Shor's words, "philosophizes experience and experientializes philosophy" in ways that lead to social and intellectual empowerment (255-56).

Before I turn to a critique of Shor's classroom literacies, I want to acknowledge how much he—as much as Berlin or even more—has influenced my own thinking about literacies and teaching. Significantly, Shor theorizes a legitimacy for students' literacy practices, and he sanctions positions for authority and responsibility for students in their learning (*When* 116 ff). Through his characteristic narrative, he offers an accessible way of thinking and talking about negotiated curriculum, classrooms, and institutions, as context-specific sites that draw upon competing versions of cultural capital, and collaborative education as interdisciplinary practices of integrated literacies across the curriculum (*Empowering* 44 ff, 187 ff). Besides recognizing Shor's influence upon me, I should also acknowledge that reading Shor's classrooms in this way has been difficult. His classroom practices are uneven, but this is so in part, I suspect, because of what he calls their contingency and specificity. In order to read his classroom practices, I have had to regularize them, which means that, as is always the case, certain instances and particular examples have had to be ignored in an effort to make connections and to draw conclusions—and this makes such a reading somewhat artificial. Nevertheless, I believe that making these generalizations about Shor's classroom practices and their implications for classroom literacies does reveal something crucial and important about literacies, legitimacy, and meaning.

My reading of Shor's classroom practices and the literacies that they sanction goes like this: in the classroom, Shor fails to enact his theoretical visions because, like Berlin's practices, Shor's classroom practices inscribe a binary between literacies-from-above and literacies-from-below; unlike Berlin's, Shor's practices explicitly authorize students' literacies, but ultimately he denies their legitimacy, which results in what Freire's calls a subjectivism that leaves the social structures of classrooms and institutions unchanged. In doing so, Shor's classroom practices tacitly deny the politics of conventional academic literaci(es) even as they ultimately authorize them as the only legitimate literacies. As a result, Shor's classrooms do not empower students, as he hopes they do, because they enact artificial dialogues that leave the social structures of classrooms and academic institutions intact, not to mention the larger social transformations that Shor's critic Irene Ward cites(102 ff). Though Ward bases her criticisms of Shor's classroom practices—that they are "limited and self-contained dialogues" which ignore the larger social world and which deny students' authority—primarily upon Shor's early work *Critical Teaching and Everyday Life*, I believe that his later works—*Empowering Education* and *When Students Have Power*—reinforce her criticisms. In addition, they reveal both the artificial binary between literacies-from-above and literacies-from-below and the contradictions between the explicitly and implicitly authorized literacies, both of which, I maintain, reinforce the conditions that critics have called contemporary crises in literacies and education.

If the major problems with Berlin's classroom practices are that, in conflating critical and cultural literacies, they invoke a context-free literacy that is imported into classrooms and imposed upon students, then the problems with Shor's classroom practices are somewhat different—that they invoke the same binary between literacies-from-above and literacies-from-below by seeming to privilege students' literacies all the while imbuing academic literacies with an ultimate legitimacy in ways that, in the end, leave classrooms and institutions relatively unchanged. First, Shor's practices seem to privilege students' literacies, almost to the extent that they deny the political realities of conventional literacies, and in doing so, they marginalize the discourses and the literacies that would enable students to acquire social and political power. For example, Shor explains, in the description of his literature course cited earlier, that he would begin with a question about students' experiences of street violence and then ask them to produce texts from interviews with their families, to write essays on violence in communities, and to produce fiction in which characters resist street violence. Only after "seeking out audiences to read the students' stories to encourage their self-image as writers" would he turn to the institutionally legitimized purpose of the course—consuming texts traditionally considered to be literature, which he would supplement with nonfiction narratives and sociological essays, which students would take to their families for their responses. After this, to complete the process, Shor would ask students to produce an additional piece of writing in response to social questions about the reduction of violence in their neighborhoods, which, with their permission, he would distribute within the community (81-82).[26]

Second, he invokes essentialist versions of literacy that ignore the power of sanctioned discourses and privileged cultures. Though Shor, in his descriptions of his practices, reveals his essentialist literacies in several practices, such as what he calls Think-Itemize-Write, dictation sequence, or, as Ward also cites, voicing,[27] I will limit myself to dictation sequence, which, as he describes it, clearly denies the cultural conflicts inherent in classrooms:

> The key feature here is connecting spoken language to written language. Dictation involves not only mental imagery, but also speaking, listening and composing, in a phased technique. The dictation sequence begins by asking students to break into groups of two. One member of the team will be dictating his or her verbal thoughts on the theme for composition, while the second member of the unit will record, on paper, verbatim, what the person speaks. Then the two change places, the recorder becoming the speaker and the speaker becoming the composer. The students are asked to gain a sharp mental picture of the things they want to speak before they begin talking to their partners, and each recorder is urged to ask the other to speak as slowly as necessary to get every word down. (131)

In justifying this practice, Shor explains that "it is important to make clear that the written language of our culture is nothing more than encoded speech" and that "[s]tudents should make a connection between their speaking language and the act of writing language on paper" (131). Though "transcribing the language of a peer," assuming that the practice includes "respectful care," may legitimize students' discourse, which, Shor maintains, "turns out to be far richer than they had imagined," it ensures that students remain confined within their "own native speech," thereby virtually guaranteeing their positions as outsiders to academic discourse communities, unable to change them or even to participate in them.

In his endorsement of students' primary and popular discourses, Shor denies the politics of literacies in classrooms and in society. Though Shor claims that, at least in theory, his classrooms do not work against "subject matter, scholarly knowledge, or intellectual passion" in their attempts "to recover that eagerness to learn" (84), this literature classroom that he has described does marginalize the very subject matter and scholarly knowledge of literature courses, as defined by academic communities. While I would applaud his efforts to connect classrooms and students' lives, and while I would agree that traditional classrooms must be changed, I believe that beginning and ending with, and devoting the bulk of the time to, activities and experiences other than those identified as legitimate by the academy is to place students at a disadvantage by denying them experiences that would enable them to reread and rewrite their classrooms and their educations. Furthermore, to marginalize the experiences that their peers would have in other sections of the same literature course is to deny them experience with the cultural capital of the academy, thereby ensuring that, to the degree that literature courses prepare them for the close reading expected of students in colleges and universities, they are at a greater disadvantage.

In his composition classrooms, this same denial is evident. As for the Think-Itemize-Write, there is seeing, and then there is seeing, and, as we all know, some ways of seeing are more powerful than others.[28] Whether or not students, in their "native idiom," have "strong speaking skills," the connections that Shor suggests they make in the dictation sequence "between their speaking language and the act of writing language on paper" (131) deny them the experiences with the conventional discourses and literacies of the academy and ensure that they will remain powerless to effect changes in classrooms and institutions.[29] Finally, Shor's practice of voicing reveals his essentialism at the sentence level, suggesting that meaning is separate from and independent of language, which he implies is merely a vehicle for its transmission,[30] and ignoring his own theoretical conclusions about the importance of cultural contexts and discursive politics. While Shor is right, I think, when he argues that "[m]ost students possess more language skills than they will display in school" and that "[t]he turn towards student reality and student voices can release their hidden talents" (130), his failure to foreground the conflicts between students' cultures, which makes these "language skills" meaningful, and the culture(s) of the academy, which makes these talents *hidden* talents, denies the politics of literacy that will prevent students' from rereading and rewriting their experiences in any way that will be granted an institutional legitimacy, which is necessary in order to effect change in classrooms and institutions.

In his haste to assert the legitimacy of students' cultures—that is, presuming that students even need to be informed of their cultures' legitimacy by their teachers—Shor overlooks the manner in which his practices authorize conventional academic literacies with the ultimate, and in some ways exclusive, legitimacy in his classrooms, which merely reinforces traditional institutional formations. While his day-to-day class activities and assignments laud the power of students' primary literacies in ways that deny the politics of sanctioned literacies in the academy, his assessment methodologies reveal that conventional academic literacies are the ones that count. In *Empowering Education*, Shor describes his use of learning contracts. Since he tells students that he would prefer those who plan to earn a D or an F to drop his course at the outset,

his learning contracts, which he distributes during the first week of the semester, only describe three grades—A's, B's, and C's:

> For each grade, I usually propose different levels of participation, attendance, length
> of papers, number of papers, project work, books to read, and so on. I hand out the
> contracts, ask students to read them, discuss them, and then ask questions for
> whole-class negotiation. Then I ask them to take them home, think them over, and
> make one of three choices: sign the contract as proposed and amended in class at a
> specific grade level, or negotiate further changes with me individually, or throw the
> contract out and negotiate a new one of their own design. (159)

On the surface, Shor's practice of learning contracts appears to invite students
to collaborate in the assessment of their classrooms, yet a closer analysis indicates otherwise, as the criteria he lists—"different levels of participation, attendance, length of papers, number of papers, project work, books to read, and so
on"—suggests. In *When Students Have Power*, Shor offers two versions of
learning contracts from a 300-level elective literature and humanities course
on utopian societies—his proffered contract and then the negotiated
version—both of which are worth examining. As for the first, his proffered
contract reveals Shor's expectations for students' performances and literacies.
As suggested by this contract, Shor expects the average student to "write 500
words on each of three assigned books" and "[d]o one Utopia project and
hand in a written report (500) words on it," as well as have "C quality on written work," in order to be assigned a C. He expects the superior student to
"write 1000 words on each of the three assigned books," "make class presentations" on "two Utopia projects, one on changing the College and one on
changing NYC," and "hand in a written report (1,000 words) on each," including "A quality on written work," as well as have "all work handed in on time"
and "be a leader in class discussion" in order to receive an A (77). Surprisingly,
Shor's expectations are thoroughly conventional, and, at least at the level of his
expectations, students must engage in conventionally academic literacy acts in
order to earn these grades. The negotiated contract merely reinforces these
conventional expectations: "C-level minimum words (500) on all written
work," written responses to "all 3 assigned books," "sometimes" participation
in class discussions, and a written project report, including "C-quality writing
on all written work" for the average evaluation and "A-level minimum number
of words (1,000) on all written work," written responses to "all 3 assigned
books," leadership in class discussion through responding to other students,
keeping the dialogues focused, and participating every class," two group projects or one project and participation in an out-of-class group, and two written
reports and class presentations on projects, as well as "A-quality writing on all

written work" for the superior grade (120). Interestingly, the major differences between Shor's proffered contract and the negotiated contract are a provision that enables students to rewrite homework assignments "for a higher grade if handed in on time and if redone one week after [the students] get them back" and a clarification of his expectations for leadership in class discussions and for the projects (120).

As I read Shor's use of learning contracts in this 300-level literature and humanities classroom, I am surprised, given both his practices of theory and classroom assignments from *Critical Teaching and Everyday Life* and *Empowering Education* (which foreground students' literacies almost to the exclusion of conventional classroom literacies), by the ways that the standards for literate performance in these classrooms imbue conventional academic literacies with the ultimate legitimacy. In other words, at least in Shor's literature and humanities classroom, the ultimately legitimate literacy acts are those that have traditionally dominated classrooms in U. S. colleges and universities: three to four page papers with specific word limits, oral in-class presentations, reports on projects, etc. Given this contradiction, the sanctioned literacies in Shor's classrooms may be even more difficult for students than Berlin's. While Berlin's sanctioned literacy resembles those that most students have already encountered throughout their educational histories, though with a different foundation, Shor's sanctioned literacy offers students contradictions that, to their credit, do not take students long to recognize and resolve, as Shor's explanation of the final learning contract suggests. Not only were the students savvy to the contradictions in his classroom, but they also saw that they were denied a legitimate role in the classroom. Despite offering students classroom experiences that may have challenged conventional academic cultures, Shor constrains them, in the end, to conventional literacy acts, as both versions of the learning contract suggest. Furthermore, his summary of their negotiations over the standards for literate performance in their classroom reveals that, if collaboration occurred, it was over "legalistic" terms, to use Shor's word, and not over substantive issues of assessment, standards, and literate performance:

> [t]he students bargained for more absences and a more lenient lateness policy. They insisted on maintaining the legal minimum of absences specified in College policy, similar to their legalistic demand for ten minutes less class time through dismissal at 3:40 instead of 3:50. I retained the discussion leadership clause for A-level students and the quality provision for written work at each grade level. The students debated and accepted the use of plus and minus grading (A-, B+, etc., instead of just A and B). The college had implemented plus and minus final grading without consulting students, so I chose to present it to them as an option they could accept or reject. They also bargained for one late assignment without penalty. (120)

As this explanation suggests, students selected relatively safe issues to negotiate, perhaps in order to conform to the teacher's expectations. Furthermore, none of these negotiations, not even re-presenting the "option" of "plus and minus final grading" for acceptance or rejection, challenges classrooms or institutions in substantive ways.

Though I am interested in the ways that Shor seems unwilling (or uninterested) in problematizing the culturally-specific standards of ideal students in terms of punctuality that reinforce students' earliest experiences in classrooms,[31] I am even more interested in the moves that Shor makes, such as "quality provision for written work," that disable more authentic collaboration in establishing the standards for literate and learning performances. In regard to this example, Shor reports that, when the students challenge the authority of "A or B *quality* on written work," he offers the following justification: "my ethos, my face of good intentions—experience, openness, fairness—jury-rigged with standards of serious thought I look for in student writing, coupled to ways for student to contest my decision and to rewrite for higher grades" (80, 87, original emphasis). What I find interesting is that such a move not only reverts to a traditionally absolute and universal authority for teachers in classrooms but also sublimates any conflict among culturally-specific standards for literate performance and learning within an ostensively collaborative practice of learning contracts.

In neither his proffered contract nor the negotiated contract does Shor create *the space for literacy differences*, which, given the legitimacy accorded to conventional academic literacies by their historical and social presence in classrooms and institutions, is necessary if he intends to produce the third idiom that he theorizes from what he believes about his classroom practices. In his classrooms, he offers no space in which a "dialogic process" actually "overcomes the noncommunication" by transforming "the students' language of everyday life" and "the teacher's language" into "a new discourse, the third idiom," that "relates academic language to concrete experience and colloquial discourse to critical thought" (*Empowering* 255-56). Tellingly, Shor theorizes of this transformation as if both discourses have an equal currency in classrooms when, even in his own classrooms, the disparity between these discourses is evident. Furthermore, the (false) dualism that Shor constructs between students' literacies and teachers' literacies forces him to suggest that students' discourses can be neither **critical** nor **scholarly**: the third idiom, he explains, is "simultaneously concrete and conceptual, academic and conversational, critical and accessible" in its transformation of "the students' language of everyday life" and "the teacher's language" into a new discourse in which "[e]veryday language assumes a critical quality while teacherly language assumes concreteness" (255-56). Such an explanation begs the question as to what Shor actually means by *critical* and *scholarly*. Contrary to the dualism that forms the basis of Shor's third idiom, academic language is about experience—just different kinds of experience from "the everyday"—and concreteness has more to do with perspective than with some autonomous quality that can be assessed outside of context. Moreover, he seems to invoke **academically critical** and **academic scholarship**, which are culturally-specific terms and features and, as Geneva Smitherman, Keith Gilyard, Helen Fox, Jane Tompkins, Victor Villanueva, and others have demonstrated, are not the only ways to be intellectual.

As with Berlin's, there seems to be a discrepancy between Shor's theorization of his classroom practices, and the literacies they sanction, and the classroom practices themselves, which authorize a very different literacy. In theorizing of the third idiom, his dualism between students' literacies and the literacies of the academy is the same dualism that produces literacies-from-above and literacies-from-below. Through his assignments and other classroom practices, Shor privileges literacies-from-below, often at the expense of those of the academy, yet through his practices of assessment and evaluation, he simultaneously authorizes these same literacies-from-above with the sole legitimacy in his classrooms. As a result, Shor's classroom literacies fail to authorize students to reread and rewrite their classrooms and their worlds in any meaningful way. For example, Shor argues that, in the practices he describes in *Critical Teaching and Everyday Life*, "reading and writing are legitimized as human activities because the class study turns towards daily life in a **critical** and **dialogic** fashion" whereby "students are not lectured about the meaning of their reality, but rather engage in a self-regulating project through which they discover and report that meaning to each other" (196). Even as Shor's self-regulating projects may enable students in his remedial writing class to produce what Shor calls "an interesting document" in the form of a new Constitution, which was published in the school paper and may have led students in this same class to plan, write, and act out a television show (199), they do not necessarily afford these students the literacies they need if they are to reread and rewrite their remedial status within the academy, and to access and to mediate the dominant discourses of the academy, both of which can be disabling for students who have already been identified as lacking the requisite cultural capital of the academy. In fact, of the nine or so language projects that he describes in *Critical Teaching*, only two of them—"The Model Classroom" and "College Re-design"—have the potential to offer students the literacies that can enable them to reread and rewrite the conditions of alienation that characterize the students that Elizabeth Chiseri-Strater describes and many of those who appear in the classrooms in which I work, the alienation that, I maintain, is responsible for the current crises in literacy and education.

Though I disagree with Xin Liu Gale's claim that conventional academic discourses must be taught before resistant discourses, I do agree with her assertions that, if students are not afforded experiences with conventional academic discourses, they will not acquire the requisite literacies and that, if they are only offered experiences in conventional academic discourses, they will have gaps, to use her word, in their education (*Teachers* 90). In Shor's classrooms, students run the risk of experiencing the worst of both worlds—few, if any, experiences with conventional academic discourses *plus* assessment methodologies that authorize these same discourses with the sole legitimacy.

Collaborative classrooms and dialogic literacies go beyond offering choices about how students arrange their desks or whether they raise their hands or if teachers use pluses or minuses, as in Shor's classrooms—and even beyond beginning with students' experiences or contextualizing canons and cultural codes, as in Berlin's—to substantive and significant shifts in classroom practices and theorizations about experiences. As Bizzell suggests early in this chapter, it is extremely difficult by a "collective act of will" to overcome the inequalities inscribed within classrooms. Something more is needed, something that will deconstruct and reconstruct classrooms in order to provide legitimate challenges to the "unilateral transfer of culture from the teacher to the students" that Shor envisions (*Empowering* 256). What is needed is not some external literacy that, as in Berlin's classrooms, is imported into classrooms and imposed upon students, nor some hopeful speculation that, as in Shor's, simply foregrounds students' literacies without concomitant and substantial changes to the social structures of classrooms and institutions. Something more is needed, so that this unilateral transfer will cease and so that a dialogic exchange will occur between two cultures in the classroom that are both *legitimate.*

In the next chapter, I shall offer some of the ways that students and I have tried to establish this something more, this something additional—though, in the end, it, too, seems to fall short of resolving the conditions that critics have been calling crises in literacy and education in American colleges and universities. Nevertheless, these efforts have been productive in what they suggest about the impediments and obstacles that must be resolved in order to come closer to "mutual transformation of academic and community cultures" that enables both "to transcend their own limits" and to produce the classroom experiences and the discursive practices that critical literacies dream about.

INTERLUDE
Read(Writ)ing Classrooms with Students I

Linda Moore

English 191A

Before entering Dr. Schroeder's English 101 class, I expected a traditional instruction on grammar and writing. However, I later learned that Dr. Schroeder uses a more modern way of teaching in which he instructs his students about different literacies and presents abstract ideas. He was very enthusiastic about the subjects presented in each class. Dr. Schroeder teaches the students about the Literacy of the Academy and compares and contrasts it to other literacies or themes. For example, in the class I attended, he and the students discussed how the Literacy of the Academy relates to the Literacy of Cyberspace or how we read and write emails. Dr. Schroeder has been teaching college students since 1992 and is currently writing a book. Therefore, he uses his experiences with his classes as the basis for material in his writing. He believes that being literate involves both reading and writing.

First, Dr. Schroeder told the class about the upcoming events and goals for the class. He was straightforward and organized in what he wanted to achieve which helped the students to focus on the class. Then, he gave them a question or an entrance slip designed to help students concentrate and make connections in writing. In the class I visited, the students were to describe the literacy of cyberspace and use the same language as that of an email. At first, they seemed confused as to what they were supposed to do, but then, Dr. Schroeder explained in more depth of what he wanted them to achieve in the activity. After completing the writing assignment the students went into their groups and discussed their thoughts about the topic. Later, Dr. Schroeder talked to each group and discussed their ideas about the literacy of cyberspace and how it relates to that of the Academy.

By using groups, Dr. Schroeder promotes collaborative learning since the students teach each other and provide new and different insights. In order to increase the productivity of the groups, a monitor watches the time and a secretary takes notes. While I viewed each group working, I saw that each person is supposed to contribute something to the discussion. Groups play a major role in Dr. Schroeder's teaching methods and the students enjoy them since they were able to interact with one another and discuss their own opinions. In addition, each group takes a turn co-teaching a generative theme such as the Literacy of Cyberspace. Therefore, each student takes an active role in the instruction of the material. Besides groups, Dr. Schroeder uses other methods of teaching which include lecture, student presentations, and skits.

During the interview, Dr. Schroeder explained that his main goal in teaching the students. He aims to have their literacy goals met, whether it is writing or reading. Therefore, the students are able to decide what they want the focus of the class to be. I found this interesting since most instructors are not as flexible in their goals for teaching the students. In grading, Dr. Schroeder not only concentrates on the final product, but also on the progress that the students achieve in the class and in their efforts and investment in the process.

In helping one of Dr. Schroeder's students in the Writing Center, I would aid them in their ideas and use of the Literacy of the Academy. From observing his class, I have found that using grounds or evidence to make a claim in writing is important. Therefore, I would help the students to use supporting ideas in order to make sound and successful arguments. Dr. Schroeder also promotes using transitions to connect ideas and thoughts. Therefore, in helping one of his students, I would make sure the student followed the laws of the Academy and used support in making a claim or main idea. I would focus on an insightful thesis with proper grammar. Also, I would ask the student to bring his other papers so that I could check for progression and achievement since Dr. Schroeder puts emphasis on the investment of work in each of the student's tasks.

Observing Dr. Schroeder's class and interviewing him was a very worthwhile experience. Before doing so, I did not realize the variety of teaching methods that each instructor has. Therefore, it is important that to ask each student I help in the Writing Center about his or her own goals and those of the instructor. From the other students' presentations, I learned that other instructors may have different grading techniques and goals for the achievement of the students. For example, since Dr. —— helped to develop the CLAST test, he instructs his students on how to pass it with the use of proper grammar and even passive voice in order to make the writing longer. If I was to help one of his students in the Writing Center, I would concentrate on grammar and not so much the ideas and evidence in the paper. Therefore, it is important to understand that each instructor has different ideas about a good paper. In the Writing Center, I will adapt my help to the goals of the student and the instructor.

EXAMINATION OF DR. SCHROEDER'S ENGLISH 191 CLASS

Kelly Barnes
ENG 191A

Upon entering Dr. Schroeder's class, I felt very confused. As a person who was not aware of his methods, the class experience was like being in a foreign country; I could hear words and topics, but I did not really understand what was being said. His class was not a normal English class where the teacher stands at the front of the classroom spouting ideas about grammar or thesis. In his class, he introduced the idea of "Literacy of the Academy." The first time I heard it used I was baffled. I passed ———— a note that said: "What is the Literacy of the Academy?!?!" After observing his classes and talking to him, though I gained a better understanding of what he was trying to teach.

Dr. Schroeder has very different ideas about how English should be taught and what effect language should have in all aspects of life. He follows the principal of Literacy of the Academy. The idea of the Academy is that if people are better at academic writing they will be better at reading, writing and speaking in all aspects of life. His students will be able to apply the concepts they have learned in the classroom not just to papers for school, but in letters, memos or any other type of writing they may encounter in their lifetime. The other goal Dr. Schroeder has is to help his students reach their own personal goals. If they want to be better at grammar, then he will focus on that area with them. If they want to work on certain types of writing, he will help them on that particular genre.

To achieve these goals, Dr. Schroeder has unique methods. He does not stand up and talk to the class for fifty minutes, three days a week. Although like any teacher, he uses lecture, but he also does skits, co-teaching and outside activities. In co-teaching, the students help him teach a genre. One of the most important teaching methods he uses is the group. In the classroom, the students are usually in groups for some period of time. He uses groups because he thinks discussion adds to the discourse of the world and by talking about their writings, his students will write more effectively. He also believes that language is a social action and talking about writing is necessary. The group seemed to be effective and the students really did do work. They were not just sitting around chatting about the day. In the group there is a secretary and a monitor who make sure the group stays focused on the task presented to them. I am personally do not like group work, but I think the groups were effective in this case.

Dr. Schroeder also has an interesting method of grading. Although he does grade in the traditional manner, such as the student writing papers and then having him grade the paper, he also places an emphasis on another area. He is not only interested in the final product, but the process the student went through to achieve the final product. When he grades the paper, he looks at how the student worked. He looks at if they participated in class and asked questions. The progression is very important and he wants to see it in their work.

Dr. Schroeder is writing a book about teaching English. He uses his class as an experiment for his book. He uses many methods to help him figure out what concepts and ideas are effective. If something works or doesn't, that is fine. Everything is a learning experience.

Going in to the writing center and tutoring a student from Schroeder's class would be difficult without having this experience. I think that when we attend the writing center we should always ask the student if they know what the goal of the paper or the class is. For example, if I were helping one of Dr. Schroeder's students I would know that progression was important and that they each have personal goals. I think it would be important to tap into those specific areas. If I were tutoring one of Dr. ———'s students I would know that grammar and the CLAST were very important and so I think my approach would be different.

From observing the class, I noticed some of Dr. Schroeder's topics were a little unusual. From being in the classroom, I felt that the students were sometimes confused on the topics and many had to ask several questions many times and in different ways to make sure they completely understood. There is a possibility that as a tutor I would have no knowledge of the topic. I think talking to the student would be very beneficial. By explaining their ideas to me, hopefully they would realize new possibilities for their writing.

With his students I would also encourage my tutee to participate in class and ask questions. Knowing how he feels about the process of writing, participation could make a difference in the grade the student receives. I would also encourage them to be clear and concise and follow the rules of the Academy.

I think this experience was very effective and interesting. I think often times as students we get accustomed to one type of teaching style. We need to remember the students we will be helping will be coming from all types of teacher backgrounds. The methods we use for one student may or may not work with the next student. I know it is not possible to know how all the professors are here at ———, but I think with experience tutoring various students we will gain valuable knowledge. I think in order to be an effective tutor one really has to communicate and make sure he knows what the student and the teacher hope to accomplish in an English class.

3   CONSTRUCTED LITERACIES

But what would happen if one no longer believed in the existence
of normal language, or ordinary speech, of the linguistic norm (the
kind of clarity and communicative power celebrated by Orwell in
his famous essay, say)? One could think of it in this way: perhaps
the immense fragmentation and privatization of modern
literature—its explosion into a host of distinct private styles and
mannerisms—foreshadows deeper and more general tendencies in
social life as a whole. Supposing that modern art and modernism—
far from being a kind of specialized aesthetic curiosity—actually
anticipated social developments along these lines; supposing that in
the decades since the emergence of great modern styles society has
itself begun to fragment in this way, each group coming to speak a
curious private language of its own, each profession developing its
private code or idiolect, and finally each individual coming to be a
kind of linguistic island, separated from everyone else? But then in
that case, the very possibility of any linguistic norms in terms of
which one could ridicule private languages and idiosyncratic styles
would vanish, and we would have nothing but stylistic diversity and
heterogeneity.

Fredric Jameson
"Postmodernism and Consumer Society"

"Normal" (or, as I would prefer, . . . "standard") discourse is
discourse that proceeds under a set of rules, assumptions,
conventions, criteria, beliefs,which in principle anyway, tell us how to
go about settling issues and resolving disagreements . . . "discourse
which embodies agreed-upon criteria for reaching agreement"
[(Rorty).] . . . "Abnormal"(or "nonstandard") discourse is, then,
discourse in which "agreed-upon criteria for reaching agreement" are
not the axis upon which communication turns, and the evaluation of
disparate views in terms of some accepted framework . . . is not the
organizing aim. Hope for agreement is not abandoned. People
occasionally do change their minds or halve their differences as a
result of intelligence concerning what individuals or groups of
individuals whose minds run on other tracks believe. But "exciting
and fruitful disagreement"—how do I know what I think until I see
what you say—is recognized as a no less rational process. . . . It can
also be, less dramatically, a practicable method for living in a situation

where dissensus is chronic, probably worsening, and not soon to be removed.

Clifford Geertz
Local Knowledge

In chapter two, I offered examples of the concerns that Freire and others have had about critical literacies in American schools[1] by considering the classroom practices of James Berlin and Ira Shor, two theorists who have done much to foster the conversations about critical literacies in contemporary American colleges and universities. As I explained previously, each of these theorists, in different ways, has made important contributions to critical literacies, and yet their classroom practices, though for different reasons, cannot sufficiently resolve the conditions that have been called the contemporary crisis in literacy. What I intend to do in this chapter is to describe some of the ways that students and I have struggled in classrooms to construct literacies and then to consider some of the ways that these efforts, as well, have been unable to resolve the crises in meaning and education that, I believe, are at the center of what others have called a crisis in literacy. Much as I did in the previous chapters, I will begin with classroom practices before turning to the versions of literacy these practices produce and then to the shortcomings, as identified by students and myself, of these practices. These failures, I believe, are revealing of changes that must occur, not only in our classrooms but also in departments and institutions, if we are to dissolve the conditions that have given rise to the contemporary crises within American colleges and universities.

In theorizing about constructed literacies, I have collaborated with students from various institutions in which I have taught and worked—urban community colleges, liberal arts colleges, and research universities in the Midwest, the South, and the Southeast—though most of the contributions come from undergraduate students with whom I worked during 1998-1999 and 1999-2000 academic years at a four-year private, liberal arts college in St. Louis, MO (religious) and another in St. Augustine, FL (independent). Demographically, these colleges had much in common. Both had around 1,500 students, most of whom were first-generation college students and came from what is often considered to be mainstream America—white, middle to lower-middle class, European-American backgrounds. Though each had an under-representation of ethnic minorities, both institutions had a higher percentage of females than males, perhaps reflecting the origins of each as private women's institutions that subsequently admitted men. In many ways, these are some of the very student cultures that, as Maureen Hourigan points out (31 ff), are overlooked in current conversations about literacies and cultures in the academy.

CLASSROOM PRACTICES

Course Outline and Schedule
Generative Theme A
English 102

Central Question: What is Academic Literacy?
Readings and Writings:
Monday (1/17) Social Contexts for Composition Courses
Reading—"Freshman Composition and Administered Thought"
Writing—Write a letter to a friend or a peer who is also taking a first-year writing course in which you explain your understanding of the article by comparing it to your experiences.
Wednesday (1/19) Literacy, Literacies, and Academic Literacy
Reading—TBD
Writing—What does it mean to write? To read? Who determines what counts as writing and reading? Why do they get to define what counts? (freewrite)
Friday (1/21) Academic Literacy (Part I): Who to Be and How to See the World
Reading—Lester (123-54)
Writing—Identify the writing and reading practices that you were asked to do last semester in all of your classes.
Monday (1/24) Academic Literacy (Part II): Who to Be and How to See the World
Reading—Lester (3-82)
Writing—Drawing upon what you can find between the lines, write a *dramatis persona* for Joe or Jill Smart, the ideal college student, and the stage directoins for the setting of Utopia U, the ideal university.
Wednesday (1/26) Alternative Discursive Practices
Reading—TBD
Writing—Compare and contrast the practices of writing a note to your parents and writing a final exam.
Friday (1/28) Continuing the Conversation
Reading—TBD
Writing—draft*

Cumulative Assignment

This text will have two parts—a collage and an explanation. In the collage, you (and others, if you'd like) are to define (academic) literacy through the use of magazine pictures, headlines, and other materials. In the explanation, each of you will translate and interpret the collage into a conventional academic argument (i.e. "Literacy is . . . .").

COLLAGE WRITE-UP

Katy Davidson

English 102/2pm

My collage consists of simple words and phrases that all have significance to the theme of academic literacy. All of the pictures and words represent some opposites and parallels to what James Lester and Richard Ohmann have to say about academic literacy.

Both Lester and Ohmann give, what they believe to be, valid and organized explanations of "Academic Literacy." Lester explains how we need to think in an organized thought pattern to be successful. He also believes that students must put aside many hours towards excessive amounts of research in order to produce a good research paper. I displayed his point of view in my collage by showing a picture of a person studying, a person typing on the computer, the word learn, and the phrase, it's a foundation. All of these things shown on my collage focus on Lester's point of view.

On the other end of the spectrum is Ohmann, who thinks students aren't satisfied with their classrooms today. Ohmann explains how students aren't getting enough out of the academics in which they attend. They have simply lost interest in the academic world. I showed examples of his thoughts in my collage by putting an example of Utopia University and some basic black white colors reinvented with blue, yellow and red colors as well.

My collage seeks to explain academic literacy through powerful words such as, wow, power, learn, and see yourself. I believe that academic literacy is being able to control situations that you may find yourself in, and in the process learning new things. I used a variety of shapes, sizes, colors and words to show that being academically literate is about being yourself and incorporating others' ideas and situations into your life. Ultimately, when a person is academically literate, they are able to use a variety of perspectives when looking at a certain topic.

Overall, I think my collage shows that academic literacy is what you make of it. It is being able to be expressive, creative and open minded. Taking into consideration what Lester and Ohmann have to say, I think that the definition

of academic literacy changes with the ages. Next year it will become even more complicated than it already is today.

In order to resist reading students' needs for them and imposing literacies upon them, I ask students to collaborate in constructing the semester by co-teaching dialogically legitimized contact zones and generative themes.[2] Over the semesters, I have learned to start with an initial theme that centers upon students' presences in these classrooms, such as a theme on the nature of literature, as defined by the college catalogue, or on academic literacy, according to required textbooks, which I will teach alone. For example, on the previous pages are the schedule that I supplied to students in a second semester composition course and the cumulative assignment from Katy, a traditional white female who was majoring in theater and who had recently transferred to the college. Besides problematizing students' presences in our classrooms, this initial theme also offers a shared experience and provides a context for the remaining themes, which are co-taught by the students and me. For instance, students and I from the same composition course explored themes on social class in America and drugs in literature, though, in previous semesters, students and I have used a wide range of themes and zones, from oral literature to masculine studies, while several, such as gender or advertising, appear to be perennial selections.

Given that each class and each semester is different and depends, at least in part, upon students, institutional expectations, myself, and a number of other variables, I will describe two different themes, one from a literature course and one from a composition course, in order to provide a better explanation of our classroom practices. I will use one theme that worked particularly well in an introduction to literature course; this was a theme that centered upon the differences between oral and written discourse. During this theme, there were six co-teachers, five of whom were women, five of whom—not the same five— were African-American, and all of whom were in their late teens and early twenties. Through our negotiations, we had decided to focus on fairy tales, on urban legends, and on signifying over the three weeks that I had allotted to each individual theme. In order to co-teach the theme, they decided to work in pairs: Mary and Beth would handle the fairy tales; Shelia and Janie would focus on urban legends; and Carl and Toni would present signifying. For my part, I would provide an introductory lecture on oral and written discourses, select some readings, and collaborate on the implementation and assessment of the theme. On the first day of the theme, we distributed a course schedule indicating our goals, and throughout the theme, we read various texts, such as traditional fairy tales from the library, urban legends from the Internet, and a selection from Geneva Smitherman's *Talkin and Testifyin,* and we produced a number of individual and collaborative texts, such as literary analyses of fairy tales and original urban legends. During one class, Mary gave a powerful Freudian reading of the implicit cultural values of gender in Cinderella, a reading that about which students were still talking when they returned for the next class. On another day, I distributed a handout in which I used conventional academic language to explain the conventions of signifying, or what Smitherman calls "the verbal art of insult in which a speaker humorously puts down, talks about, needles—that is, signifies on—the listener" (188-21) and to experiment with my own efforts to transplant what Jeff Foxworthy and others have called "redneck jokes" to sig on students and teachers:

> You know you're a good student when . . .
>   . . . your professor blames his secretary for losing work that you never
>   submitted.
>   . . . your intuition tells you which teachers don't have an attendance pol-
>   icy and when to show up for the mid-term exam.
> On the other hand, you know you're a bad student if . . .
>   . . . your textbooks crack when the clerk opens them in the buy-back
>   line.
>   . . . your grandmother has to die three different times in order for you to
>   pass fall semester.
> And finally, you know you're a bad teacher if. . .
>   . . . most of your students call you by the same wrong name.

In a second semester composition course, a theme that illustrates this process is a theme that students and I did on gender and epistemology. In order to prepare for this theme, the co-teachers submitted a draft of their course schedule to me, in which I wrote my own presence, and then we uploaded the following version to the online syllabus that, as a class, we were producing as we, both literally and figuratively, constructed the semester. Though the co-teachers—all white females—and I struggled to negotiate our roles in the theme, our final version reflected a number of different contributions.[3] For this theme, Janie, a conscientious writer who had found success with her writing from the previous semester at a community college, and Anne, an education major, scavenged the library for readings, such as "Is Biology Destiny?," and Maria, an English major, in consultation with a peer who was pursuing a degree in women's studies, selected poems by Dylan Thomas and Sylvia Plath that challenged stereotypical social beliefs about gender. To their selections, I added readings from *Textbook,* which, as the textbook

I required for the semester,[4] reflected my efforts to include institutional discourses, and the introduction from *Women's Ways of Knowing* to raise the issue of gendered epistemologies. Throughout this theme, the co-teachers took control of specific classes by conducting class discussion on the poems, which they found frustrating, and moderating the guest speaker, whom Angie and Linda, the same students who supply the interludes following this chapter, had recruited from the social sciences department. As for my role, I conducted various activities on conventional academic concerns, such as the practices of academic critique or the linguistic basis for gendered metaphors. Together, we responded to the students' cumulative assignments.

Course Outline and Schedule
Generative Theme B
English 102 2 p.m.

Central Question: What Is the Relationship Between Gender and Thinking?
Readings and Writings:
    Monday (1/31) Introductions
        Reading—
        Writing—
    Wednesday (2/2) Stories, people, and Gender
        Reading—*Textbook* (chapter one)
        Writing—Freewrite connections with gender.
    Friday (2/4) Biology and Destiny
        Reading—"Is Biology Destiny?"
        Writing—Pick a popular song that supports or challenges the view
        expressed in the article, and rewrite the lyrics so that they respond to
        the article.
    Monday (2/7) Men, Women, and Knowing
        Reading—excerpt from *Women's Ways of Knowing.*
        Writing—Write a dialogue between two people that demonstrates the
        contrasts between masculine and feminine epistemologies (i.e. ways
        of knowing).
    Wednesday (2/9) Gender and Text, Thoughts, and Things (part one)
        Reading—*Textbook* (45-75)
        Writing—Five questions about the relationships between gender and
        texts, thought, and things (see reading).
    Friday (2/11) Draft
        Reading—None
        Writing—draft ii (submit)

Monday (2/14) The Experience of Gender/ The Gender Experience
   Reading—collection of poems (distributed)
   Writing—Write a poem that recreates the experience of gender or the gender of experience.
Wednesday (2/16) Gender, Metaphor, Thought, and Text
   Reading—*Textbook* (76-126);
   Writing—Critique three metaphors, analogies, parables or advertisements on their treatment of gender and meaning.
Friday (2/18) Gender and Metaphor
   Reading—Reread *Textbook* (91)
   Writing—Imitate or parody Sontag's text with respect to gender and its metaphors.

Cumulative Assignment:
Creating an advertisement designed to appeal to a masculine, feminine, or androgynous, and then using academic discourse, explain and justify your ad.

As these examples illustrate, students and I, sometimes successfully, sometimes not so successfully, negotiate the themes, select readings and generate assignments, and participate in the design, implementation, and assessment of each theme. Though I insist upon certain assignments and request certain texts, the students and I, to greater or lesser degrees depending upon their initiative, interest, and independence, co-teach the theme. In doing so, sometimes we will ask students to experiment with popular practices, such reading *Seinfeld* or other situational comedies for what they say about gender in a theme on gender in social settings. (One of the conclusions of one group was that Jerry's and Elaine's appeal came from the ways that they merely exchanged conventional gender roles and that George and Kramer served as foils for this exchange.) Other times, we will expect that students experiment with the practices of particular contact zones, such as producing their own advertisements in a theme on how advertising works on college audiences. (One group of first-year students in a first-semester composition course produced a commercial in which the requests for a date from the main character were repeatedly rejected because each person he called, including, in the closing scene, his mother, preferred to spend the time writing for our course). Still other times, we will use popular practices to explore conventional academic concerns, such as writing parodies of drug slogans in order to understand intertextuality, context, and citation ("Say N_2O to Drugs" from a second semester composition course) or juxtaposing different readings of texts for insight into narrative sequence

(Raymond Carver's short stories and Robert Altman's *Short Cuts* from an introduction to literature course).

At the conclusion of each theme, I will often produce a text in which I explore convergences and divergences that I have encountered throughout the theme, which I will distribute to students and post in the calendar of the online syllabus. Here is a example from the initial theme from a second-semester composition course:

Academic Literacy:
What It Is and What It Ain't
English 102 (11 a.m.)

In addition to going though the typical beginning of the semester processes we have spent the first three weeks talking about academic literacy. For me, there have been four important conversations that have been on-going throughout this first theme. One of the conversations has been trying to define good writing and to understand who determines what makes good writing, why they get to make these decisions, etc. Another conversation has been about the histories of literacies and of composition classrooms in America. A third conversation has been about whether or not we should talk about an academic literacy or academic literaci(es), such as a functional academic literacy, a cultural literacy, etc. A fourth conversation has been over how certain ways of writing an reading offer us certain versions of who we should be and how we should see the world.

As this theme is coming to a close, I have been trying to juxtapose, or set side by side, what textbooks and teachers say academic literacy is and how students experience writing and reading in the classroom and in the world outside of it. To help us make this comparision and contrast, I would like to offer these lists:

	Academic Literacy *(textbooks, theory, etc.)*	*Academic Literaci(es)* *(students' experiences, etc.)*
Practices	Universal ways of writing, reading, and thinking for everyone in every situation (e.g. *critical* reading or *five-paragraph* essay)	Specific was of writing, reading, and thinking that are different depending upon the teacher, the course or the assignment
Who to be	Rational minds communicating to other rational minds (e.g. the	Generally passive participants who allow education to be done to them in spite of the

critical thinker)		expectations to use the languages of the academy
How to see the world	Objective reality based upon Truth, Knowledge, and Meaning (e.g. the answer, right and wrong, etc.)	Contingent reality based upon versions of truth, knowledge, and meaning that are different for different classrooms and specific teachers

Though textbooks and theories posit, or put forth as truth, a uniform version of literacy that is expected to work for all students each semester in every classroom, students are generally too smart to buy it. Instead, they often recognize that, as nice as a uniform and universal version of academic literacy might be for them, what counts as legitimate, or acceptable, ways to write and read are subject-, and sometimes even teacher-, specific.

So what should we be doing in a first-year composition course?

* * * * *

For those of you who are looking for ways to experiment in your writing and reading, I want to make these two general suggestions as practices with which to begin:

    a. appropriating (i.e. taking for one's own):
- mosaic—constructed wholly with materials taken from other sources
- patchwork—words, phrases, utterances are inserted in original text

Texts that appropriately use the words, phrases, sentences, and utterances from other texts in their own. A mosaic text is one that is made up entirely of others' languages. A patchwork text uses language from others' as parts of their own, generally in ways that go beyond merely citing secondary sources.

    b. blurring:
- merging—combining two independent forms to create a new one
- embedding—one form is placed within another

Texts that blur create new shapes out of old shapes. A merged text is one that combines letters and academic essays, for example, to create a new category, or genre, of discourse. An embedded text is one that inserts songs in plays, for example, to create a new definition of an old category, or genre, of discourse.

* * * * *

Q: How does academic literacy shape us?

A: It shapes us by offering particular versions of writing and reading, and, in the ways that these practices are defined, it offers us particular people to be and certain ways of seeing the world. *Critical* reading, for example, tells us how to be *critical* (e.g. looking for contradictions), as well as tells us who is not critical, and offers a version of the world in which the **real** meaning, or the actual meaning, exists and can be obtained. But what happens if we won't have a problem with contradictions, even when we see them, or if we don't believe in a world where **real** meanings exist?

Q: How can someone actually be academically literate? If so many of the practices are universalized then to be literate is actually more literate in all areas not just academic.

A: If I understand your question, I think you've got a good point. For many people in American society, being academically literate is the same as being literate. For these people, having an education means you're **smart** and **intelligent**, both of which, you've probably discovered by now, may not be true. (It may be true that you grew up in the right homes, or the homes that best represent the literacies that they're testing in school.) I see a difference between academic literacy and social literacy, as evinced or demonstrated in the jokes about nutty professors. If so, then there is a contradiction between the universalization of academic literacy and the notion of literacies.

Q: Where are Knoblauch's 4 types of literacies, subcategories of academic literacy or are they on their own?

A: They enable us to talk about versions of academic literacy—a *functional* academic literacy, as opposed to a *cultural* academic literacy.

Q: Is academic literacy a way if thinking or way of writing or both?

A: Both, and more (a way of valuing, believing, understanding, reading, speaking, etc.).

Q: Why are we spending so much time coming up with an answer if there is no real answer?

A: In part, I guess, because teachers and textbooks often act like there is an answer. There is an answer, I think, just not a nice, neat, clean one. Academic literacy is the ability to control the discourse(s) of the academy. Now all we need to do is define the discourse(s) of the academy.

At the same time, the co-teachers and I will respond to the students' cumulative assignments with descriptive evaluations to assist students in the event that they decide to include a particular text or project in their portfolios. In addition to co-teaching the semester and participating in generative themes, the students are asked to produce a series of formal (i.e. public) texts, which often emerge from the cumulative assignments. In terms of these texts, students are required to complete a prescribed number of drafts, which, depending upon the ostensive focus upon discursive consumption or production, can range from two to five or more. The requirements for these drafts are minimal: that students have a draft each time one is scheduled; that students start a set minimum of new texts (depending, again, upon the ostensive focus of the class); and that the drafts can be connected, in one way or another, to any of the themes that we have explored. Again depending upon the class and the semester, students will elect to produce various texts with a range of functions, some more conventionally academic and some less so, to which their peers and I will respond with feedback. Generally, my responses to formal texts focus upon ways to make these formal writings more experimental, or risky, by bringing together competing discursive practices that we've experimented with as a result of particular themes or specific contact zones. Near the end of the semester, the students and I will negotiate the contents of their portfolios. In addition to selecting from various texts and experiences, the students will also write a narrative of the semester, in which they are asked to synthesize their experiences and to serve as an introduction to the portfolio. Finally, they will write a critique of a peer's portfolio as the final exam.

PERFORMANCE

As a way of understanding what students and I are doing, I have begun to talk of constructed literacies as the literacies of contact zones. Given the ways that we experiment with competing discursive practices, our classrooms tend to be sites where becoming literate amounts to learning to control discourses that mediate and that emerge from the cultural clashes of contact zones. For example, the co-teachers and I asked students, in a theme on social class in America from a second semester composition course, to experiment with a variety of discursive practices, such as rewriting newspaper articles, summarizing movies, comparing and contrasting two articles, and generating a dialogue between two historical figures, and then, as a cumulative assignment, we instructed them to "[w]rite a short story that illustrates your answer to the central questions (i.e. 'What is class in America?'), and then translate the story into an academic argument." As her cumulative assignment, Jamie blended together historical figures (Henry George and Joseph Medill) and texts on class in America (quotes from George's *Progress and Poverty* and Medill's testimony before the Senate Committee on the Relations Between Capital and Labor[5]) from a previous assignment during the theme, with local geography (a Spanish fort, a popular tourist attraction) and her experiences as a college student ("two-for-one shooters and dollar drafts" at "Murphy's College Night"), along with popular symbols (e.g., a yacht and a blow-up raft) into a text that depicts and explains her evolving position on social class in America:

What Is Social Class in America?

English 102 Portfolio— Jamie Meyer
Cumulative Assignment: Theme B

Henry George and Joseph Medill are seated on one of the Fort walls overlooking the bay beneath. Their feet are dangling over the saltwater, as they both just stare of into the distant horizon line. There is complete silence as Medill sits with an outrageous hangover from the night before, his head pounding. George sits with concern for his acquaintance, who had a nervous breakdown on the previous evening when George took him to Murphy's College Night, to observe the uncountable students drinking their earnings away just as they breathed the air. Medill broke down last night and gave in to two-for-one shooters and dollar drafts in his last resort to ease his pain of disappointment and disgust. He has given up on his argument that wasting earnings to indulge in alcohol and other amusements is "the chief cause of the impecunious condition of millions of the wage classes of this country."

A state of the art yacht sails by in the deeper water as a middle-aged man is struggling to paddle against the currant in his blow-up raft boat below them. George now breaks the silence to the temple-throbbing and now completely sarcastic, Medill.

George: "You know Joe, 'the wealthy class is becoming more wealthy; but the power class is becoming more dependent. . .'"

Medill: "-Yeah, more dependent on alcohol, that is. . . "

George: "Oh come-on now Joe, you don't think that an ice-cold beer every now and then isn't part of that 'free, independent spirit' that has marked our kind in the past?"

Medill: "Hank- are you blind? It is never just *one* ice-cold beer! 'Too many squander their earnings on intoxicating drinks, cigars and amusements, who cannot afford it.'"

George: "Property and land are the issues here, Joe. 'The private ownership of the land has created poverty when wealth has increased from industries.'"

Medill: "Henry- you're killing me. You said so yourself, 'There is no luxury, but there is no destitution. No one makes an easy living, nor a very good living; but everyone can make a living.' This living needs to be saved! 'The possession of property among the masses is really due more to saving than to earning.'"

George: "Joey, 'the gulf between employed and employer is growing wider.' 'Those who are above the point of separation are elevated, but those who are below are crushed down.'"

Medill: "Hankie, it is the employers that are the 'private owners' of the land anyway, so I guess the resolution is to just donate any leftover earnings to Murphy's on Thursday nights, to ease the pain of our 'rent swallowed' lives."

George: "I am simply stating that 'the equal right to the use of the land is as clear as their equal right to breathe the air- it is a right proclaimed by the fact of their existence.'"

Medill: "My dear Henry, 'a penny saved is a penny earned.' Private ownership of the land exists and isn't going to change overnight, face it! As far as I'm concerned, 'the power of waste is vastly greater than the power of production.' Land can be bought with saved pennies, you know, so for right now that's all this 'power class' needs to get straightened out! But in the meantime, the private owner of Murphy's is making out allright."

THWARP!

-Medill throws a stone into the bay, and the two of them watch the man below still struggling to paddle against the current.

Translation

So, what is social class in America? My answer to this question at the beginning of the theme was an optimistic statement that "to some degree, America is a classless society." Now after reading texts from *Negotiating Differences*, as well as learning other views from class discussions, I would have to say that America is definitely divided into classes: the upper class, or those "seated on the top of the coach (Bellamy. 480)," the middle or "power" class, which is the largest class and contains the most variety in terms of types of labor and ways of life, and lastly the lower class, or "the rope pullers (Bellamy, 480)." President Clinton would disagree with me according to his talk about the strong, "equal opportunity to compete" in America's economy. I agree that there *are* opportunities out there for *everyone*, but the separation of classes puts a *limit* on these opportunities as being *equal* to all.

Henry George and Joseph Medill, in my dialogue, discuss the problematic issues of classes. George believes that "private ownership of the land creates poverty when there's an increase in wealth from industry (George, 511).'" Medill feels as though "The power of waste is vastly greater than the power of production (Medill, 582)," and that "the possession of property among the masses is really due more to saving than to earning." I agree somewhat with both of them in that the private ownership of land can sometimes promote unfairness to those who pay rent. The private owner can charge an unfair amount, and sometimes there are so may private owners in one area, renters only have the option of paying an unfair price. Hence, "the wealthy class becoming more wealthy; but the power class becoming more dependent (George)." However, I also must admit that I have been to Murphy's on Thursday night and have waken the next day to realize that perhaps I should not have *wasted* a certain amount of my weekly earnings there! If I had saved my money in certain situations rather than spending it on material items or evening "amusements," I could very well have put my money to better use.

According to Bellamy, "the worker is not a citizen because he works, but works because he is a citizen (495)." Bellamy feels as though "the value of a man's services to society fixes his rank," and that in all fairness, those who work in society should basically live equally. I don't agree with this entirely since I believe that there are definitely different levels of work, and different levels of pay, thus not *everyone* who works should live equally. Bellamy did recognize however, within *Looking Backward*, that the scenario with "those on the top of the coach" and "the rope pullers" indeed "was a pity, but it could not be helped, and philosophy forbade wasting compassion on what was beyond remedy." In other words, you cannot change the fact that classes exist, and you cannot change what society has known traditionally, at least on a whim.

Within each of these texts we have read throughout this theme, each author has identified a problem with social class in America. I do agree with certain aspects of each as I have illustrated above, however, I would have to agree the *most* with a quote from Council, in that "nature everywhere teaches that differences and distinctions must exist (463)." America is a land of opportunity and everyone has some form of chance in working their way up in the world. Social class in America does exist, and although life within classes may not always seem fair in every light, the class system will not disappear overnight. Opportunities are not necessarily equal to all, however, each individual as a member in society today, needs to recognize opportunities as they present themselves. It is very important for individuals to seize them in order to move up in society, even if it means "paddling against the current." Opportunities *are* out there for everyone.

Though it is possible to read the ending as Jamie's inability to escape the narrative of equal (individual) opportunity that is part of the American Dream, what her submission both shows and tells about social class is revealing of her experiences in that theme. Within the context of the semester, her use of utterances from other texts, which she has inserted within the utterances of her characters invokes the conversations that we were having about citation and dialogic discourse, and the sheer presence, at the end of the twentieth century, of these nineteenth century historical figures sitting and talking in a gaudy tourist attraction as they recover from a night at a local college bar, using their own words and the words of the author raises a host of questions, including issues of history, class, age, gender, textual ownership, etc., not to mention the less conventional issues that surface from her translation and the more conventional issues that emerge in her academic argument, any of which could serve as responses for rereading, rewriting, and rethinking. For Jamie and other students, becoming literate in our classrooms amounts to attempting to control the discursive practices of the cultural clashes within the parameters of the inscribed contact zone. In shifting the focus from functional academic literacies, or the minimal abilities to read for the main point or to write a five-paragraph essay, and from cultural academic literacies, or the abilities to distinguish evidence from claims or to provide legitimate supporting details, to the literacies of contact zones, or the abilities to mediate and negotiate competing discursive practices, constructed literacies foreground the ways that classrooms are (and have always been) sites of competing versions of cultural capital, or the linguistic currency with which people, namely students and teachers, conduct their social relations through literacy practices.

Unlike more conventional uses of the contact zone that have been, or can be, assimilated by the academy, the contact zones of constructed literacies are legitimized (i.e. identified and/or delimited) through dialogue between students and myself. As I indicated in the prologue, Mary Louise Pratt has defined contact zones as "social spaces where cultures meet, clash, and grapple with each other, often in contexts of highly symmetrical relations of power . . ." ("Contact" 34), and perhaps more than any other, Patricia Bizzell is responsible for the popularity of the contact zone in English studies. Through her scholarship and in the textbook she co-authored with Bruce Herzberg, Bizzell has advocated reconfiguring both literary and composition studies around cultural conflicts, such as "the New England region from about 1600 to about 1800 . . . in which different groups of Europeans and Native Americans were struggling for the power to say what had happened in their relations with each other;" or the Japanese American internment and the conflicts of cultural identity during World War II; or the policies and protests surrounding the Vietnam War in the 1960s and 1970s (Bizzell, "Contact" 739; Bizzell and Herzberg, *Negotiating* 609 ff, 795 ff).

Most recently, our disagreement over the nature of the contact zone has to do with its size. If I understand her position accurately, Bizzell argues for larger, rather than smaller, contact zones because of her belief that larger contact zones invoke historical contexts in ways that smaller contact zones cannot. Though I recognize the importance of the historical dimensions of contact zones, I also believe that, for today's students who often are fully conversant in postmodern America, the historical trajectory has often been so flattened as to be virtually nonexistent—which is not to say that history is unimportant to these students, but to say that conventional ways of invoking have become irrelevant. Additionally, there is some sense, as I indicated in my critique of *Negotiating Difference* in chapter one, that the potential for these larger contact zones for transformation of education in America has been negated when they resemble conflicts that have already been institutionalized as legitimate sites of study within academic institutions themselves. Within the zones that Bizzell has identified, the outcome for English departments, for example, amounts to doing what they are already doing a bit differently, such as widening the scope of early American literature surveys or using a heterogeneous instead of a homogeneous cultural reader, not doing something differently entirely different. In this explanation, the contact zone is appropriated by institutional formations in ways that require minimal disruption in day to day activities. Furthermore, and perhaps more germane to issues of literacy crises, these larger contact zones, with the more recognizable history, generally possess an external legitimacy, one that has not been authorized by particular students in specific situations. If critics or teachers identify, ahead of time and outside of the classroom, the contact zones that will occupy the entire focus of students throughout the course of the semester, then they have, in effect, merely exchanged one external cultural context for another, which is imported into classrooms and imposed upon students—a strategy that, though perhaps less destructive in that it, by definition, recognizes difference, nonetheless ensures that the conditions that have given rise to the contemporary crises in meaning and education in America are maintained.

In an effort to resist the ways that the contact zone has been assimilated by the academy to construct students as passive participants even before they arrive in classroom, students and I collaboratively identify, delimit, and, in so doing, legitimize contact zones that form the content and curriculum of our classrooms. In doing so, the classroom itself becomes a contact zone, replete with competing cultures—academic cultures and students' cultures—and its own history. And then, within the classroom-as-contact-zone, the semester unfolds as a series of contact zones. Besides legitimizing contact zones collaboratively, the students and I also co-teach zones, which, given their roles in establishing the contact zones, only seems appropriate. (Students are, in fact, authorities on literacies about which I will never be an authority.) Somewhere and at some point, students and I will negotiate generative themes—or the approaches that will enable us to access the cultural conflicts. (The theory is Freire's, but the practice is not.) Last semester, generative themes had three aspects—a central question, writings and readings, and a cumulative assignment. The central question provides an

organizing principle. The writings and readings enable us to experiment with
consuming and producing a range of competing discourses. Finally, the cumulative assignment asks students to bring together competing discursive practices in
the production of a text. During the initial theme that I teach alone, the co-
teachers will draft a schedule for their themes, which we will negotiate into its
final version.

The result is (more or less, sometimes more, sometimes less) a collaborative
curriculum that the students and I have legitimized together, and the semester
becomes a series of shifting zones in which students experiment with a range of
discursive practices, some that emerge from the cultural conflicts of specific
zones (e.g. ways of interpreting oral discourse from a theme on oral literature or
feminine arguments from a theme on gender in schools) and some that come
from the classroom as a contact zone (e.g. formalist ways of reading or writing
academic analyses). Within the conflicted cultural contexts, the students and I
explore generative themes that we have created. Unlike Shor, I do not distinguish
among generative, topical, or academic themes. Rather, I have situated Freire's
original sense of generative themes within the context of postmodern America.
As Freire defines it, a generative theme is "the present, existential, concrete situation, reflecting the aspirations of the people" that serve as "[t]he starting point
for organizing the program content of education" (*Oppressed* 76-77). In appropriating Freire's generative themes, I have interpreted them as more than merely
concrete objects and situations, to include dominant ideas, attitudes, knowledges, institutions, and so on. I seek to identify the ways that generative themes
are such only with the conflicts of competing versions of cultural capital, both
academic and non-academic, conflicts that can be generational or geographical,
ethnic or existential, class-based or gender-based, and so on, with the only pre-
requisite that these conflicts come from the intertextuality of students' and
teachers' experiences.

In addition to exploring and experimenting with literacy practices within
specific contexts, contexts that have been collaboratively constructed, I ask students to synthesize their experiences at the conclusion of the course into a narrative of the semester, which serves as the introduction to their portfolios.
Here, students bring together the competing literacies of zones/themes in an
effort to construct the literacy of the classroom, which they do by theorizing
from these experiences in way to account for the classroom within the institution and their lives. Obviously, conventional academic narratives—"All this
semester, we learned to write the academic research paper"—rarely appear.
Instead, students must situate academic literacy within a context of the classroom that included a range of other literacy practices. In an effort to account
fully for the semester, they will contextualize their narratives of the semester

with their expectations prior to the beginning of the term, the official institutional descriptions from course catalogues, the formal explanations from the required textbook, the experiences of their peers in other sections of the same course, and so on.

Introduction to My Portfolio
Sara Yates
Eng. 102

Hello, and welcome to Virtual Class Games, your one stop virtual game shopping for kids of all ages. We thank you for your letter inquiring about some of out more advanced educational learning products. At this time, our number one leader in the field is what we call "English Comp. 102." With the purchase of this product magically you, the buyer, are transformed into a first year English student at Comp. College. Virtual Class Games personal virtual college for only the brightest of students.

Unlike many products similar to this one, "English Comp. 102," allows the player to have almost complete control over their class conclusions for each section. This is due, in part to the mechanical devises we have installed into your virtual teacher. No longer will specific guidelines be given to player. Instead, they must think for themselves if they wish to pass and move on to the next game in the educational series, what we call, "Graduating."

Over the course of only four months this game plunges into questions only the student can answer on a personal basis. To help students on their quest for knowledge, "English Comp. 102" is divided into four sections throughout the semester. Each phase entails different worldly questions we all must ask such as; what is academic writing? Is there class conflict in America? How does a person form their gender? And finally, the age-old question: should there be a mixing of church and state?

While adjusting to their new scholastic surrounding, many players can find this program challenging. Why? First, as I have stated before, "English Comp. 102" main goal is to make the student think for themselves. This entails a new style of teaching where the player is not given an obvious black or white answer. Although a player may come away from each contact zone with different answers for each of these questions, the class will try to come to an extended conclusion for each zone. This is done through group and class discussions, free writes, homework assignments, collages, plays, readings, short story writings, movies, handouts and much much more. Many are not used to this and can feel uncomfortable with it, but only at first. Also, not only is "English Comp. 102" an educational tool but a learning game as well. As the semester progresses, the game will change and mold into a structure suited for the players. Ideas that seem to have confused students in the past are dropped from the database, while ideas that students comprehend are given more time to be discussed further. By the end of the semester students will come away with their own answers to each of the questions.

Also, if you order within the next two weeks, we will include, at no extra cost, the co-teacher program and the "Works of Writers" disk. Both of these programs allow the student to more fully understand the contact zones and be able to digest increased amounts of information comfortably. With the co-teaching program, players will be allowed to work hand in hand in the creation of a schedule for one of the contact zones. This will entitle the player to adapt readings, homework assignments, and projects, which he or she sees as relevant for the zone. Alongside the co-teaching program, you will receive the "Works of Writers" disk. This includes writings like *What Rights Do We Have* and *The Education of American Women*, from such known authors as Henry George, Anna Julia Cooper, Margaret Fuller, and articles from the *Joplin Globe* and *Kansas City Star*. The "Works of Writers" disk will open a world of writing to the student on the issues discussed during class.

For these and many more reasons we feel our "English Comp. 102" class far out does any other programs in the same field , but don't take our word for it:

> "Through this course I have found that there will always be a question on top of a question. Just as I think an answer is found on a topic raised, the teacher or classmate provokes a new question to the answer I have found. This has made me think harder when trying to create an answer, and has made me understand that until I have completely understood a discourse I will always need to strive to complete my answer."
>
> Sara Yates

> "After completing only four months of Virtue English I feel I understand English as a whole a lot better. Although I have always loved to read and write I'm now starting to realize that English entitles more than just that. To truly grasp English you must first understand that there are not always correct answers to subjects. Thanks Virtue English."
>
> Marilla Shoemaker

> "Although I found myself many times confused during this English class I have come to find the style is far better then any I have had before. For the first time I was able to express my creative side when it came to drafts and cumulative assignment. Through this I have found

my strength and weaknesses in English. While I still am working on my ability to completely understand a discourse, I know that others are as well. I need to remember that there never can be only one answer to an academic argument."

Sarah Merick

"Just as many of my class mates, I too found myself many times confused by this class. I feel this was partly due to the style of teaching and to my own understanding of the issues. While the class did sometimes leave me in bewilderment, due to the fact the questions were not fully answered. I now know the teacher did this so that I would have to answer the questions for myself and to teach me that I will not always find an answer to my question. Although some issues we touched upon I thought were somewhat boring, such as academic writing, I know they are important if I wish to understand English. While I leave the class still somewhat hazy on issues such as; is there a thing which is not truly a research paper, I believe the teaching style effective. With daily discussions and cumulative assignments I was able to see what other felt on a topic express. Also, I was able to express my views in experimental ways, such as through collages and portfolios. For the first time I was given more freedom in an English class than ever before. This I feel has better equipped me for other classes I will take in the future."

Sara Yates

In what resembles an infomercial more than a conventional narrative, Sara accounts for both the individual and the social in her virtual college. Early in her advertisement, she accounts for the various themes/zones, the ongoing efforts to make the literacies and learning context-specific, the range of literacy practices that surfaced throughout the semester, and her peers' experiences with the testimonials. Such an experientialist account of understanding is generated through negotiating between people and the classroom, and as such, it preserves the notion of reasoned thinking,

As a teaching assistant responsible for his own classes, he is approached by another graduate student, not teaching at the time, who asks to observe his classrooms in order to fulfill a requirement for a graduate course in composition pedagogy taught by the director of composition. The director has yet to observe him personally, so he readily agrees to this request with the understanding that he will receive a copy of his peer's response. He never receives it.

During finals week, there is a knock on the door of the

truth, knowledge, as well as relevance and context, without appealing to the extremes of foundationalism or antifoundationalism.[6]

In classrooms, constructing literacies tends to invoke a version of culture as both social and individual, which goes beyond both Berlin's and Shor's classrooms. In *Poetics*, Berlin defines culture as "both signifying practices that represent experience in rhetoric, myth, and literature and the relatively independent responses of human agents to concrete economic, social, and political conditions . . . , a polysemic and multilayered category, best considered in the plural" (xix). For Berlin, culture has two centers: the "practices" that are used to "represent" culture in the forms that are legitimized as valuable and the "responses" of humans to their social, economic, and historical conditions. Somewhat differently, Shor appropriates several definitions of culture in his classrooms, as "the ability to perceive meaning in experience and to act on that meaning" and "the outcome of educated action and active education." These connect culture and literacy acts "in the Deweyan sense of the ability to perceive and to act on meaning in your social experience, and in the Freirean sense of culture being the power to use thought, discourse, and action to understand and change your conditions, which Lev Vygotsky explored as the developmental or 'bootstrapping' potential of reflective language" (*Empowering*

cluttered office that he shares with five or six other TAs.

"Can I speak to you for a minute?" asks the man who observed his class. He settles into the chair next to the desk and sighs. "I want to apologize," he says, "I've done something wrong that I wish I hadn't."

Both wait for what he is going to say next.

"Do you remember when I asked to observe you?" the man says. "Well, the director of composition told me to observe you. Actually, she told me what to criticize and what to say, even before I came to your classroom. I needed the grade, so I did it. Which is why I never showed you my report."

Another TA who carpools with him volunteers that he is being mistreated but says that she can't comment further because she needs a good recommendation from the director. The department chair says that unless the director of composition formally complains about his teaching, the chair will not conduct an investigation—which, the chair feels, would be worse for everyone.

No one can tell him whether he should ask the director for a letter of recommendation or not.

❧

In a graduate linguistics courses he is teaching on Standard English and competing discourses, he asks students to translate not from Black English into SE but from SE into BE, and he is humbled to

137; *When* 219). For Shor, culture amounts to the ability to "perceive" meaning within social experience and to use literacy practices "to understand and change" social reality through reflecting upon experience. In classrooms of constructed literacies, I define culture as both determined, in the sense that it emerges from historical and social contexts of students and teachers, and as generative, in the sense that students produce new hybrid cultures through connecting experiences as they reread and rewriting their conditions. As such, culture becomes both a set of discursive practices and experiences and a method of making connections as a basis for meaning.

Obviously, constructed literacies have emerged in response to my reading of the conditions that critics are calling a contemporary crisis in literacy in America. Though negotiating and exploring contact zones and generative themes, constructed literacies disrupt conventional classrooms by legitimizing the use of primary and popular discursive practices, which, in the ways that students integrate these with conventional discursive practices of the academy, can give rise to constructed discourses and constructed knowing.[7] In recognizing the ways that all literacies emerge within contexts of conflict and difference, and as they are constructed from the discursive practices of specific classrooms-as-contact-zones, constructed literacies shift the focus from

discover how much better at this the students are than he is. In a new, almost visceral way, he experiences the privilege of academic discourse, as he sits at a small desk, hiding behind his oxford dress shirt and colorful tie. In his next mental breath, he wonders what might happen if suddenly the naturalized discourse of the academy were no longer the coveted white, middle class SE but, say, the BE that Gilyard and Smitherman write so eloquently (about). How would classrooms change? And how many of us would be out of jobs?

As a visiting lecture-adjunct at a small, liberal arts school, he is asked to apply for the newly created position of director of composition, which is being offered under a temporary contract. He declines, citing the work to be done on his dissertation, but agrees to consider the position when the college conducts a national search next year. The ad in the local newspaper turns up one candidate who has the credentials for the position. She is hired, and he calls her at home to welcome her and to express his relief at having another rhet/comp person in a department dominated by literature people and literary ideas. On the phone, she confides that she has been uninvolved in the field for some time while adjusting to a new role in her personal life. She says that she needs his traditional definitions of literacy to the literacies of relevant contact zones, or sites of cultural conflict, which have been authorized by students and teachers. In this process of collaboration, teachers serve as institutional and disciplinary voices, and yet these voices engage with the voices of students, as representative of their own cultures and literacy needs. As such, the practices of our classrooms become context-specific, which is not to suggest that they never resemble conventional classrooms but rather that, when they do, they do so, in part, because students' literacy agendas have constructed them in that way. For example, contact zones that emerge from gender conflicts regularly appear in our classrooms, and though we often use feminist theory and feminist texts in the process of trying to understand these cultured conflicts, the important distinction between, say, a feminist first-year composition course and a contact zone of gender in one of our classrooms is that, together, students and I have legitimized the conflicts of gender as part of the curriculum. Nevertheless, I am not trying to suggest that everything that transpires in our classrooms reflects students' input, and in part I'm amazed at how difficult it is to authorize students' voices in dialogues over the nature of classrooms and the curriculum. However, I do want to suggest that, insofar as the students and I are successful in constructing literacies, we have been able to collaborate upon

help to understand what has been happening over the past ten years.

Later, as director, she denies his request to continue teaching literature as well as composition in order to facilitate the remaining revisions of his dissertation. Instead, she assigns his literature section to a grad student working on her secondary ed certification with a concentration in geography.

While conducting an observation in his classroom, the new director intervenes in a collaborative learning activity and then argues in her observation that the collaborative learning failed. One of the students afterwards asks him why she interfered.

The first conversation with his new chair in a cluttered office. He is told that the current director of composition has resigned, that an interim director has been appointed, and that he will be assuming the duties in the fall. He had been hired with the understanding that he would be working on a Writing Across the Curriculum program, not directing the composition program. Yet he can't decline the duties since there is no one else who will do the job.

Publicly, the new interim director has assured both the chair and the dean that she does not want the job, and not only because, as a former real estate salesperson with an M.A. in literature, she is, in her own words, unqualified for the classroom in ways that are not available in more traditional classrooms. And the degree to which we approach a greater, as opposed to a lesser, equality is the degree we have been successful in constructing literacies and classrooms rather than having them constructed for us to use and to occupy.

As the literacies of contact zones, constructed literacies often legitimize a range of discursive practices.[8] Given the context-specific condition of constructed literacies, it is somewhat inconsistent to prescribe the discursive practices outside of specific classrooms and particular semesters. Having acknowledged the contingency of these literacies, then, I can report that some of the conventional (i.e. academic) discursive practices that students have experimented with in various classes over the past several years to produce and consume texts are: class discussions; academic and scholarly essays; journal responses; canonical and noncanonical primary texts; final exams; textbooks; large and small group discussions; and lectures. At the same time, they have also engaged in a range of non-traditional discursive practices to produce and consume magazine and newspaper articles; imitations/parodies of academic texts; situation comedies; songs and poems; editorials and documentaries; fairy tales; urban legends; the dozens; commercials and experimental newscasts; newsletters and newspaper articles; plays and skits;

the position. Privately, she explains to the new professor that she actually intends to retain the position, at least through promotion review in the spring, because she thinks it is the only way that she will ever be promoted from instructor to assistant professor.

The new professor's advisor compliments him on the way that his classes prepare majors for graduate school. But over the course of the year, the interim director counsels unhappy students from his classrooms and fans the fire of one problem personality, even taking the student's complaints to his advisor. The interim director gossips with another member of the small department, who confides that the professor won't be rehired. She complains to the chair about him. She never speaks to him directly about her complaints.

The interim director abruptly resigns and swears the chair to secrecy about her reasons. Over grilled sandwiches at a nearby diner, the chair encourages the new professor to sign a contract in which he agrees to assume the duties of the composition director, even though it will be some time before the duties are negotiated. However, the new professor must agree not to write any memos or make any telephone calls without the chair's prior approval.

At a curriculum committee meeting, the WAC proposal is tabled, after which one member asks whether such a move will advertisements and proposals; and most recently, websites and collages. In addition, I have encouraged students to experiment with mosaic (i.e. constructing a text entirely out of other texts), with patchwork (i.e. inserting pieces of other texts within the student's text), and with blending and embedding genres as ways of reconciling the competing literacies of contact zones.[9] In classrooms, these competing discursive practices serve one of two different functions—critique and performance—both of which often appear, in one form or another, in postmodern theory and postmodern classrooms.[10] As critique, these discursive practices seek to deconstruct, or dismantle, texts and

send the wrong message, merely keeping the new professor's hopes alive. After the meeting, the chair of the committee, who argues for an exit exam in place of a WAC program, apologizes for what he calls "the bloodbath" and offers to buy him a drink. Before the new professor can respond, the chair of the committee says, "If anyone is going to work harder, it's the English department."

The new professor is walking with his tiny daughter, so he can politely decline.

So much for the legitimacy of being an insider with a Ph.D.

discourses, both inside and outside of contact zones. As performance, these practices generate alternative texts, participating in competing discourses and alternative versions of culture, to fill the deconstructive gaps. Together, critique and performance work in dialogue, which both enables students to construct order and meaning and provides them with multiple perspectives from which to read, or understand, contact zones.[11]

There is a growing recognition of the advantages of experimenting with multiple discursive practices in the classroom, particularly in the ways that these challenge conventional academic literacies.[12] For example, James Paul Gee suggests that narrative itself challenges the topic-centered texts of conventional academic literacies ("Narrativization"), and John Schilb advocates the use of autobiography as a way to legitimize personal experience (*Between* 170 ff). In a similar way, using practices that have an increasing legitimacy within the academy can offer significant alternatives for students. For instance, Lester Faigley invokes the use of microethnographies, which, he thinks, insist that students consider agency and situate themselves within cultures (*Fragments* 218). For another example, the license to use Patricia Bizzell's hybrid discourses (which exhibit variant versions of English, non-traditional cultural references, personal experience—what she calls offhand refutation and appropriative history, humor, and indirectness as a direct challenge to conventional academic discourse ["Hybrid"]) could be extended to students. Nevertheless, all of these practices have an external legitimacy that, especially if they are imported into classrooms and required of all students, can alienate students in just the ways that more conventional academic practices can. Though I would want to resist reductive characterizations, I would agree in general with Miriam Camitta that, particularly in the ways that these practices are more often than not tied to local contexts, popular literacies can be nonhierarchical, nonhegemonic, and noncanonical, and as such, they not only can facilitate proficiencies in the literacies of power within the academy, but also, and perhaps more importantly, can empower students to legitimize their experiences in classrooms.

The conflicts between academic and popular literacy practices can be used to develop alternative perspectives on each other.[13] Often, the co-teachers and I ask students, in light of the political contexts of literature and composition courses, to use translation as a way of shifting between literacies and experimenting with the boundaries that lie between them. For example, we created a cumulative assignment for a theme on competing gender constructions in the first semester of first-year composition in which we asked the students, either collaboratively or individually, to create a collage of the social meanings of gender out of magazine advertisements. Advertising is a language with which the students were familiar, as their texts demonstrated, and one that is extremely relevant to social meanings of gender. Then each of them was to translate the collage into academic discourse individually. Linda, Angie, and the rest of their group submitted this collage:

In her individual response, Linda translates the seemingly chaotic images of competing genders, which she acknowledges as complicated, into accessible prose:

> The collage that Justin, Angie, and I created for gender and sexuality theme appears to be very complex. But in truth it has only three main ideas.
>
> Idea one: You will notice that the top right side of the page portrays women in aggressive roles with the cutout of a woman yelling at a man and the one with the women holding a gun. Whereas the men in this section are doing ballet and one is holding a baby. This was done to illustrate the not so traditional side of gender and sexuality.
>
> Idea two: This idea is found through out the poster, men and women in more traditional roles. For example the picture of the man with all of the money shows power and success traditionally associated with men. Also as the picture right next to it displays a women in maid attire, giving off a more servantorial role. Along with these are the picture of men and women together, in an apparently happy and loving relationships; there is one almost in the middle of the poster and one on the left side.
>
> Idea three: This like the second idea can be found all over the poster. It is the way the other not so traditional roles are placed on the page. All of the gay or lesbian couples are upside down and by doing this we show that they are a very integral and important part of our society but going against the main stream.
>
> To sum up our poster I will use the quote at the top "At some point you just know who you are." The people on our poster are all very different but that is the only norm in our society, everyone is different, there are no set gender roles or responsibilities it is the individuals choice as to who or what they are!

As Linda's submission suggests, her collage has provided her with a way of articulating the conflict between individual and social meanings of gender ("'At some point you just know who you are'" and traditional and nontraditional roles), which was a constant tension throughout the theme. Virtually all of the readings advocated a predominantly, if not exclusively, social definition of gender, and the guest speaker, a female philosopher from the social sciences department, argued against *masculinity* and *femininity* as useful terms for considering gender and in favor of individually determined constructions. Within this context, it is possible to read Linda's translation as textualizing this conflict between the individual and the social (e.g. **"the** picture of **men** and **women** together, in

an apparently happy and loving relationship**s**"). Given such a reading, Linda's submission disrupts the continuity of conventional academic discourse, not unlike some postmodern feminist discourses.[14] While I wouldn't suggest that Linda is deliberately engaging in postmodern feminist practices to disrupt the sexism of a phallic academic discourse, I am suggesting that one productive response to Linda's submission would be to connect her translation with postmodern feminist texts and that the competing literacies—popular, academic, and other—foreground these conflicts and challenges in accessible ways.

Using translation also enables students to explore the ways that literacies encode certain versions of who to be and how to see the world and to generate alternatives to these inscribed subject positions and versions of the world. In classroom, translation can establish a dialogue among competing practices and discourses—a dialogue that, according to James Sosnoski, enables conflict and competing practices in ways that conventional academic discourses cannot (207). Again, Linda's submission can serve as an example. In her submission, Linda has translated from the popular practices of gender in advertising to a complex declaration of gender in society that recognizes difference of sexualities and gender and the similarity of heterosexual and homosexual "not so traditional roles" (or what Danny Weil calls the politics of difference and solidarity), which are part of critical multicultural literacies (32). In other words, she is able to introduce sexual inclination into the gender equation, and, at the same time, she offers an alliance between unconventional heterosexual gender roles and (perhaps stereotypical) homosexual gender roles. One way to theorize about these dialogues is to see them in terms of internal and external discourses, designations that are provisional and that change depending upon where one is situated. (In this theorizing, I have read and appropriated Bakhtin as provisional and contingent.) For many students in the classroom contact zone, "internal" discourses are the discourses of the academy, the discourses of power within classrooms from which they have traditionally been excluded. For these students, "external" discourses, on the other hand, are the discourses that students bring with them into the classroom. These external discourses, though internal perhaps to students, have been traditionally denied by the dominant academic literacies. In classrooms, the internal discourses, which Bartholomae and others insist that students must appropriate or be appropriated by, are the products of sanctioned ways of reading, received knowledges from teachers, etc. In these forms, interal discourses generate a zone of distance, which keep students separate from and outside of the culture(s) of the academy. As possessing a historical legitimacy with the academy itself, these internal discourses often resist mediation and exclude students and their literacies, demanding that students either accommodate them or suffer the consequences. Unlike internal discourses of the academy, the external discourses of students, as outside academia proper and nearest students in linguistic proximity, can be used, through dialogue, to rupture the ostensive uniformity and universality of academic discourses by situating students and their discourses as legitimate participants in academic culture-making, thereby providing spaces in which students can use competing discursive practices as a way of generating constructed discourses.

Through dialogues between external and internal discourses, students can use multiple discursive practices to rewrite the sanctioned versions of who they should be and how the (academic) world is. For constructed literacies, the dialogues generated through translation foregrounds the ways that students can use literacies in what Freire calls "the process of becoming—as unfinished, uncompleted beings in and with a likewise unfinished reality" (*Oppressed* 65). The way that this "ideological becoming"—to use Bakhtin's characterization— occurs is through the act of negotiating through and among various discursive practices, acts that Don Bialostosky suggests make "ideological development" not an "accidental outcome" but "the deliberate goal of reflective practice" (191). Stacey, a member of the women's softball team and a first-year student in a composition course names this process as the act of becoming "individualized." When I asked her to clarify the theorization of her experiences in a theme from the conflicts between the cultures of home and school, she sent me the following email:

> What I meant by students do not get to talk about knowledge is that in most classroom settings students are not allowed to speak their minds and tell how they feel about ideas. Students can not disagree with their teachers and therefore students are not allowed to talk about knowledge. I believe that if students were allowed to speak more freely that the student would be come more individualized. This would allow the student to think more critically which would reflect in their writings or any other work that they completed. I think that if students were allowed to speak their minds that they would learn more about not only the subject but also the people around them.

As Stacey's clarification explains, she has begun to challenge conventional subject positions for students and the business of traditional classrooms as she has struggled to mediate between competing discourses and competing cultures. Being asked to shuttle back and forth between these discourses and to bring them together in order to navigate throughout this theme enables Stacy and others like her to learn more and, as Freire suggests, to search for significance in their own experiences (*Education* 140).

In legitimizing the discourses that students bring with them to the classroom and in situating them in dialogue with conventional discourses of the academy, constructed literacies authorize alternative ways of being and seeing the world within classrooms.[15] Recent work by Ellen Barton on the discourse of the medical profession has suggested that, through literacy practices, doctors, nurses, and patients negotiate an intersubjective reality (410 ff), and the situation is the same in classrooms. Through and with, and only through and with, the discourses that have legitimacy in classrooms, students and teachers negotiate their own versions of the world. By problematizing the classroom in the initial theme, we have been able to rupture the purported continuity of the curriculum, of teachers' authority, of institutional and disciplinary history, and so on, thereby challenging the denial of difference of academic literaci(es)[16] and creating spaces in which students can construct alternative versions of who they are, or should be, and how the (classroom) world is, or ought to be. In the legitimacy that is accorded to the literacies in which students are already proficient, students acquire the authority to theorize about their experiences and to experientialize their theories, as well as the theories of others.[17] In an introduction to literature course, Melanie, an African-American student who listened thoughtfully throughout the term though not contributing unless she was asked directly, decided, on her own, to focus one of her formal texts not on a literary work or an author, as is often the case, but upon her own experiences with literature. (In my initial theme that semester on what literature is, I struggled to connect any proffered definition, whether from textbooks, the discipline, the institution, the catalogue, or students' experiences, to particular ways of reading, trying to foreground how definitions of literature are contingent upon presuppositions about what it means to read literature.) In this piece, she theorized about her experiences with literature in such a way that called into question the theories about literature that she had encountered previously. After describing several of her experiences in high school and connecting them to her experiences this semester, she theorizes the following assertion:

> My high school instructor kept me from realizing the fact that literature could be fun. Instructors have a lot of control over how students perceive literature, which is why if the student feels as though the literature instructor is bad it can ruin his or her chances of ever enjoying literature. That's what happened to my chances of understanding literature and being able to understand it.

She concludes her essay by writing that "[c]ollege literature beats high school literature by far in every aspect," thereby linking her assertion to the site of instruction. Though we might want to question whether or not the site of instruction, itself, is the source of this difference, I can see the ways that she is using her literacies to reread and rewrite her experiences in powerful ways. For example, she reassigns her previous problems not to some cognitive deficit, as she originally suspected, but to her former teacher and to the institution.[18] Perhaps more importantly, Melanie did not limit herself to her experiences but extended her explanation, or theory, beyond them to a theory about the world.

In a similar way, Daniel, an international student in his late twenties, manages to reread and rewrite classrooms and education. By his own admission, Daniel managed to drop his first-year composition course until as a junior he appeared in my classroom and then, the next spring, when he reappeared in my second-semester classroom. In a formal text, Daniel rewrites both his previous semester and the conditions of education in a formal text, which he entitles "Academic Literacy: a lifestyle, a concept, a philosophy, or just mechanics?":

> Apparently we have started to dig deeper into the meaning of Academic Literacy this semester. The Academic Literacy we explored last semester had mostly to do with mechanics and the process of writing and thinking, but now we are looking for answers about its history and the people and thoughts behind it. We question who has the right to determine the limits and ways of this way of writing, reading, and thinking.
>
> I believe that scholars in the 19th century started to put structure into the Learning system and felt there was a need to somehow synchronize the ways of educating the people. Because if this was not done there would be different "schools" of teaching, and this would separate people into different groups rather than bring them together as a nation. By setting standards and rules they could not only bring the academic citizens together, but also justify themselves as being scholars, and make sure people could communicate in the same ways.
>
> At the time Literacy was probably just a way of communicating or a standard of communication. It is probably now in the 20th century that the scholars of today have incorporated well thought out mechanics and thinking processes. For example, critical thinking, which is today encouraged, while it is in the early stages of the Literacy concept probably was highly unwanted (because the scholars back then thought highly of themselves and most likely did not want to be questioned).
>
> As a conclusion I would like to say that the concept of Academic Literacy was created by scholars at some point in the 20th century, it has evolved into a lifestyle for some, and nothing but standardized mechanics for others. For me, being a graphic designer and art lover, it is nothing but a correct way to write the English language. Back home in

> Sweden, Swedish is Swedish and nothing else. Here in America English
> has numerous styles and there seem to be no certainty in which English
> is the correct English.

Through the ways it explicitly invokes context, Daniel's text challenges conventional academic discourse, which strives to encode much of context in its syntax and then deny the rest. Yet he brings together universality and uniformity (e.g. "mechanics and the process of writing and thinking" and "answers about its history") and contingency (e.g. "the people and thoughts behind" academic literacy and "the limits and ways of this way of writing, reading, and thinking"). In constructing his subject position, he foregrounds his positionality (e.g. "Apparently we" and "I believe that"), and yet he offers his perspectives as universal accounts, all the while eliding the basis for his assessment. In his efforts to theorize from the readings and experiences during the initial theme, he articulates a relationship between education and social stratification, and accounts for this relationship with a multivalent motivation, yet he struggles to contextualize his experiences at home even as he offers theories about the differences between my agendas for English I and English II. Nevertheless, he offers a theory of academic literacy (i.e. as functional literacy) that is different from his literaci(es) in Sweden (i.e. a cultural literacy) and from the version of (academic) literacy that I offered throughout the semester (i.e. a way of writing-reading-thinking-seeing-valuing-believing-being) and subjects the theories offered to him to his experiences, both home and abroad. In so doing, he constructs new positions for himself in the classroom (e.g. outside-insider, or someone who, though claiming a different culture than that of the United States, nonetheless possesses insight, a secret, about the highly stylized literacy of academic institutions) and of the world (e.g. culturally-specific universal standards for literate performance).

As Daniel's text suggests, the theorizing of experiences and experientializing of theories that results from problematizing the classroom extends, in the initial theme and in subsequent themes, beyond the academy to students' cultures and worlds in ways that enable students to reread and rewrite themselves and their worlds outside of the classroom. In constructing their literacies, students use the literacy practices of the worlds beyond the classroom to problematize the academy. In an exit slip after examining substantive reasoning in a theme on the conflicts between home and school literacies, Kati, a second-semester composition student writes,

> I think Toulmin's model works more with a written argument than a
> verbal one. When I'm fighting with my parents, it would be stupid to stop
> and think of a claim, evidence, and warrant to back up my side.

> However, I think it could be quite helpful, say, if I was trying to sell a product over another. I often write down what I have to say if I need to argue with someone over something or explain to them why I feel the way I do about it.

In her response to the day's class, Kati both problematizes the content of the classroom by theorizing from her experiences and then problematizes her own theory (i.e. that substantive reasoning is unproductive for verbal arguments). Students also use the literacy practices of the academy to problematize the world beyond it, as Angie, a student from a second-semester composition course, does in a draft of a formal text:

> The second theme that has been covered in Freshman Composition relates gender and thinking. The theme has been based around the assumption that men think differently than women. Is this true? I don't think we have found any concrete evidence that supports this theory.
>
> The readings that we have covered so far relating to gender have not been very enlightening. We have read "Is Biology Destiny?" and the introduction to "Women's Ways of Knowing." These two readings refer to men and women being different. It is very possible that they do think differently, but these two readings did not do a very good job of supporting their opinion.

After explaining her reasons for using substantive reasoning to deconstruct the texts "to see if the writer really knows what they are talking about," she asserts that "[s]ometimes the warrant does not connect the claim and grounds at all" and that "[t]he readings we had so far in this theme have had this problem." In her analysis of *Women's Ways of Knowing*, she explains that, in light of the grounds offered in the introduction—that women have historically been excluded from psychological analyses—the claim—that women and men know differently—cannot be justified. "This would mean the warrant is that because women know differently than men, they are not used in psychological theories. This may not be the cause, and it may not be true at all. How do we even know if they think differently? Without knowing this, it is impossible to say that that is why they are not used. It is a circular argument." Though she limits herself to two of the readings from the theme, Angie uses one of the academic literacy practices she has seen to deconstruct a piece of what has been, unbeknownst to her, a powerful book for many in feminist studies and that has been cited regularly, in both academic and popular presses, as an authority for gendered epistemological differences.

Within the contexts that I have theorized, the goal is to enable students to reread and rewrite their worlds through their literacy practices. Sarah, a student writer from a second semester composition course who announced her intentions to become an editor, does this in her essay "The Attempt." In her text, Sarah opens by questioning what, exactly, college writing courses and college in general, prepare students to do. In the first sentence, she writes, "When we finally reach the end of our four or more years in college, will our capacity of literacy prepare us for the transition into society?" In the next paragraph, she explicitly invokes a chapter from Richard Ohmann's *English in America* entitled "Freshman Composition and Administered Thought," and then she uses it to justify her own experiences in classrooms. In an earlier draft of this segment, Sarah limited herself entirely to her experiences trying to negotiate among textbooks, teachers' expectations, and her interests, and in her final version, she has struggled to authorize these experiences in ways that an academic audience would find credible:

> There are many things to be aware of before walking into a classroom with an assumed opinion of what we will learn, what we will enjoy learning, and what we will learn by truly enjoying ourselves. For example, how can a student ever do a piece of "decent writing" by segmenting the process consciously into word choice, sentence analysis, etc. (Ohmann 137). It's a harsh reality that a piece of writing is the only visible product of the freshman course (Ohmann 135). The authors know that writing and thinking interlock in perplexing ways, and they have some earnest things to say, but really the textbooks are about tidying up and transcribing thought, not thinking (Ohmann 136). It is practically pre-destined to accept that our professor will be teaching from a text that is so very structured to the point of the structured society they are preparing us for, (supposedly.) The professors want us to demonstrate what we can do with our verbal skills, our outlines, our thesis'; our style, and our tone. The student has to write something out of a storehouse of subjects, but then fit a theme to a subject to transcribe a ready-made subject within the right scope for the paper, not "too broad or too narrow" and especially not too broad (Ohmann 137). Thus they make no allowance for the essentially creative process of exploring a topic (Ohmann 138). It is strict discipline and non-dimensional training that has created our interesting writing into nonsense babble that seems to just fulfill the requirement. Professors prepare us to write with underlying restraints that do not allow us time to think about what a subject actually means to us, and for us to write about it. They put borders and corners and bottoms and lids on how far we can go in length, matter, and detail, and about what our writing is

supposed to divulge to an audience instead of what our writing is revealing about ourselves. Good writing is filling up a subject of pre-established dimensions (Ohmann 137). But to us as students everything we create through literacy is considered "good writing" no matter how broad or how narrow we weave our messages within our writing. We limit ourselves from exposing our creativeness by just giving the professor, and responding to the professor with what we have learned, instead of our experiences and honest thoughts of what we truly want to say. The reason for this is the student has no compelling interest in an initial subject, but wants to write a theme (Ohmann 147).

"At this point," she writes at the beginning of the next paragraph, "we find ourselves questioning, what *is* real learning?" and later she writes about the inconsistencies between the subject positions that students occupy and the ones that are prescribed for them within classrooms:

We are all ornamented and characterized by our strong opinions, thoughts, beliefs, creative ideas, and goals. There are some, or let us say few, professors who can understand and also accept our personal views. But, structured books, and previous English courses, and the outside world of writing interjects between us and those few professors by threatening us to be nice, and not honest, and not creative, and overall limited in our service of writing for everyone else but ourselves.

She concludes her text by considering how, when "the teacher remains in the background, holding the status of a resource person . . . we students take over *because* of our interests." In doing so, she asserts that

[w]e finally realize who we are to the point that the repetitive system of a grading scale from the past declines in value and we gain insight into constructing a grade for ourselves. And in that lovely revelation we uphold the limits we originated for ourselves. And in the end, individually we will have finally learned to break away from the structured system of society and past English courses. We will have finally learned to tear off the outer coating of ignorance we have grown, to confidently reveal who we truly are through our re-education of literacy.

To be sure, some of what I consider to be the more important arguments—that different narratives authorize different versions of who we can be, and not some essential self, and that one person's ignorance may be, within a different narrative, another's wisdom—didn't take root, at least not at this point and in this text. Nevertheless, this text is effective in the ways that it rewrites the conditions of students and teachers in classrooms. In her account, textbooks and teachers inhibit students' efforts to actualize themselves and, in so doing, resist students' intentions for education. (Surely not all students share Sarah's agenda for herself, but more do, I suspect, than I often realize.) In the ways that textbooks and teachers prescribe textuality and practice, they are restricting and confining students—imposing "borders and corners and bottoms and lids"— and the most appropriate function of teachers is to facilitate students' efforts to resist "structured society and past English courses" in order to construct versions of themselves (my interpretation of Sarah's text) that resonate more clearly.[19]

CRITIQUE

As Stacey, Melanie, Daniel, Kati, Angie, Sarah, and others use the literacy practices of contact zones, as both critique and performance, in order to theorize their experiences and experientialize their theories in ways that enable them to reread and rewrite who to be and how to see the world. Given the ways that constructed literacies emerge from specific students and teachers and specific classrooms, they resist the totalizing tendencies of other context-free versions of literacy. In situating the power to define the curriculum, as establishing contact zones and generating themes, within dialogues between students and teachers, constructed literacies foreground difference and encourage students to bring together competing discursive practices as a way of mediating and negotiating contact zones. As the literacies of negotiated contact zones and collaborative generative themes, constructed literacies recognize cultural conflict and linguistic difference, and they encourage students to construct new discourses through bringing together competing discursive practices. In so doing, constructed literacies invite students to integrate their own literacy needs with the curriculum of the classroom in ways that legitimize alternative forms of cultural capital.

In spite of the ways that constructed literacies emerge in response to the conditions that critics are calling a contemporary crisis in literacy, the practices of our classrooms are not without their own shortcomings. In the absence of the absolute legitimacy of conventional literacies, the classroom practices of constructed literacies must struggle to generate a provisional legitimacy and contingent standards, which establish an authority for interventions in order to repair breakdowns. One of the places that classrooms can break down is in the dialogues over texts and among discursive practices, as the following example illustrates. Throughout one entire semester, a first-year student who was working with a text on gender in society for a second-semester composition course, persistently refused to respond to experiences and texts that challenged the assertions she was making in her own writing, and there was nothing that her peers or I could do to authorize these challenges. In spite of holding a black belt in taekwondo and living at home where she worked in her mother's dojo, this student insisted on a dualistic reading of gender in American society, in which her alternative was a reductively simplified equality between the sexes. Both her peers and I challenged her readings of the contact zone by suggesting that it ignored the reported experiences of her classmates (and even her own experiences) and the texts throughout the theme, and yet her final draft demonstrates her refusal to reread her position:

> In today's society, emotions are considered a weakness by those in society and those that show them are considered feminine. Men are taught from babyhood to be independent, strong, and to support their family and hold down a job. Women are taught to be dependent on the men, to grow up and take care of her family, to get married and settle down. Maybe she can hold down a job, but that is rare.

She goes on to explain that, in her alternative, "female-dominated society," emotional displays in public would be "a strong point," men and women would assume equal financial responsibility, and "one or both of the parents could work" in order to support the family. Despite our efforts to suggest that her reading of gender, while perhaps reflective of her individual experiences, ignored the larger social experiences of her peers and additional variables such as class or ethnicity, we were unable to generate enough authority for our challenges to her reading of the contact zone.

Similar to the ways that classroom dialogues break down over texts and among discursive practices, they can also break down between and among students. Often, these breakdowns occur when students are co-teaching themes. Sometimes, I am not aware of these breakdowns until after the fact, and even when I stumble across them as they are occurring, I am often at a loss as to how to authorize their repairs. In a first-year composition course, one student—a European-American male—describes the problems that he and another—a European-American female—had with a third member, an African-American female student: "As much as I like [this student], I don't think she is deserving of too much praise. In all actuality, her contributions to the group were pretty nonexistent. Anytime we would try to include her in our ideas and ask her what she wanted to do, she either had little to say or would leave before we could get to discuss things together." In the rest of his assessment, he cites their peer's inability to keep commitments for meetings or her refusal to participate in class discussions and activities.

Even among more homogeneous groups, the dialogue among peers can be difficult. In a different section from the same semester, one student who was concerned about problems during their theme waited to approach me until after the theme had concluded. At her request, I emailed each of the others from her group—four white women who were approximately the same age—to investigate further (though the student asked me to protect her anonymity):

> I wanted to ask some questions about your generative theme. If memory serves me correctly, you all had originally decided to look at gendered discourse (i.e. the discourse of men and women), and your library assignment was centered on this contact zone. What changed? How did you end up doing political discourse? And how were assignments/responsibilities for group members determined?

The contradictions and conflicts in their responses suggest the degree to which dialogue had not occurred. The ostensive leader of the group offered this response:

> In my recollection our group at no time was going to do men and women interaction. Our library assignment was done on political discourse. That is what we as a group decided. As for dividing things up for the assignment, they knew what was needed and they offered to take care of some things, and what they didn't do I did because I wanted a great grade for this generative theme.

She concludes her response by acknowledging that her comments "have been blunt" because she is "getting discouraged" over all that she had to do. The response from a third member of their group seems to contradict the ostensive leader's response:

> I am not quite certain how it changed from gendered discourse to political discourse. We were meeting in the library, however when I got there, I didn't see the rest of the group so I decided to do some research on my own. A little while later, we found each other and I was informed that the rest of the group decided on political discourse instead. There was enough material on either that it didn't matter to me which one we did. I was a bit irritated that I had to start over with the research, but that's the ways things are sometimes.

After offering some details about the way that the leader of the group dominated discussions and unilaterally made decisions, she concludes her response much differently: "I felt that there was a lack of organization in how the jobs were divvied out. No one gave out jobs. It was like you either found something to do, or [the leader] would do it for you. I should have probably been more assertive, but it's just so hard to speak up at times." The last member of this group never responded.

These classroom dialogues also break down between students and myself. Rare is the student who will resist—not reject[20]—classroom practices and renegotiate terms that meet his or her literacy needs. In spite of stating explicitly at the outset that facilitating students' literacy agendas is one of my express goals for the semester, students and I rarely negotiate substantive changes in the semester. Occasionally, students will suggest that we eliminate a peer critique session, as students from an introduction to literature course have done, or they will negotiate a reduction in the length of reading journals from two pages to one, as students in a second semester composition course once did. However, many more students reject the classroom rather than resist in meaningful ways for changes. For example, one student missed at least five classes, rarely contributed to class discussions when she did attend, and failed to submit three-fourths of her assignments in spite of repeated efforts by her peers and me to engage her. Her rejection was so pronounced that neither of the two phone numbers that she gave me to use in order to inform her about her eligibility for the final exam were hers (or anyone who had heard of her).

Though students rarely ask questions, they consistently complain, as I cited in the prologue, about what a former chair calls "a lack of clarity." After sixteen weeks of collaborating with me in constructing literacies in and of our classroom and listening to me describe literacies as context-specific practices, students regularly complain about assessing each other, claiming that they do not have the requisite authority. In these and other ways, it is clear that, somewhere, somehow, the dialogues between students and me, not only as a literacy practioner but also as the representative of the institution and of disciplines, are less than expected. To this day, I have yet to discover a way to *require* students to participate in dialogues with me, with the institution, with the discipline. When I problematize standards for literate performance and ask them to engage in dialogues between texts and among themselves, many students insist that I cannot ask questions about what it means to read or what makes for good writing because, they assert, they have come to me for the answers. When I ask students to collaborate with each other in consuming and producing discourses and in constructing and teaching the semester, many protest that they lack the necessary authority or credibility because, the say, many years of school and training are necessary before one can talk about others' texts or to teach about literacy practices. When I acknowledge my situatedness within the world and inside the classroom and encourage students to negotiate the semester in order to facilitate their own literacy agendas, many of them say to me that grades cannot be negotiated because, they claim, only I can know what they need to know and only I can identify the difference between, say, an A- and a B+.

Given the ways that, in order to resist universalized standards for literate performance, constructed literacies legitimize context-specific and contingent ways of writing, reading, and thinking, they rely upon dialogues and collaboration that, almost by definition, lack standards to which we can appeal in order to repair breakdowns in our classrooms. It is less that dialogue and collaboration lack standards and more that dialogues are governed not by rules to which we can appeal but by "certain principles" that are generally acquired through practice and provide only a general direction instead of explicit instructions.[21] Perhaps, in spite my assertion that constructed literacies can resolve the conditions that critics have called the contemporary crisis in literacy, there is some degree to which the practices of constructed literacies cannot alone resolve the crises in meaning and education that I believe are behind these assessments of literacy crises. If these crises are crises in the legitimacy over conventional standards for literate performance, then maybe, at least for some students, their encounters with constructed literacies produce the same, or similar, crises. Maybe for some, the original anxiety that over conventional literacies is simply exchanged for an anxiety over the authority and credibility of constructed literacies. If so, then these (and other) shortcomings are also problems of legitimacy. And if so, then, in the dialogues between texts and over ways of writing and reading, the issue becomes which way is the legitimate way, or the more legitimate way.

In the dialogues among peers, the question centers upon the legitimacy of students to teach and to assess each other, even to teach and assess the teacher. In the dialogues between students and myself, the conflict is over the legitimacy of curriculum and classrooms in which students had a hand in producing. (And for some, there is an obvious crisis in the legitimacy of a teacher who, for whatever reasons, resists the role of omniscient and omnipotent authority in his or her classroom.) At the same time, I believe that establishing standards, though necessary, can be tricky because the act of establishing standards, at least within classroom contexts, seems to constrain what can transpire. I believe that asking students to work together on texts and teaching can induce chaos because, in doing so, teachers must relinquish autonomy over their classrooms. And I believe that authorizing students can be difficult, for, within the historical and social contexts of colleges and universities in America, doing so requires a special blend of presence and absence, all of which must be negotiated within institutional contexts, which include powerful constraints, such as teacher evaluation methodologies designed to identify the absence of predetermined outcomes or tenure-review boards expecting to find certain kinds of evidence.

In the forthcoming interlude, you shall hear from Angie and Linda, two students from this chapter who appeared in same composition classroom with me in consecutive fall and spring terms. Both of these students were in the same group each semester, and both of them experienced my efforts to respond to the institutional critique that was being made of my classroom practices and, by extension, constructed literacies. Following their interlude, I will turn to what I believe the strengths and shortcomings of constructing literacies with students suggest about the positions for students and teachers within classrooms and about the narratives of education that dominate literature and composition classrooms.

WHICH DIRECTION IS SCHROEDER HEADED?

Angie Ulmann
English 102 J

Being exposed to the same teacher for an extended period of time can result in many things- some good and some bad. I have taken English 101 and 102 with Dr. Schroeder, and by choice, surprisingly. I found through the first semester that I had developed a love/hate relationship with his teaching style, but there was enough of the love to have me sign up with him again for my second and final semester of Freshman English.

Dr. Schroeder has some very interesting views on all sorts of topics—some I agree with, some I do not, and some I have yet to comprehend. A few of his other students agreed with this whole-heartedly. He is not a very traditional professor and has different expectations for his class than the average college professor. His classes are based around the themes, or contact zones, in which we try to distinguish the different literacies involved in society. Everything within that boundary is structured as the semester proceeds by supposed co-teachers finding readings and thinking up writings and cumulative assignments.

When I was in Schroeder's class for the first semester, we took some standardized tests to see where we as students should be placed. I had the opportunity to switch to an accelerated class, but decided to stay with Schroeder out of curiosity and laziness. The first few days of class was spent with us trying to clarify what academic literacy was, along with understanding what Schroeder expected of us for the semester.

For the first week or two it was difficult for the class to understand what Schroeder was about and what he wanted from us. After leaving class, my class would debate what he was trying to get across to us. It was also very difficult trying to figure out what he wanted us to understand about Academic Literacy. When most professors ask a question, they are looking for a specific answer. That is what Schroeder didn't like. He said that society like to simplify complex things. He wanted us to think for ourselves instead of working in the invisible box society has constructed for itself.

The academic literacy theme this semester was different than it was last semester. We started at the beginning again with the theme because there were new students who were not accustomed to Dr. Schroeder's different ways of looking at things. I felt (along with the other students who took him last semester) that we had an advantage because we knew where he was coming from, so we were much less confused. It was a good way to get me back into the mindset of Schroeder's class.

Although the theme was the same, we approached it very differently the second semester. We concentrated more with the reading and writing expected in academic literacy instead of discussing classroom behavior and the teacher's influence on the students. We also had a different introductory reading that I did not appreciate as much as our reading the first semester by Paulo Freire. We did, however, write in more diverse texts than the first semester where we basically did free writes as responses to readings. Instead of free writing we answered specific questions. I didn't like this quite as much because I felt I was being constrained to think about certain things. Last semester I could write freely about the reading, which I found very productive. Another difference is that for the most part this class seems to have caught on much faster than the last class, which is a great relief.

A big change made from the first semester is the way we dealt with the curriculum from the start. Learning contracts are a new idea and students from last semester agree that the way they were used was not productive. This could be because the students either don't know how to deal with them or try to manipulate them. I know I am not happy with my learning contract because even though I set the standards and feel I have met them the best I can, I don't think I will get the grade I signed up for. Friends of mine also felt so strongly about this that they thought about renegotiating their contracts.

Another change is that we no longer have permanent groups or pick our themes within our group. We are to sign up for the theme that interests us the most and work on it with the other people who chose it. This was not a positive change because there seemed to be less unity and more conflict within the group. Our permanent group last semester posed no problems as we all learned to work together.

These are definite changes within the class, and there are many more that didn't make a noticeable difference. One very negative change that I saw this semester was that Dr. Schroeder had resumed much more control over the class. Students new to Schroeder this semester came to me and asked if co-teaching was this much of a farce last semester. We no longer co-taught our theme, but stepped back as Dr. Schroeder conducted it. Maybe we needed

more direction than last semester, but it seemed to be the teacher taking over
again and the students passively obeying.

I have compared the activities we have completed from one semester to
the next, and I am obviously more frustrated with this semester and feel it was
not as productive as the last. Dr. Schroeder tells me that frustration with
writing is a sign that the writer is improving. If so, I just hope that someone
else can see that I have improved, because it doesn't seem that way to me.

MY SEMESTER

Linda Crisman
English 102 J

Friday January 17:
I had my first English class today. I have a feeling things are going to be
different than last semester. I'm looking forward to learning more, but it's going
to be weird. We have a bigger class this time and there are different people in
it. I think it is just going to take some getting used to. Dr. Schroeder told us
today how the themes were going to go. With more people we are going to
have bigger groups, and we have to sign up for the theme we are going to co-
teach, plus we have to sign learning contracts. This semester is going to be
different.

Friday January 28:
Surprisingly the first theme about academic literacy went well. After not getting what we were talking about last semester I understand now. I'm not sure if
it's because I have heard the terms before or if it's just clicking this time but I
get it. Karoline, one of my classmate that had Dr. Schroeder last semester
also, found this academic literacy theme much more interesting. And Angie,
another one of my classmates that has been in both of my classes with Dr.
Schroeder thought that it was easier going into it [academic literacy theme].
The first reading "Freshman Composition and Administered Thought" was
hard to understand but after the group discussion on Monday I get it and
Angie and I agreed that Richard Ohman took too long to explain his point. The
Lester readings were interesting because I view them as the absolute
opposite of what Dr. Schroeder believes and teaches us. This semester might
not be as tough as I thought it was going to be.

Friday February 18:
I was wrong. This theme was the one I co-taught and it was very
discouraging. Angie said "It wasn't productive," and I have to agree with her,

we had too many people working together it was hard to find common ground we all had different ideas about how the theme on gender was going to go, and it got frustrating. Karoline thought that we used the Text Book too much in our theme and didn't get a chance to make our theme interesting. I liked it better when we our group of four got to pick what we were going to teach. I got more involved that way. One of the nice things about this semester's themes is the outline of what we are doing it allows me to be prepared more easily.

Friday February 26:

I'm sorry to say but I didn't really get a chance to participate in journal week. For some reason my draft didn't get to everybody, so I didn't get feed back, but that paper isn't going any where, and that's a big problem of mine right now none of my drafts are going any where. I think I'm not into the themes like I was last semester but I'm trying.

Wednesday March 15:

We just finished the theme on drugs. I think it went well, it was much different then the one last semester, but this one was better. The co-teachers had interesting readings, which made for interesting discussions, Angie also thought the readings were productive. She was impressed with one of the co-teachers in particular, "John Flor had good ideas." We had to associate drugs with other things such as society, religion, and medicine. Also the outline of what we were doing was clearer, and the central question was defined. Where as last semester I didn't even know what the main topic was. I knew what we were going to talk about therefore it was easier for me to get involved.

Wednesday April 5:

Well they say practice makes perfect and even though the last theme on capital punishment wasn't perfect it was by far the most productive of the semester. The co-teachers had a mini theme that went along with cp, it was an advertising campaign done by Benetton Clothing Company. This campaign, called "We on Death Row," used men on death row to sell clothing. While I have never seen one of these ads outside of this class it is said that Benetton Clothing Company have magazine ads, billboards, and of course a website which I have viewed, but only because of this class. Also we watched all of <u>Dead Man Walking</u>, a movie about a man on death row and a nun that befriends him before he is put to death, this gave me an interesting perspective on cp. Watching <u>Dead Man Walking</u> made cp personal for me and after reading the Benetton ads my feelings towards cp became stronger. Because each, <u>Dead Man Walking</u> and the discussions on the Benetton ad lasted more than a day I was able to get involved with the issues and express how I felt. I thought it was a nice way to end the semester, where as Angie thought this theme was only semi-productive. She was able to generate her own thoughts but would have liked to debate more, "nobody changed my mind."

Friday April 7:

Over all this semester is different for the most part, it is working for me. I was expecting things to be how they were last semester but there not and that in itself is an amazing learning experience. I think that if they were the same I wouldn't get as much out of each day as I do, although it's not the same it is better this way.

Sources Cited

Ullmann, Angie. Personal Interview. 12 April.

Westaway, Karoline. Personal Interview. 12 April.

4 REINVENTING THE UNIVERSITY

> For all that, there *is* something to cultural literacy. One has to know
> how to be heard if one is to be heard. Those who rail the loudest
> against cultural literacy can afford to. They already have it. How, then,
> to exploit it without being subsumed by it?
>
> Critical literacy, like that espoused by Paulo Freire and others, will
> lead to change, we're told. And I agree with that too. But what are the
> students to be critical of? How do they come to know what to be criti-
> cal of? Why not cultural literacy, the national culture? Play out the
> polemic; develop the dialectic.
>
> Victor Villanueva, Jr.
Bootstraps

> But how would a critical literacy about "the" national culture lead to
> change in a postmodern America? An America where the cultures are
> almost as divergent as the people who live them? Why not academic
> literacies, the academic cultures? Students rereading and rewriting
> themselves and classrooms—play out that polemic, if you genuinely
> want change.
>
> Christopher Schroeder
ReInventing the University

As I have been arguing throughout, the contemporary conditions that are
being called a crisis in literacy are more productively described as part of larger
social crises of engagement and meaning. In offering this reading of literacy
and learning, I have rewritten what critics are calling the contemporary crisis
in literacy in such a way as to foreground it as merely a symptom of a larger
crisis in legitimacy, not only in American educational institutions but also in,
and as a result of, the dominant cultures of American society at large. Based
upon my experiences in college classrooms, both as a student and a teacher,
and upon current scholarship, I believe that the cultural capital of the academy
has increasingly less relevance and legitimacy for students and teachers, even
those who, like myself, from what is often called mainstream America—a
white, male, European-American middle class.

If so, then the contemporary crisis in literacy is more a crisis of sanctioned
literaci(es), and of the ways that these standards for literate performance
endorse an increasingly specialized and irrelevant version of cultural capital.

Many, such as Elizabeth Chiseri-Strater and Paula Salvio, have written about the alienating effects of classroom literacy practices, practices that deny the cultural capital of lived experiences that students bring with them into the classroom. Using postmodern terms, I would argue that the contemporary crises in literacy and legitimacy in American schools and American society are less an inability to read and write (though I do not want to deny the real problem of those who cannot, in fact, read a warning label or write a letter in their defense), and more the result of a mercantilization of knowledge, which critics as diverse as bell hooks and Jean-François Lyotard have discussed, in which the standards for literate performance in schools have ceased to hold meaning for a growing majority of people. In these contexts, what have been called failures in literacy are often political and cultural differences,[1] and the literacy practices in which students are proficient are of little use in school settings.[2] Hence, they are labeled illiterate by the people who have the power to construct them as such.

As parts of larger social crises in meaning and legitimacy, the conditions that critics are calling the contemporary crisis in literacy cannot be resolved by new conferences, journals, books, or other responses designed to address increasingly specialized aspects of literacy and education,[3] for not only have these responses failed to alleviate the conditions of literacy, but they also, I maintain, have exacerbated the larger crises of meaning and education in American society through institutionalizing an increasingly rarefied cultural capital as the criteria for social credibility and authority. If we are going to escape these crises in meaning and legitimacy in America, then we must generate alternative understandings of literacy and education for the increasingly multicultural classrooms—and I mean *multicultural* in both the institutionally identifiable cultural differences, as well as those that, in lacking an institutional legitimacy, are not as recognizable—as we struggle to respond to the literacy and educational needs of specific students and particular classrooms. Such literacies would be literacies in which subjects who are written and read also write and read, and who, in writing and reading, participate in the negotiation of knowledge and intersubjective reality, in which all discursive practices are contingent and provisional and discourses are contextualized within the communities that accord them meaning. Juxtaposed alongside the uniformity and universality of conventional academic literacies, these literacies would also be literacies of disruption and complication, predicated upon ongoing acts of emerging consciousness and resistance in which being literate amounts to entering into dialogue with others and with texts within zones of difference.

As such, these literacies would be literacies of difference, literacies that politicize what it means to write, read, and think, and be written, read, and thought, not just academically but socially. And at the same time, they would foreground their own discursive practices in efforts to acknowledge the ways that all literacies privilege some and discriminate against others and the ways that education is always and everywhere political. At the same time, these literacies would be collaborative literacies, versions of literacy that are legitimized through the collaborative praxes of particular students and teachers within specific institutions and particular semesters. In classrooms, these alternative literacies would generate different classrooms and different versions of educating. In legitimizing the literacies and the cultural capital that students bring with them into classrooms, the business of classrooms is transformed as sites, as Andrea Fishman writes, not merely "to prepare our students to enter mainstream society, but rather to help them see what mainstream society offers and what it takes away . . . [what students] may gain by assimilating and what they may lose in the process" (38). We can accomplish these ends, I believe, when we juxtapose the literacy practices that students bring with them alongside the sanctioned literacy practices of the academy. This allows us to examine the convergences and divergences and to negotiate alternatives among them for intellectual work because the patterns of language and discourse used are both in accord with and mutually reinforce cultural capital and cultures.[4] In recognizing and mediating the conflicts among competing versions of cultural capital, these alternatives would not reject any literacies outright, including conventional academic literaci(es), but would seek to fashion alternatives out of their interplay.

To do so, the modernist standards and cultural values of conventional literacies and traditional classrooms must be supplemented, not merely replaced, with additional standards and values, postmodern values that involve critiques of traditional epistemologies, alternative sets of practices, and awarenesses of larger social conditions.[5] Even as these classrooms problematize realist or objectivist discursive practices, they could encourage students to appropriate, parody, and refashion traditional ways of writing and reading, to mix forms and strategies, to engage audiences explicitly, and to raise self-reflexive questions. While they problematize traditional positions for students and teachers that are based upon transcendental objectivity, stable subjects, and dominant metanarratives, they could offer students positions of positioned rationality informed by a sense of truth as persuasion while acknowledging the importance of difference, multiple and constructed subjectivities, the influence of historical and social situatedness, and the potential of dissensual communities. In lieu of decontextualized classrooms and fragmented worlds, these classrooms could offer to students the local and the spatial, particularly in the forms of provisional and contingent epistemologies and narrative struggles and in the implications of the local and the spatial for their classrooms and their communities.

In the end, however, it is not the legitimacy of postmodernity, in whatever flavor, that animates these literacies and these classrooms, for such a legitimacy would be tantamount to exchanging one version of literacy and one set of values for another. At the same time, it cannot solely be the legitimacy of students' cultures that generate these literacies and these classrooms, for beginning and ending in students' lives would ignore the political realities of schools and society (as in Shor's classrooms) in an effort to allow students, alone, to authorize the classroom. If constructed literacies are going to resolve the conditions that critics have called a contemporary crisis in literacy, then they must offer legitimate alternatives to literacies, whether modernist or postmodernist, that institutionalize universal values, and to literacies that relativize all standards and values, and to literacies that make the study of these standards and values the object of study. In short, constructed literacies must be context-specific and contingent, they must that recognize historical and social contexts and the lived experiences of students and teachers, and must be authorized as legitimate neither by cultures from above nor by cultures from below. Instead, legitimized by the interplay of cultures, they must emerge within institutions and disciplines and among students and teachers in particular moments in space and time, places where students and teachers, working within particular histories and specific institutions and certain traditions, converge to make sense of their experiences and their worlds.

In what remains, I want to begin exploring these context-specific and contingent conditions of constructed literacies, and then I will turn to the implications that these have for classrooms and what they could say about reinventing the university. If we can find ways to generate these context-specific and contingent literacies in collaboration with students, then we can go a long way toward restoring the social and intellectual legitimacy not only to English classrooms but also, I dare suggest, to education in America. In constructing literacies, students and teachers will reinvent the university one classroom and one semester at a time.

CONTINGENT AND CONTEXT-SPECIFIC LEARNING AND TEACHING

Near the end of a second semester composition course, I asked Carolyn, a student from a private high school who had worked with me the previous semester as well, to offer an explanation, based on her experiences both inside and outside of our classrooms from both semesters, of student's roles in classrooms:

i am not too sure if students should be completely involved in the development of knowledge in the academy. in one way, i think that they should be involved because they are as much, or even more involved than their teachers in the learning process. another reason why they should be included is that it would develop the way that we speak about knowledge in a discourse that is more familiar to students. this would make it much easier for students to learn because they can relate better to it. the reservation that i have is that it can not be denied that teachers have generally seen more of life and in that way are more knowledgeable about life in general. in addition to this, teachers have also been exposed much more to the learning process (both by being students themselves and also by teaching) and can bring more to the discussion just from their own personal knowledge. i have no vision of what this would look like. call me a pessimist, but i do not believe that this will truly be happening any time soon.

Though Carolyn is struggling over her thoughts and mired in an either-or alternative, she does raise several interesting observations in her response. First, she authorizes students, in light of their role in classrooms and the goals of education, with a credibility and a legitimacy that they are not often accorded. Second, she privileges teachers' experiences, both inside and outside of classrooms, over their disciplinary knowledge as the basis for their authority in classrooms. Third, and perhaps most importantly, she invokes an implicit, and mutual, respect for the differences between students and teachers. Each of these observations is important, I think, to the classrooms that seek to dissolve the conditions that have given rise to what critics are calling the contemporary crisis in literacy. Such classrooms must recognize the unique authority that students bring to classrooms, including an authority on literacies in which teachers will never be proficient. At the same time, such classrooms privilege experience, rather than content and knowledge, and the value of teachers is less in the disciplinary knowledge that they carry around inside their heads and more in the experiences that they can provide for students. In addition, such classrooms must rely upon a mutual respect for differences and a recognition of the dignity of both students and teachers.[6]

Within classrooms that recognize the unique legitimacy of students, the power of experiential learning, and the importance of difference and dignity, the acts of learning and teaching are transformed from transmitting the knowledge of universal academic literaci(es) or certifying students in the cultural capital of the academy, or even from liberating autonomous subjects, to facilitating multiple literacy agendas and discharging responsibilities and obligations. Such a revision, or "rephrasing," to use Bill Readings's term, constructs classrooms as "sites of *obligation*, as loci of *ethical practices*" and establishes the practices of teaching and learning as *"network[s] of obligation"* (154, 158, original emphasis). As such, the acts of learning and teaching, once resituated within specific contexts of competing literacies and social relations, become contingent upon what Readings calls *"the question of justice"* (154, original emphasis) and can only be performed through dialogue. Given the ethical imperatives of the classrooms that Carolyn struggles to envision, these more resemble what Irene Ward has called functional dialogism, which brings together the ideological becoming of internal dialogues (expresssivist dialogues) and the external dialogues (social constructivism) towards empowerment (radical pedagogy) without denying narrative provisionality (postmodern dialogues) (192, 169 ff).[7]

Within this context, the classroom practices of constructed literacies are characterized by a contingency and a context-specificity.[8] More specifically, the acts of learning and teaching are contingent, as Carolyn's response appears to imply, upon the provisional standards of ethical discourses, which, according to James Paul Gee, are that some discourse would **harm** someone is always a **good** reason, though not necessarily a **sufficient** reason, not to use it; related to the first, Gee argues that students and teachers have a responsibility to **acknowledge** the ways that discourses and literacies **privilege** some over others.[9] Governed by these provisional standards of ethical discourse, the practices of teaching and learning, as Carolyn's response also seems to suggest, manifest themselves within specific contexts of certain classroom and particular semester. In this way, the classroom practices of constructed literacies begin with students' literacy agendas, including any desires to develop proficiencies in conventional literacies. In a second semester composition course, Jackie, an African-American student who worked several jobs in addition to school, articulated her literacy agenda for our second semester composition course:

> When I get through with college, I plan on working in a daycare facility for a few years. After I feel that I've gained enough knowledge from working in that setting, I plan on opening up my own chain of daycare centers. In order to do that you have to be able to speak a business language to parents, employees, and the people that you're trying to buy the land from to build your center on. You also have to be able to speak an English language that makes you seem to be more intelligent than you actually may be. I seriously doubt that parents would trust me and my center if I spoke the same language to them as I do with my friends and associates.

In addition to exploring this literacy agenda in the initial theme on standard language literacy, on masculinity, femininity, and the discourses of work, and other themes that semester, Jackie also discovered, in the course of readings and writings in the theme on work, additional literacy needs, such as naming the actions of a fellow employee as sexual harassment, which she did through conversations over a text she produced with her peers and with me. (Freire writes of naming the world for one's self as one of the most fundamental literacy acts.) After using her literacies to name the world for herself, she was able to inform her employer and to obtain professional help with what turned out to be a history of sexually abusive situations.

Along with the revisions in the practices of learning and teaching come corresponding shifts in the positions that teachers occupy and narratives of education in classrooms of constructed literacies, both of which are always, to a large degree, contingent upon the students and specific to individual classrooms.[10] As Jackie's situation suggests, teachers spend more time listening to students and their explicit and implicit literacy agendas, to the literacies and discourses that they bring with them into the classroom, and to the convergences and divergences between the cultures that are present in the classroom and the cultures of the academy.[11] Such listening must begin in students' experiences and students' lives and must go beyond hearing to include a willingness to change and be changed. In an email conversation over dialogues with students and their discourses, Peter Elbow explains that any such dialogue "would surely have at its center the willingness and openness of participants to be *changed* by the process. Thus an emphasis on really listening—but that's not enough. Only if people play the believing game (even if not using that formulation) are they allowing themselves to be changed" (RE: dialogue). In constructing literacies, these cultural transitions transform both students and teachers, a condition to which Terry Dean attests in "Multicultural Classrooms, Monocultural Teachers," as both students and teachers extend beyond contact zones in which they are comfortable and authoritativeies to ones in which they are neither. In classrooms, the practices of constructed literacies, as, bell hooks explains, with all engaged pedagogies, do not "seek simply to empower students" for change, but are sites where teachers, too, "grow, and are empowered by the process" (*Teaching* 21) of engaging their students at the multiple levels of their lives both outside and inside the academy. In this way, teachers resemble Henry Giroux's border-crossers, or positions characterized by the abilities to be "not at home in one's home" ("Paulo" 198), with the major difference being that these teachers must have multiple homes.

Even as teachers must be willing to assume positions of change, they must also be willing to institute change, both in their students and in the institutions in which they work, through the ways that they construct literacies with, and alongside, students. In addition to modeling the acts of constructing literacies, teachers also generate a legitimacy through the literacies they construct in the classrooms, a legitimacy that, I have discovered, is important to students as well as to teachers. These positions are simultaneously positions of difference and solidarity, as teachers situate themselves within the differences between the students and themselves, as Marian Yee does when she explores her positionalities as Chinese, as a woman, and as a teacher (24 ff), and at the same time, seek solidarity through striving to facilitate students' own literacy agendas. Both of these are evident in Ellen Cushman's definition of empowerment as "(a) to enable someone to achieve a goal by providing resources for them; (b) to facilitate actions—particularly those associated with language and literacy; (c) to lend our power or status to forward people's achievement" (14).

When teachers, as co-learners in the classroom, construct literacies *with* students, they model the process of bringing together competing discursive practices to mediate contact zones. When teachers construct literacies *alongside* students in the classroom, they are also legitimizing classrooms in at least two ways. First, teachers legitimize classrooms for students, who often need help understanding how what they are doing, and often what they're not doing that their peers are, is credible and productive intellectual work. Second, they often must legitimize classrooms in the event that they will be asked to justify the intellectual work of their students to department chairs, deans, and other administrators who make teaching assignments, renew contracts, and decide on tenure. In this way, teachers must also cross borders, in order to assume multiple perspectives and satisfy different, and often competing, functions.

As for revisions to the narratives of education that dominate these classrooms, they, too, are defined in contingent and context-specific terms. The presence of teachers' willingness to change and be changed necessarily transforms the business of the classroom from static transactions to dynamic interactions. In these classrooms, the intellectual work is fundamentally contingent and context specific. (Irene Ward, Patricia Comitini, and others point out that the practices of collaborative/dialogic learning are often at odds with its theory [Ward, *Literacy*; Comitini 283].) In theory, we believe that the practices of collaborative learning constructs students with full agency and legitimacy to generate their own ideas and to interact with each other over ideas and texts. In practice, what often happens is that students are put into groups with the outcomes preordained—in which case collaborative learning becomes another banking mode of education (monologue placed within students' mouths). After reading Ohmann's "Freshman Composition and Administered Thought" and Bizzell's "Academic Discourse and Critical Consciousness" during the initial theme on academic literacies in a composition course, I asked everyone to conduct electronic conversations in which they explored the conditions in which student writers found themselves. In the following excerpt, Carolyn, who was introduced earlier, and Amy, a white student who, at first, was uncertain whether to trust the practices of constructing literacies, explore the legitimacy of resistance for students:

> Jennifer,
>
> Do you think that students can write without conforming to their teacher's preferences? Would they have to suffer any consequences? I think that they can up to a certain point. Teachers have standards to grade by so what would they use if their opinion and say in how to write wasn't used by the students? So much is controversy. Those who have authority to change "English in America" need to act on their statements that things need to be changed in this subject area. Maybe one of the things discussed should be this question of allowing students to have the upmost freedom to write what they want how they want. What do you think? Please write back.
> Amy

> amy—
>
> in response to your email [to Jennifer], i would have to say that in the real world, students do not have the freedom to write whatever they choose, in whatever style they choose. however, that does not mean that students can not break free from tradition and write freely, without teacher's restrictions. but doing this would most likely cost the student something, which is usually his grade. teachers generally want students to write the way they do, or the way the academy does, and so they use this as their standard for evaluating student writing. i wasn't clear what you meant in the third sentence about teacher's standards. but i definitely do understand what you mean about so many things being in controversy. i think that the freshman English course is a perfect example of the teacher's desires butting heads with the desires of the students. they have opposing expectations and goals for the class that develops a place of conflict (contact zones). i know that i am not really defending myself when i say this, but i do not think that the solution is to let students have the "utmost freedom" to write in the way they wish. i hope that i responded to at least some of what you wanted! write me back if you wish to keep up the discussion.
> carolyn

> Carolyn,
>
> I understand why you said that the solution is not to let students have the "utmost freedom" but is there a solution? Should students just

accept the situation they are in? I mean it's not really fair to grade a student, especially at the beginning, on something (academic discourse) that is not really taught. But, I guess that's just part of being involved in this discourse. What do you think? Please write back.

Amy

In these exchanges, Carolyn and Amy exhibit three of the four discursive functions of what Kay Halasek calls dialogic intellectual scholarship (*Pedagogy* 14): they clarify issues, such as autonomy, expectations, and assessment; react to their experiences in classrooms, including teachers' opinions and standards for writing; and initiate speculations about alternatives, such as what a classroom free of teachers' "opinion and say" about what counts as writing might look like or whether students should be given restrictions, even as they fail to generate legitimate options, which is the fourth figure (though it might have appeared in the missing response[12]).

Clearly, it would be relatively easy to legitimize the intellectual work that Amy and Carolyn have done in any number of ways. In the first comment, Amy raises the question of whether students are always beholden to their teachers and tries to conceive of a classroom free of teachers' "opinion and say" about what counts as writing. In the second, Carolyn theorizes from her experiences that the cost of resisting conventional standards for literate performance might be significant and speculates about the relative benefits of a classroom with no limits. In the third, Amy questions whether students should simply acquiesce to the conditions of the classroom in spite of how unfair she thinks it is. As one possible response, I could encourage them to experiment with alternative practices, such as beginning with this dialogue and blurring or merging genres, as well as to include a section in which they speculate about what the resultant text enables them to do that more conventional texts would not. In terms of legitimizing the intellectual work for them, I would focus on each interchange. Building on the first interchange, I would be respond by asking what a classroom free of teachers' "opinion and say" might use as the basis for the inescapable grade, who should generate these standards, and so on. Referring to the second, I would recognize the seeming contradiction between students' not having the freedom to write and their abilities to break free, as well as the conflicting desires between students and teachers or the as yet unarticulated explanation behind why students should not be given the "utmost freedom" to write. In the third, I would ask for more about the point at which students opt out of resistance and buy into teachers' agendas. As for making the connections to disciplines and to institutions, the options are also plentiful: foundationalism, antifoundationalism, and authority; resistances and departmental policies; case studies of resistant students; mini-(auto)ethnographies of resistant classrooms; etc.

As much as possible within the exigencies and constraints of specific classrooms and institutional demands of individual departments, the curriculum of constructed literacies becomes contingent upon the intertextuality of the literacies and discourses that students bring into the classrooms and the literacies and discourses of the academy, and it is generated from specific literacy agendas (including the disciplinary and institutional agendas) and particular literacy needs, both personal and public. In these classrooms, what results in legitimate literate performance will emerge from the selected zones and explored themes, the students' interests and levels of engagement, the pace and rhythm of the semester, and so on. As students participate in determining the standards for literate performance, they must come to terms with fundamental literacy questions that, in traditional classrooms, are naturalized into a supposed universal legitimacy—questions that emerge within specific contexts, such as what does it mean to read? or how does a writer develop credibility? in these classrooms, what does it mean to read academically? or how does a writer develop credibility for an academic audience?

In many ways, students' experiences in investigating contact zones and exploring specific themes prepare them for the final literacy act of the semester, which is reading and writing their classroom. As we have been doing all semester long in themes from conventional and unconventional contact zones, I ask students at the end of the semester to theorize their experiences over the past sixteen weeks and to apply their experiences to theories.[13] More specifically, I ask them to reflect upon their experiences, both the experiences they have had in our classroom andas well as other experiences that appear relevant to them, in order to account for them in with a (semi-)coherent explanation, or theory. At the same time, I ask them to apply their experiences, again both inside and outside of our classroom, to theories, whether their peers' accounts of the semester, such as interviews with students from our course or from another section of the same course, or the theories of practicing professionals, such as Louise Rosenblatt's theories about efferent and aesthetic reading or David Bartholomae's explanation of students' requirements to appropriate, or be appropriated by, academic discourses. In so doing, students must read and write the semester, as they mediate competing cultures, including the culture of the academy, in their efforts to construct the literaci(es) of our classroom.

When students and I have been able to construct literacies of our classrooms, being literate amounts to recognizing the benefits and the costs of reading, writing, and thinking within specific contexts, including the context of the classroom. And, if they desire, it includes reconciling the cultural conflicts of these contexts in a way that exploits, not erases, these conflicts to generate alternatives—alternative texts, alternative practices, alternative literacies—that enable them to do what they want without unacceptable costs. In identifying the politics of literacies and in negotiating alternatives, students are able to bring their cultures to the table and to fashion classrooms out of the interchanges between these cultures, thereby imb(r)uing classrooms with legitimacy. This legitimacy is not a legitimacy that is externally imposed and not a legitimacy that comes entirely from their experiences, but a contingent and context-specific legitimacy that emerges from the interactions of students' cultures and the cultures of the academy. These are the efforts of creating spaces which allow students to move beyond the cultures of their lives and the cultures of schools that Gee suggests.[14] These are the practices of the third idiom which Shor theorizes.[15] These are constructed literacies.

REINVENTING CLASSROOMS

In "Postmodern Teachers in Their Postmodern Classrooms," James Sosnoski writes that, in resisting romanticization, radical discourses must be normalized (i.e. domesticated or "denominalized, made credible" or "reduced to [the] lowest common denominator") in order to effect change, which occurs "piece by piece, in a local and ad hoc manner" (200, 218). What I think he means is that critics must translate these critiques into shared discourses in order to build bridges. (Sosnoski's explanation makes me think of the intellectual work that Villanueva, drawing on Gramsci, attributes to the new intellectuals, positions in which the organic and the traditional can be fused into a counter hegemony (132).) Sosnoski explains (domesticates his explanation, I guess) by situating it within a context:

> With respect to universities, I advocate rebuilding through total and continuous piecemeal remodeling. For example, English 111 as I taught it last year changes to the extent that I import and therefore domesticate the ideas of others. Granted, if I alter my course in a way that bears no relation to what other intellectuals are doing, the program (building) will likely remain the same because changes I make by myself are miniscule. If the program remains the same, so does the department and the university. However, if many courses change in parallel ways, programs change, departments change, and so on. (200)

Though I wonder how he could alter his course in ways that have "no relation to what other intellectuals are doing" (is there ever anything **new** under the sun?), I think his, and Villanueva's, emphasis upon connections is valuable. So here is my effort to make connections between what I am doing in my critiques of textbooks and pedagogies and my performances of constructed literacies to what other intellectuals, such as Pat Bizzell, are doing, in the hopes that, as Sosnoski writes, making these connections will link what my students and I have been trying to accomplish and what other intellectuals are also trying to do. (But isn't this connecting what we're always doing when we cite sources, why, in the best sense, we value those academic writers who cite sources?) Various critics, such as Bruce McComiskey and John Trimbur and Patricia Comitini,[16] have theorized about the kinds of changes in disciplinary and departmental structures that constructed literacies would generate, and yet the one who comes the closest, and the one whose differences might be the most revealing, is Patricia Bizzell. In an effort to talk about the implications that I see in constructed literacies for classrooms and, if Sosnoski is right, departments and institutions, I will connect them to what Bizzell has done, and is doing, looking first at the similarities and then the differences. Finally, I will present two themes, one from a literature classroom and one from a composition classroom, in order to see what they suggest in way of reinventing departments and institutions, which ought not to be the inflexible formations that Bartholomae constructs them as but which ought to change, and be changed, by those readers and writers who pass through, who, some (I) might say, construct them.

BIZZELL'S RHETORICAL LITERACIES, ENGLISH-CULTURAL STUDIES, AND EDUCATION

Though Bizzell devotes much of her professional writing to using theory as a way of understanding her teaching,[17] she most explicitly describes her classroom practices and their implications for the discipline in two texts—"'Contact Zones' and English Studies," in which Bizzell describes an alternative configuration for English classrooms and for the discipline, and "Marxist Ideas in Composition Studies," in which she offers a reading of the theories that inform her composition classroom. Separately, each of them can be read to understand her literature and composition classrooms, and together, they provide a snapshot of the discipline as a whole.

Bizzell offers a version of literacy, which she calls rhetorical literacy, to students. In literature classrooms, the discursive practices of rhetorical literacies are what she calls "the skills of analyzing and imitating rhetorical arts of the contact zone," such as critique, parody, comparison, and others, while in composition classrooms these discursive practices—negative and positive hermeneutics (though perhaps one and the same)—serve as "methodologically sophisticated and ethically informed modes of social analysis of language use in the construction and control of knowledge."[18] As for the subject positions and versions of the world, rhetorical literacies privilege positions characterized by what Bizzell calls a critical consciousness, which, at least in later essays, amounts to accommodating multiple academic epistemologies while negotiating differences in and through the discourses of others and the world. Rhetorical literacies invoke a contingent reality of contradictions and tensions in which discourse communities challenge one another for hegemony and for the right to define knowledge and reality and in which shared contexts generates meaning from discourses.[19]

In terms of learning and teaching, Bizzell is fairly explicit on the ways that these practices of rhetorical literacies would transform classrooms. For teachers, the position that Bizzell's theoretical practices offer is what she calls the public intellectual, whose function is to facilitate shared discourses within communities both inside and outside the academy.[20] (Again, we see the importance of connecting beyond the classroom.) According to Bizzell, the public intellectual assumes a rhetorical positionality with "multiple allegiances," which engages in collective political action, such as "arguing about what we should read and write, arguing about what canon we want to endorse instead of pretending we can will away the power of canons."[21] Such teachers maintain explicit connections between their practices in the classroom and their practices of theory—she calls these connections "an affective link between our work and the classroom"—that provide them with both the legitimacy to act and the skepticism to investigate their own ideologies.[22]

Given the way that Bizzell insists that classroom practices remain connected to larger social concerns, her practices give rise to an alternative configuration of English studies, in particular, and of education, in general.[23] The alternative version of English studies would bring the disciplines of literary studies and composition studies, along with their various sub-disciplines, "into productive dialogue with one another" in social spaces where cultures clash. Building upon Pratt's notion of the contact zone, Bizzell defines a contact zone "in terms of historical circumstances" and as "circumscribed in time and space, but with elastic boundaries."

> In short, I am suggesting that we organize English studies not in terms of literary or chronological periods, nor essentialized racial or gender categories, but rather in terms of **historically** defined contact zones, moments when different groups within the society content for the power to interpret what is going on. As suggested above, the chronological, geographical, and generic parameters of any contact zone are defined on the basis of including as much material as possible that is **relevant** to the **issue** being contested. **Time periods** can be **short** or **long**, **literatures** of different **groups**, **languages**, or continents can be considered together, all **genres** are admitted, and so on. (739)

Rather than enrolling in either literature or composition courses, students in Bizzell's classrooms would encounter both in the same course, a course that was writing-intensive and that included reading of literature in the broadest sense. The advantages, according to Bizzell, are recognizing differences, implementing multiple cultures in English studies, and blending composition and rhetoric into literary studies.[24] In more general terms, her practices give rise to what she calls the rhetorical education of the whole person "in culturally **endorsed** values, through reading, writing, and speaking," not demanding that students conform to transcendent, universal values but deconstructing dominant discourses for contradictory values and offering alternatives through rhetorical justification.[25] In focusing on social tensions and contradictions, Bizzell's rhetorical education would function as a cultural criticism: "Cultural criticism should work to reveal the inequities in the social world around us—beginning, I think, with the most immediate site, the school itself—and also to help students imagine liberatory alternatives to the unjust status quo by drawing on the knowledge they possess from their membership in groups at some remove from those who enforce this status quo." Within a classroom informed by the cultural criticism of a rhetorical education, students and teachers would be encouraged to break the rules and to violate academic conventions.[26]

Obviously, Bizzell's rhetorical literacies and my constructed literacies have much in common. Both versions of literacy appropriate traditional and alternative discursive practices, and both use these practices to dismantle and reassemble texts and discourses. Both acknowledge the ways that the positions for readers and writers are constructed and constrained by the discourses available to them, and both endorse positions of cooperation and resistance, centered upon difference. Both refuse to dismiss academic epistemologies and versions of the world, and both acknowledge the social conditioning of discursive practices and contextual theories of discourse and meaning. Nevertheless, there are some substantive differences between rhetorical literacies and constructed literacies. As I suggested in previous chapters, Bizzell's use of contact zones remains rooted in the historical narratives authorized by academic institutions, and in turning to academic narratives for legitimate contact zones, Bizzell opens the possibility that the academy can, and, in some instances, does, appropriate the radical discourse of contact zones. (Perhaps this condition is what Villanueva means by the dangers of specialization and academization, leading to a hegemony by consent.[27]) In these instances, the legitimacy of these zones is dependent upon the institutional authority of the academy and comes from somewhere beyond specific classrooms, not from the authority of students as credible participants in their own education nor from the dissensual community, artificial though it may be, of specific classrooms.

The potential dangers of this external legitimacy and institutional authority are evident, I think, in the contested terms that Bizzell describes her practices:

historically (what amounts to a recognizable history?); relevant (what, and who, counts as relevant?); issues (how is the issue defined or by whom? gender differences in the nineteenth century, as restricted to heterosexual females, and the ways that males were implicated, or to include hetero- and homosexual females and males?); time periods (historical, that is, asynchronous, or simultaneous, synchronous?). Many have argued that literature, groups, languages, and genres are merely complex social relations and, as a result, must be recognized as such within these groups. If the academy does not legitimize them, it cannot recognize them, and then, at least in the ways that Bizzell describes her practices, I am unsure that these could be admitted even if she were so inclined. Endorsed by whom? (as if they can be separated from the contexts in which they exist.) Now, I know that she would not want to be seen as invoking decontextualized cultural values, yet, as she suggests with the elaborate exploration of virtue and values that follows her phrase *culturally endorsed values*, she recognizes that teaching is always "value-laden," and the importance of "incorporat[ing] into [her] persuasive arguments the values and circumstances of [her] students."28 (Though, as far as I can tell, the values begin and end with hers, and she retains the right to determine which become incorporated.)

To be fair, these questions are the questions of authority and legitimacy in the classroom, questions about Bizzell's classrooms that others have also raised.29 Also to be fair, she acknowledges the importance of bringing students into the act of altering the classroom: "I have to devise pedagogical mechanisms in our work together, for example, through finding ways for students to change the agenda of a course in progress or to take its lessons out into nonacademic contexts."30 Though some might say that these are merely issues of semantics, my questions have to do with why students have to *change* the agenda of a course, rather than participating in its construction, and why they must take what, the discourse suggests, are already determined lessons beyond the classroom. Read the Interludes in this book. These questions of authority and legitimacy are the questions that Constantine raised in his evaluation of my classrooms, the same issues that some students who have worked with me complain about. After observing my class in the fall, Constantine wanted me, in the spring, to assume more authority; Angie and Linda thought that more authority for me in the spring meant less for them. As for Bizzell's practices, she appears to begin with the legitimacy and authority of institutional(ized) cultures, which can be modified, as necessary, in response to students. As for the practices of my classrooms, I try to begin with the cultures and values that have legitimacy and authority for students' and use the conflicts between these cultures and the cultures of the academy to read and write the classroom as a contact zone.

Classrooms, however, lack the requisite history, Bizzell explains, to be a contact zone—they may be "located within contact zones" or they may be "places where contact zones overlap" but they would not be contact zones themselves.[31] (However, according to Villanueva, this becoming is what Gramsci saw to be the original opportunity of the American condition—"formulating a uniquely American history."[32] But no, Victor, constructed literacy is not a denial of what you call internal colonialism, not an effort to institutionalize a naïve "melting pot sensibility"[33] but rather an attempt to (re)instill a legitimacy in education by beginning with students' worlds. Students are smart enough to code-switch, but what if they didn't have to? What if a classroom asked them simply to begin with these discrete cultures, these cultures that they've learned to switch back and forth between, and then to extend somewhere outside of the limits of each to a position from where they can theorize about their experiences—inside and outside the classroom—all the while not losing that ability to experientialize these theories in lived life?)

And so the conversation goes, as we read and write the worlds that students must traffic in as they buy and sell their way through the academy.

CONSTRUCTED LITERACIES, ENGLISH STUDIES, AND EDUCATION

Early in an introduction to literature course, D.J., a white male in his late teens or early twenties and an avid rock and roll fan, approached me at the end of class one day to ask whether I thought that songs could be considered poetry. During the course of the conversation, I suggested that he and his group members—two women and two men, all of whom were white, middle class college students in their late teens and early twenties—consider using this question as the center of their generative theme. The next class, he reported to me that all of them agreed that it would make an interesting theme, and without much formal debate, we decided to build a theme around D.J.'s original question. Throughout the course of our conversations, we made plans for the theme. For example, the co-teachers decided to assign a reading entitled "The Minimalist Styles of Raymond Carver and Suzanne Vega," which D.J. located on the Internet, because just before their theme began, we had finished a theme in which Raymond Carver's short stories figured prominently.

In co-teaching the theme, we discovered that, as we expected, the primary cultural conflicts were those between academic culture, which would generally dismiss songs, and students' cultures, which, they attested, would see songs as poetic, if not poetry. Though many of the students in our class were first-generation college students and agreed with the co-teachers that songs were poetic, if not poetry, there were other cultural conflicts, such as ethnic differences about what prototypical examples of music were, that challenged us to think in different ways about music and poetry. For one class, we decided to juxtapose Meatloaf's "Paradise By the Dashboard Lights" and John Dryden's "Why Should a Foolish Marriage Vow," both of which raise questions about the relations among love, sex, and marriage. During class, we would play the song and project the poem with an overhead projector, and then the co-teachers would facilitate small group discussions over the similarities and differences, which I would bring together at the end. As homework, we would ask each student to produce a written response, after class discussions, about the similarities and differences between these two texts. Though the similarities enabled D.J. to read them both as arguments on these issues, he focused primarily on the differences, as he explains in this excerpt from his homework:

> I think that the Meatloaf song "Paradise by the Dashboard Light" was an excellent compliment to discussing this poem. However, they have some critical differences. First, the Meatloaf song features both a male and female persona while the poem only presents one side of the relationship. Second, the song mainly takes place before the "foolish marriage vow," while Dryden's persona has 20/20 hindsight vision. Again, I believe that the persona is copping out, but if both parties feel that nothing was left to gain but pain, then he has a valid point.

As this excerpt suggests, D.J. is bringing together competing cultures as a way of understanding the texts through the language that he uses. Through, for example, connecting *persona* with *copping out* and the popular allusions to the exercise slogan "No pain, no gain," D.J. is establishing overlapping cultural contexts in a way that permits him to read the differences and similarities between Meatloaf's song and Dryden's poem, a way that, importantly, would be difficult, if not impossible, to articulate in either of the discourses individually. (What is the academic translation of *copping out*?) Furthermore, I believe that the ways that D.J. is situated squarely within these overlapping contexts enables him to name significant gaps, if you will, in the texts, such as gendered differences in perceptions of relationships, which he reads in the song but not the poem, and historical differences between the persona in Dryden's poem and the characters in Meatloaf's song. In each, D.J. seems to be acknowledging the importance of situatedness in meaning and understanding, and not only in what he explains but also, I believe, in what he is doing with the discourse of his homework, thereby reinforcing the legitimacy of multiple cultures.

As the cumulative assignment, the co-teachers and I decided to ask students to generalize from their experiences throughout the theme in order to justify an answer to the central question about the literary status of songs. In one of the more interesting responses, April, a white female student who was devoutly religious and also a member of the school's softball team, uses discursive practices with which we were experimenting during the initial theme to answer the question. As the beginning of "Are Poetry and Song Lyrics Poetry?," April reminds her readers—her co-teachers and I—that, in the initial theme on literature, I wrote to them that "'learning to appreciate literature is . . . learning how to read'":

> What this statement means to me and from what I understood he felt as well, was that learning how to read literature means learning how to read from many different points of view in order to grasp all possible meanings. This generative theme has basically done that very thing. It has given me a new way to look at poetry and song lyrics, which I believe is literature.

She writes, "First, I will talk about the reader's response point of view," and then she invokes the class discussion on Meatloaf's song and Dryden's poem:

> I felt that was probably one of our best discussions, every group seemed to come up with a new and different interpretation. No group's interpretation was wrong. In fact, we could have given solid evidence that would have supported each idea discussed. I felt Dryden did not give too much information. He allowed the reader to fill in the gaps and we all filled them in differently. Some thought the poem was written for today while others thought it was written for then. Some felt he was in a marriage and expressing his desire for a release from the marriage while others felt that he was writing to a woman who wanted him to get married.

Later in her text, she uses "[t]he formalist point of view," which, she explains, "is the exact opposite of the reader response," to interpret several songs and poems that we discussed in class, such as "Blackened," by Metallica, and "Alone," by Edgar Allan Poe. At the end of her text, April concludes by generalizing, from the experiences she cited earlier in her text and others, about song lyrics, literature, and ways of reading:

> I feel that both music and poetry are literature. Many song lyrics probably started out as poetry. I feel that when the music is added, it gives us, the listener, one less gap to fill in. It gives us the mood of the author. I believe that any type of thing that is an expression of a person can be considered literature. I feel that when people begin to pick apart the work of another's work, it loses the title of literature. We can guess what someone is trying to say, but unless that person decides to reveal his/her meaning we really don't know. I think that is part of literature,

> revealing feelings or emotions indirectly. That is why I consider song
> lyrics and poetry literature.

In this text, April is mediating among cultures through bringing together competing discursive practices in order to theorize from her experiences and experientialize dominant theories. After acknowledging the history of our classroom by connecting the current theme to previous ones, April authorizes her perspectives in ways that would be considered legitimate by academic readers. Nevertheless, she does not accommodate academic culture unequivocally. In juxtaposing reader-response and formalist ways of reading, she problematizes academic ways of reading literature, which she illustrates through using canonical and noncanonical texts. At the end of her text, she invokes the previous dialogue she established between academic ways of reading as she offers explanations of the origins of song lyrics, the function of music, about reading literature, and about the nature of literature itself. Though some of her theories (e.g. "part of literature" is "revealing feelings or emotions indirectly") are perhaps more plausible to academics than others (e.g. "Many song lyrics probably started out as poetry"), through reading and writing her experiences in our class, she has fashioned her own version of the world.

The cultural mediation that took place throughout this theme on poetry and song lyrics also occurred in students' more public writing. To facilitate our discussions during the theme, the co-teachers produced and distributed a handout, "Special Types of Diction Used in Poetry," detailing such elements as parallelism or denotation/connotation, which we used one day when we considered the lyrics of Metallica, one of the co-teachers' favorite groups. After leading a class discussion that day that juxtaposed Edgar Allan Poe's "The Conqueror Worm" and "Alone" with Metallica's "Blackened," D.J. decided to use that discussion, as well as others in the theme, in producing one of two public pieces of writing for the semester that, similar to what he had been doing in his journal, reads and writes against what he believes to be the beliefs of his readers, both his peers and, ultimately, the academy. In the beginning of his text, he brings together literacy practices that resemble those of popular cinema and music videos and the academy in a way that provides a dual experience of his text:

> Edgar Allan Poe: world-famous writer and poet, reputed for his works of
> the psychological, macabre, and grotesque.
> Metallica: world-famous musical group that sings dark lyrics concerning
> psychosis, pain, misery, and death.
> At first glance, these two artists could easily be lumped together as
> conveying the same messages. However, although the rhetoric of

> Metallica and Edgar Alan Poet have many similarities, Metallica's lyrics
> are actually cynical of the attitude in Poe's poetry.

The use of juxtaposition that characterizes popular movies with the syntactical subordination of academic writing offers a complicated experience of convergences and divergences that, similar to his journal entries, ultimately privileges differences. In bringing together these practices, D.J. addresses the cultural capital of his readers—his peers and myself—all the while challenging their disparate beliefs. Later in his text, he invokes academic ways of reading—rhyme schemes and motifs, points of view and personae—in order to generate internal tensions within both cultures. "Edgar Allan Poe," he writes in the conclusion,

> was a brilliant writer and far ahead of his time. However, his poetry often
> lacked reason to its grotesque rhyme and many times led to a persona
> wallowing in self-pity. The lyrics of Metallica have been an excellent
> source of tough love for the manic-depressive rants, as they point out
> the foolishness of being trapped in such a private hell. In fact, assuming
> literature is didactic, it could be argued that Metallica's songs are more
> representative of literature than Poe's writings. Metallica teaches us
> about misery. Poe simply dwells in it.

Again, the language of D.J.'s text—"lump[ing] together" Poe and Metallica with the "rhetoric" of their texts or the "grotesque rhyme" of Poe's poetry and the "tough love" of Metallica's lyrics for "manic-depressive rants"—evinces the cultural mediation that D.J. is doing. Not only does he establish an intertextuality with the convergences of Poe's own manic-depression and private hells, to which Metallica's lyrics speak, but he also challenges the multiple audiences of his text, who would read this text in his portfolio. Within the terms that he establishes in his text, D.J. argues that Poe's poetry lacks socially redeeming value, which, given the power of the established canon and the printed word, his peers might not expect, and that Metallica, and not Poe, is a better example of literature, which academic readers might not expect, and not, as his peers might believe, because Metallica expresses generational angst but rather because Metallica condemns it.

In addition to a theme from an introduction to literature course, I want to describe a theme from a second-semester composition course on masculinity and literacies, which a pair of co-teachers—Kyle and Ryan, two white males, both of whom were on college sports teams—proposed. During a conversation about their theme, Kyle explained that he and his partner thought that too much time was spent in college talking about women's issues and that they wanted to give time to what they considered to be men's issues. In the process of producing the theme, the co-teachers identified four areas on which they wanted to focus, which they labeled "Man v. Man Relationship," "Man v. Women Relationship," "Man in the Business World," and "Man at School," and over the three weeks of their theme, we read a number of texts, such as "When Your Wallet is Thicker Than His," an article from a popular magazine which they found, and "Teaching and Learning as a Man," a piece on masculinity in classrooms by Robert Connors that I selected. In class, we engaged in a number of different activities. For example, we decided to spend a couple of days analyzing *Seinfeld* episodes for popular versions of masculinity, and co-teachers conducted an informal survey of their classmates, based upon the Heinz dilemma, in order to consider gender and ethics. On another day, I outlined academic arguments about the features of masculine discourse and about gender bias in classrooms. Upon concluding the theme, the students were to produce a script for a situation comedy or other television show based upon competing versions of masculinity as the cumulative assignment. Appropriating the characters from a cartoon show, Jerry submitted the following text:

The Tick and his sidekick Arthur sit atop a building on their evening patrol of the city.

Tick: Evil. It's out there Arthur. Lurking, creeping and being o so nasty. (sniff sniff) I can smell it too. C'mon sinister beings, show us your wretched hides.

Arthur: Tick, we've been at this for seven hours now. I'm sure if evil were going to happen tonight it would have done so by now.

T: Arthur, we're superheroes. Something always happens.

A: Oh sure, you mean like the same something that has not happened every other night this week?

T: You know chum, it's impatient pessimists like you who suck the life right out of crime fighting.

A: Well I'm sorry but I just think our time could be better spent by . . .

Before Arthur can finish his sentence, he is interrupted by the sound of wailing sirens.

T: Ha Ha! Bite your tongue stalwart sidekick, the fun is about to begin. Everybody, into the pool!

The Tick and Arthur follow the sirens to a nearby bakery where they find the evil Breadmaster. Tick approaches the officer.

T: Excuse me officer, but what seems to be all the commotion?

Officer: Oh Tick, we're so glad you're here. It's the breadmaster, he's destroying every bakery in the city.

T: Egad! Fear not, law enforcing citizen. We shall thwart this devious dough maker and keep his evil yeast from rising again.

The Tick and Arthur go racing into the bakery where the Breadmaster is about to wreck a wedding cake.

Tick: Evil doer, unhand that fresh baked goodness, or be prepared to deal with the cold hard forces of justice!

Breadmaster: In your face super goon!

The Breadmaster picks up the cake and hurls it at the Tick, smacking him right in the face.

Tick: Oooh Chocolate.

As the Tick stands around licking the delicious cake off his face, the Breadmaster makes a break for it.

A: Tick, he's getting away!

T: Huh, . . . Not on my beat mister. Spoooooon!

The Tick goes charging after the Breadmaster when he notices a bunch of gingerbread men on the counter.

T: Oh Arthur, check it out! Keen! Look at how cute they are too. Hello Mr. Gingerbread man, how are you?

A: Tick! Quit playing around and get the Breadmaster before it's too late!

T: Sorry.

Picking up the plate of gingerbread men, the Tick goes racing after the Breadmaster.

T: Let's go boys, we'll stop this villainous lot together. Charge!

The Tick takes a mighty lunge and lands atop the fallen villain.

T: Breadmaster, your sour-dough has just collided the sweet taste of justice. Now it's back to the oven with you.

In come Arthur and the police.

A: Tick, is everything O.K.?

T: It is now, Arthur, for evil's cross-eyed stare has been straightened through the corrective lenses of goodness.

Officer: Thank you Tick for saving our city once again.

T: Don't mention it fellow crime stopper, yet I can not claim all the praise. The real heroes here are the city's gingerbread population. Those adorable icing smiles and cute candy buttons are enough to strike fear into the hearts of evil everywhere. Say where are our heroes anyway?

The Tick looks around to find a dog has eaten all but one gingerbread man, which is being held in his mouth.

T: Ahh! Mr. Ginger! Hang on man, daddies on his way!

The Tick runs off chasing the dog.

Significantly, even before the theme began, Jerry and I had a conversation about the Tick t-shirt that he had worn to class, and I asked about the sublimated sexuality in the cartoon, which my wife, an art therapist and a Tick fan, had pointed out to me. During the theme, several students suggested that the characters from *Seinfeld*, particularly Elaine and Jerry, challenged conventional definitions of masculinity. After the co-teachers discussed the result of their survey, others argued that stereotypical versions of masculinity failed to account for all of the men in our class. As his text indicates, these and other conversations about masculinity form the context in which Jerry is working to rewrite stereotypical definitions of masculinity in two obvious ways. First, Jerry has appropriated the conventional superhero narrative as a way of rereading and rewriting both academic and popular versions of masculinity. For example, the character of the Tick in his alternative narrative is simultaneously vigilant in his watch for crime and distracted in his pursuit of the criminal, successful in his defeat of the Breadmaster and imperfect in his inability to save the gingerbread men, independent in his efforts to save the city and collaborative in recognizing his "fellow crime stopper" and "the city's gingerbread population," who are the "real heroes." Second, Jerry has blended together what have been identified by academics as features of masculine and feminine discourses in both of the characters.[34] For instance, the Tick's language displays both the tendencies to interrupt more (masculine) with the tendency to use questions not merely for information but also as a way of deferring to others and establishing solidarity with others (feminine). Arthur challenges (masculine) the Tick's assertions that something always happens and yet uses *you* and *we* as ways to recognize their relationship (feminine). In these and other ways, Jerry uses the discursive practices of a cartoon show in order to critique stereotypical definitions of masculinity and to offer an alternative.

As in his cumulative assignment for the theme on masculinity and discourse, Jerry also engaged in cultural mediation through rereading and rewriting in his formal, more public texts. In the second text he started that semester, he again appropriated popular culture to rewrite the classroom. Here is the opening from that text:

> Earlier this semester, I developed a text which read in the form of a short story. Stealing an idea originally presented in Superman comics and later in an episode of Seinfeld, I explored the possibility of a bizarro world. This bizarro world takes what is known, and then reflects it in a whole new reality where everything is reversed. In this case, the bizarro world was set in a college rhetoric course. What had been reversed in this situation was the expected standard of how one should write in such a class. To the main character, the highly structured and focused writing we all learn growing up. The teacher in this alternative existence

> believes otherwise. In her mind, the only way to produce successful
> writing is through a loose, uninhibited manner and that the structured
> academic style her students possess is ineffective and should be forgot-
> ten. The student then finds himself in a situation where he must decide
> between adopting this new style or refusing it, keeping true to the
> discourse of the writing he knows best.

As with all narratives, there are multiple ways of reading the initial text that
Jerry invokes in this introduction: a simple allegory about the dangers of losing
something of value; a symbolic narrative in which the alternative classroom
is—in bizarro fashion, the inverse of academia at large; a parallel narrative to
the bizarro worlds, from *Superman* and *Seinfeld*, in which the hero, or the anti-
hero in the *Seinfeld* version, exists in simultaneous realities until he reconciles
them; and so on. In spite of turning to an unnecessary dualism, Jerry has managed, in the initial text, to appropriate a discursive practice of comic books and
sit-com shows in order to rewrite the classroom and, in this text, to generalize
from his experiences producing that text would lead to new positions for teachers and new ways of seeing the classroom. In doing so, he manages to problematize teachers' expectations, conventional academic discourses, and other aspects
of academic culture. Through the intertextuality that Jerry establishes in the
beginning of his text, he foregrounds the conflicts between academic cultures
and students' cultures, conflicts that include legitimate positions for students
and contradictory versions of classrooms. What his narrative problematizes
implicitly, however, becomes explicit later in opening of his second text:

> Returning now to our world, let us take a closer look at the teacher's
> suggestion. It is safe to say that her wish to eliminate academic style of
> writing is illogical. While perhaps for her class purposes it may be
> acceptable, from an overall standpoint it can not be done. This
> academic writing is at the core of all student writing and may not deem it
> to be important, it is what others have come to expect and demand from
> their students. But with that aside, is her proposed style all that bad?

From this point, he proceeds to explain how his original text, along with the
commentary in his second text, describes the experiences that he and his peers
have had in composition classrooms as they work to become "more accomplished writers," and he concludes this section by asking whether "the teachers
loosely structured style" can be "a successful method for developing student
writers."

By resituating what was, in the initial text, largely an individual narrative
within a social context of classrooms and institutions, Jerry raises questions of

standards and legitimacy. At this point, the page abruptly ends, and when readers turn to the next one, they discover that Jerry elects to respond to the implicit question from the previous section—can such an alternative style generate productive student writers? Much to my surprise, and I suspect the surprise of other readers, the next three pages are (deliberately) handwritten:[35]

> *For most students I think this would place them in a far more comfortable position or situation. I hate having to sit down and write. Most all students do, at least from my experience. Its not even a matter of me not enjoying writing. Personally, I just hate typing and / also with the process of free writings, students are sometimes assigned to write about subjects that they may find dull or all around unappealing. the freewriting will allow them to take that subject and look at it from numerous new angles until they can develop their own take on the matter, one which they can place some interest in. / back to my previous thought before I was so rudely interrupted by that stray thought, typing is just a pain. I cant stand having to write some formal essay and then to type the stupid thing. Through free writes, students can approach their writing in a more laxed manner. Many times, when were comfortable with what we writting, we can go on and on, often to say much more than we would in a typical essay.*

In producing this section, Jerry brings together, both materially and discursively, competing literacy practices in speculating about how this alternative classroom might enable students to overcome alienation from the classroom literacies and official curriculum. In doing so, Jerry has produced a section that both critiques conventional academic literacies and performs his alternative. For example, the use of his handwriting disrupts the centripetal illusions of uniform academic texts, in which even the differences of utterances from other texts and other writers are denied in the universal font and type, and the use of dashes disrupts the conventional coherence of academic discourses. At the same time, Jerry uses this section to foreground the interconnections among technology, comfort, intellectual safety, and fluency, and through it, he legitimizes his experiences in classrooms and of other students.

After suggesting in his own handwriting that his alternative classroom would enable students to engage in the learning and thereby decrease their alienation, he proceeds, in the next section, to acknowledge the legitimacy of conventional academic discursive style, which is typed:

> When writing, students should want to do it. It should be a process
> which is done for ourselves. Taking a subject and addressing it in
> freewrites I think lets us first take a broad look at the subject before we

> break it down in many aspects. Finding then an aspect which makes
> sense to us, the student can see a link of importance and will look at the
> writing with an attention to relevance and meaning of what they are
> going to say in their writing.

Through this text, Jerry has rewritten the positions that students take in class-rooms as having an agency and a control over their learning, and he has rewritten classrooms in such a way that does not deny or dismiss conventional academic cultures but that advocates for relevant and meaningful experiences in them. In his alternative classroom, lectures would be "rare," and "discussion groups" would transform the space into "a forum of ideas." Nevertheless, he is quick to recognize the futility of antifoundational, or relativistic, classrooms: "Even through freewrites, your mind will not give you all outlooks on your topic. Through the class period, students and the teacher as well, would bring up their ideas they have been wondering about and would try to develop new ideas in a way which pro-duce feedback, not always posative, for the student." In doing so, he acknowledges the contingency and specificity of these alternative classrooms. As such, the alter-natives that Jerry generates brings together the individual and the social, thereby obviating many of the critiques that have been leveled against expressivist theo-ries of learning.[36] At the same time, he seems to be suggesting that the authority originates in students' lives and that the dialogue between students' external lit-eracies and the literacies of the academy can be used to critique and perform.

As these themes suggest, classrooms in which students and teachers construct literacies exploit competing discursive practices in order to struggle over defini-tions of reality, culture, and social legitimacy within specific social and historical contexts and to articulate alternatives to conventional academic culture(s). Though these classrooms can resemble more conventional classrooms, they are different insofar that the legitimacy to authorize them comes initially from stu-dents' cultures and students' experiences, which are dialogized within the context of conventional academic cultures and traditional academic discourse(s). As a result, political terms, such as **relevance** and **history** and **legitimacy**, are defined in collaboration with students, rather than by some set of values external to, and outside of, particular students and specific classrooms. In shuttling between action and reflection—both students', their peers' as co-teachers, and teachers'—these classrooms challenge conventional academic cultures with hybrid alterna-tives that rewrite students and teachers. In juxtaposing their own histories within the academy with their current experiences with specific students and particular classrooms, teacher can objectify their positions within the institution and can create the space in which both students and teachers can act out of the agency that, according to Ellen Cushman, comes from disrupting lives with literacy.[37]

Since, as Tom Fox argues, practices can exceed social structures and, as such, can lead to change from the inside out,[38] constructing literacies can produce challenges to departments and institutions. In these classrooms, constructing literacies encourages legitimate challenges to the academy in postmodern America—challenges that, as Richard Miller, after examining the failures of universalized efforts towards educational reform, advocates in *As If Learning Mattered*, work primarily at the local level, "tinkering on the margins of the academy" (212). However, unlike the agenda of "tinkering on the margins of the academy," which situates the agency primarily within teachers, the agenda of constructed literacies invokes students' abilities to reread and rewrite the worlds of the academy through reading and writing its discourses. Through their experiments with competing discursive practices, students assume positions from which they can exploit the contingencies of language, self, and community as they reread and rewrite their classrooms, powerful positions of Freire's literacy agenda resituated within specific postmodern contexts of individual classrooms and particular institutions. Those who manage to reread and rewrite classrooms assume positions that resemble Richard Rorty's creative redescribers who aspire to private acts of perfecting the self and public acts of reducing cruelty, and they exploit this private-public split in articulating new narratives for literacy and education in specific colleges and universities.[39] Within this agenda, the role of teachers is to legitimize students' rereadings and rewritings and to connect them to other revisions in order to facilitate the local changes that Miller insists are, as the history of educational reform suggests, are the only changes we can legitimately hope to make (193 ff).

LEGITIMACY, STANDARDS, AND CONSTRUCTED LITERACIES

For me, what remains as one of the most pressing questions has to do with standards, legitimacy, and the practices of literacies, for, as I argued in my assessment of Shor's classroom practices and sanctioned literacies, and as Tom Fox argues in *Defending Access: A Critique of Standards in Higher Education*, standards for literate performance are a means of establishing legitimacy and exercising power. More specifically, how is it that literacy practices become authoritative and legitimate? With respect to

When I arrive in a classroom at the beginning of the semester, I often forget that their own experiences with teachers and classrooms have situated students in particular positions within certain models of educating, positions that often construct them as outsiders seeking legitimacy through the practices they have come to know, if not to love—the lecture, the exam, the grade. For some, their desires to become insiders requires that traditional academic literacies, the answer is fairly obvious—history, tradition, institutional authority, etc. But what about these alternative literacy practices, the ones that I am suggesting we experiment with as students and teachers construct literacies? Where does their authority, their legitimacy come from?

The issues of discourses and authority are also Xin Lu Gale's central concern in her powerful and insightful book *Teachers, Discourses, and Authority in the Postmodern Composition Classroom.* To explore discourses and authority in contemporary classrooms, Gale offers a rereading of Richard Rorty as a way of acknowledging the similarities, as well as the differences, among "normal" discourse, which, for Gale, is conventional academic discourse, and "abnormal" discourses, both students' and teachers'. In light of her rereading of Rorty, Gale argues that both students' discourses and teachers' resistant discourses are abnormal discourses, which, quoting Rorty, she defines as the result when someone is ignorant of or rejects the standards of normal discourse (73). Nevertheless, student discourses, which she calls Nonresponsive Abnormal Discourse, display a "lack of intentional rebellion against the rules or major concerns of normal discourse" and that, while teachers' discourses "can be also reactive and oppositional to normal discourse," they cannot, in the end, escape conventional academic

they rewrite themselves as outsiders in their own cultures, as Richard Rodriguez did. These students often resent constructed classrooms and seek at every turn to transform them and me into known commodities by demanding teacher talk, prescriptive assignments, and letter grades. To the degree that I can accommodate these literacy agendas without compromising my intellectual integrity, I try to give them what they want. This semester, I'm working with a group of graduate students from a different discipline, and almost across the board, they bring different contexts to our classroom from the ones that I bring. Early in the semester, I named some of these differences, such as cultural conflicts between social sciences in the academy and social services in the world, and invited them to name them for themselves. Then I tried to create some space in which they could assume more comfortable positions. Four of them—a Secret Service intern, an Indian student who participated in a literacy study in a third-world country, a former social worker who is just beginning graduate school, and a career police officer with two kids—have elected to engage in the process, while the rest, for the most part, have retreated. For other students, desire for insider status amounts less to rejecting their own cultures and more to recognizing the economic and social realities of academic culture—a discourses for their "creation and existence" (80, 82).

As a result, and also a result of the other half of teachers' responsibilities to assist students in cultivating conventional academic discourses, Gale advocates what she calls "a two-level interaction." Her "primary interaction" in classrooms is between students' (Nonresponsive Abnormal) discourses and conventional (normal) academic discourses, to which the "secondary" interaction between teachers' (Responsive Abnormal) discourses and students' discourses is subordinated, since the first can never interact with the second "without the intervention" of normal discourse (88 ff). Gale argues that turning "the secondary interaction into the primary interaction threatens to deprive students of opportunities to experience and interact" with conventional academic discourse(s)—opportunities that, she believes, are necessary in order to produce resistant discourses—and that, in addition, "the direct interaction" between students' discourses and teachers' (resistant) discourses "without a preceding interaction" between students' discourses and conventional academic discourses "would leave a gap in students' education, a gap that makes the production Responsive Abnormal Discourses impossible" (90).

The teachers' Responsive Abnormal Discourse, be it feminism, deconstruction, critical pedagogy, or cultural stud-

necessary evil for these students that comes at an exorbitant cost. These students often resent our classrooms and look for ways to obtain maximal returns with minimal investments. They refuse to do the freewrites, have nothing to say in class, forget to do the reading, and push their learning contracts beyond the limits of patience and time. When a classroom is comprised of these students as was a first-year writing course last spring with a disproportionate number of athletes and surfers, I'm pushed into a position from which I must exert more control, and as much as I can, I try to make the ordeal as painless as possible without neglecting a responsibility to call attention to the contradictions in the academy's expectations for students to invent the university. I've often been surprised at how difficult it has been for students to buy into constructing literacies and classrooms, and yet as the examples from students in here suggest, students rise to the challenge of constructing their own literacies and classrooms in inconsistent ways. With the ways that constructed literacies can challenge students' educational histories, and given the high stakes involved in these insider-outsider positions, these resistances I've seen seem to center upon issues of trust. Last semester, in response to negotiations over learning

ies, interacts at a secondary level with students' Nonresponsive Abnormal Discourse, not only to ensure that the conversation is not stopped and students' sense of wonder is not suppressed, but to reveal how the knowledge of normal discourse can be used for democratic goals in teaching and how the dominant ideology and culture can be effectively resisted with words.

As a result, "students' interaction with the canonical texts should constitute major reading, writing, and collaborative activities," she argues, not towards the ends of "reproducing imitative texts and repeating the found truth" but towards "keeping the conversation going in schools so that students who speak Nonresponsive Abnormal Discourse will not be silenced and denied opportunities to create Responsive Abnormal Discourse" (91).

There is much in Gale's book that I find useful in thinking about authority, legitimacy, and standards for literate performance. For example, she does a wonderful job of drawing upon Bourdieu and Passeron to identify the various sources of teachers' conventional authority—an "arbitrary power" comprised of "pedagogic authority," as specific social relations to language and culture naturalized within academic institutions institutionalized, a representative of the institution, and "personal authority," or "charisma and idiosyncrasy" (8-9 ff). Also, she is adept at identifying the omnipresence of conventional

contracts, a graduate student wrote after one class, "i am very disappointed in this journey which i misunderstood to be much more of an agreement and an exploration rather than a typical academic dictatorship." After we had a chance to talk face-to-face, she wrote,

> i must apologize for being "over the top". although i did acknowledge your previous email stating your contract was negotiable, i misunderstood your purpose in sending it at all. i interpreted it as your expectations and i was upset because i knew i could not meet them in our given time frame and i am working very hard and taking your class to heart . . . "to heart" meaning: i think about what you say, pair it up with what i thought i knew, chew it over. i look into other sources. i talk about what i am learning with friends. your class is reinventing my whole perspective of everything. i may even pursue the study of rhetoric further. to think i would only get (or by your expectations should get) a C—that my experience, which has been very meaningful to me, was average— was upsetting.
>
> i also see now that i have endowed you with a great deal of trust. i trust that you are sincere in encouraging us to speak our thoughts—even if they disagree with yours. i trust that you really want our input and i trust that there is a

academic discourse(s) in classrooms and the ways that students' and teachers' discourses "are related to each other and to the dominant discourse" (74). Nevertheless, there are several elements, I think, of Gale's educational agenda that prevent it from resolving the conditions that critics have called a crisis in literacy and meaning. As I read Gale, the biggest problem I have is with how she seems to make assumptions about students' and teachers' desires and, in so doing, imposes her own cultural values upon them. In the process of justifying her alternative, she appears to assume that all students want to produce resistant discourses, or what she calls Responsive Academic Discourses, and, by implication, that all teachers do (or should) desire their students to produce resistant discourses. They don't.

And perhaps shouldn't. Many students with whom I have worked have complained about learning anything other than how to find the meaning of a poem or how to use MLA documentation. While many of us (teachers) professionally and personally value the resistant discourses of feminism or Marxism or cultural studies, I am unconvinced that we should impose these (cultural) values and desires upon students, many of whom may have very different literacy agendas—to do so amounts to one more in a long line of intellectual violences. At the same time, there are those students, though far fewer, I

freedom to our responses. (which after this evening i see i can absolutely trust these things)

when i read the contract i felt i had "been taken for", that i was making a fool of myself. it may not come across but talking in class is not easy for me and talking about this subject in particular is very scary because of the personal journey i had mentioned to you about my father's teachings.

i guess i am in a very vulnerable position and that is where my "over reaction" came from.

If graduate students, as provisional insiders already, struggle this much, then I can only imagine the struggles of undergraduates who have yet to obtain even provisional insider status. And yet this semester, it is not the graduate students but the at-risk first-year students who are much more willing to collaborate on constructing our classrooms and our literacies. Some days, it's hard to remember students' educational histories, and the desires they engender, especially when these histories and desires are so different from mine, and yet contingent literacies and provisional classrooms insist that these histories and agendas become legitimized and are credible. Moreover, constructed classrooms must emerge from within the cultural tensions of tradition and change, for the institutional realities mandate that students have admit, who profess to reject conventional academic discourses regardless of the costs. Right now, I'm thinking of Jimmie, a first-year writer and ceramics major from the prologue, who told me, "I wouldn't talk the talk even if I could" and the countless numbers who drop out of college because of the costs of appropriating, or being appropriated by, academic discourse(s), students whom Gale surprisingly acknowledges (102 ff). To suggest, as Gale does, that these students, in rejecting conventional academic discourses or withdrawing from school, are rejecting "a more fulfilling life" (103) is presumptuous, a form of intellectual paternalism. While I personally might agree that intellectual work can lead to greater satisfaction and fulfillment, I, again, am reluctant to impose my cultural values upon students—those first-year students cited in the prologue, for example—for whom education is often less about developing personal philosophies and more a means to economic success, which, they believe, will bring its own fulfillment and satisfaction. While I believe that I have a responsibility to challenge these students' cultural values, I do

requisite experiences, as well.

On these days, I wonder whether the effort of confronting these educational histories and constructing literacies is worth the effort, and a part of me wonders what it would be like to use a stock set of lesson plans and readings from one semester to the next. On other days, I think that constructing literacies elicit too many other psychological and cultural issues, and even as I wonder at the emotional intensity often attached to learning, I wonder whether what I'm doing in the short sixteen weeks with them will make any difference. And then I'll get a message from one of the students, such as I did recently from a student who writes, ". . . thank you for making my spring semester of last year one of the most enjoyable learning experiences I have ever encountered," and then I'll feel more confident, at least for now, that it's worth the effort.

Maybe Tom Fox is right—staying around may be half the battle.

Now, let's see, how does one reinvent the university?

not believe that I should require that, for at least the duration of the semester, they accept my own cultural values in lieu of their own.

Besides imposing cultural values upon students, there are two other disagreements that Gale and I seem to have. Though she suggests otherwise, her classroom practices seem to posit institutions as inflexible, monolithic, and static social apparatuses, impervious to influence and change, whereas I believe that, as nothing more than people and discourses that comprise them, institutions are subject to change anytime the people or discourses of them change. Institutions manifest themselves in the texts, such as questions on the admission form and the descriptions in catalogues of degree plans and in diplomas, and cannot exist apart from or outside of the people and the discourses that give rise to them. Consequently, changes in the people and the discourses will generate corresponding changes in institutions. Second, Gale seems to advocate a determinist version of resistant classroom discourses, insofar as no resistant discourses of the classroom can come into existence except in relation to conventional academic (i.e. normal) discourse. For example, she writes that resistant discourses, or what she calls Responsive Abnormal Discourse, "depend on normal discourse for its creation and existence" and has a "parasitic and derivative" relationship to normal discourse and that students' discourses, or what she calls Nonresponsive Abnormal Discourse, "is related to normal discourse *innocently*, aware of the latter's awesome presence and power, but unaware of its content and secrets, a relationship resulting from the writer's lack of interaction with normal discourse" (80). Such a reading of classroom discourses, however, can occur only within conventional academic contexts, with their educational histories and disciplinary traditions, whereas within a different context, such as a collaborative classroom that inscribes itself within different contexts, these discourses would quite possibly assume a different existence. Furthermore, such an assessment of classroom discourses threatens to reinforce a dependent relationship between students' and teachers' resistant discourses and the dominant discourses of the academy such that these abnormal discourses, to use Gale's term, are always and everywhere defined in response to normal (i.e. conventional academic) discourses. And before any reader accuses me of denying the seeming omnipotence and omnipresence of academic contexts within classrooms—sites that, clearly, are defined within institutions (this accusation is my criticism of Shor's classroom practices)—let me clarify what I mean: it's not that students and teachers can ever escape academic contexts, unless they disassemble and reassemble their relationships outside of the academy, and even then it would be difficult to ignore the history of their relationship that brought them together in the first place. On the contrary, it's more that students and teachers, while acknowledging the existence of the academic context, can agree that other contexts have more relevance and, therefore, are more legitimate contexts in which to assess literate performances.

I want to explore this notion a bit further by turning to students' accounts of their experiences. After the 1999 academic year, I moved, as a result of the occupational hazards of being an adjunct, a thousand miles away to take a full-time job.[40] However, Jerry knew that I was trying to write about literacies and teaching, and he was eager to help me understand what he had experienced in our classroom during the spring of 1999. Since I was (and am still) struggling with these issues of authority, legitimacy, and standards for literate performance, I decided to ask him for his perspective. In an email, I wrote,

> I guess I'm stumped, right now, with this notion of legitimacy, authority, and standards, or what counts as official and valuable business in classrooms. Let me explain what I mean. In conventional classrooms, teachers lecture, students write official academic essays and are examined with multiple choice and short-answer tests, and everyone knows that what is happening "counts," or has legitimacy, because there is a tradition of education that makes academic essays and multiple-guess tests valuable. (I guess I could say that the history of education in America _ authorizes _ the practices of academic essays and standardized tests, or gives them a certain authority.) And the practices of academic essays and standardized tests bring their own standards with them.
>
> The problem that I'm trying to sort through right now is that these traditional standards and traditional ways of defining legitimacy, or what counts as official signs of learning, won't work to judge what happened in our classroom. For example, your essay in which you combined handwriting and typing couldn't have been judged by the same standards as a teacher might judge a traditional academic essay, right? What standards would we need to use? And where would they come from? And what makes these standards count, or legitimate? And who authorizes them, or makes them have authority?
>
> I guess that my second question has to do with the essay to which I referred earlier. Combining handwriting and typing is a brilliant idea, I think, one that completely surprised me and delighted me—how did you come to the conclusion to combine handwriting and typing? How did you know that doing so would be okay, or acceptable, or would "count" (i.e. have legitimacy) in our classroom?

Shortly after I sent him this message, I received the following response:

> Well, for me, I would think that legitimacy and value come from what is learned. Quite honestly, if something is learned, it has value and is therefore legitimate. Of course for us to see its value, the person must be able to show this new knowledge with a good understanding and prove to us it is relevant. But we must also consider whether the information is relevant based on the user. Certain things may not have relevance for a person when learned. In that case did they really learn

it? If it has no impact, the person will not expand on it. However, suppose we take an idea and completely alter its current state until it can be seen in a manner which can be better utilized by the user. The learned info in this new context will give the idea worth with the holder and allow them to further apply this knowladge. It now has value and is legitamate.

When developing the text with the type and written portions, I did not allow myself to view the paper under typical academic standards. I was suggesting a world which opposed the general form of academic discourse which is used over and over in every class. Since I was trying to work outside of the typical style of academic writting, I did not find it to make sense that I should follow typical academic standards. True I was writting about the idea of a class without typical sturcture, but as I did so, I made myself believe that it was that type of class I was writting for to begin with. I did not write with an authority in mind because it was the authority I was in opposition too. I think thats all I have for now. Let me know what you think and if it makes sense.

jerry

P.S. Tell your wife that I am wearing my Tick shirt right now because "I am mighty" and that I ate my frosted flakes this morning with a "Spoon!"[41]

There are several important dimensions, which Jerry identifies in his response, that comment upon these issues of authority, legitimacy, and standards. In his response, Jerry seems to be suggesting that authority and legitimacy are generated through performance and are contingent upon particular people and emerge from specific contexts (though he does seem to confirm what Gale argues about the presence of normal discourse). What is significant, I think, is the way that Jerry, at least to himself, exchanges the contexts of conventional authority, or "the typical style of academic writting," for one that he believes has more relevance, which he calls for in the first part of his response. Now, I don't read Jerry's response as calling for standards that are entirely contingent and context-specific, for he does invoke a social dimension—the "us" to whom this new knowledge must be shown to be relevant. At some point, solely individual standards begin to lose their existence as standards, anyway, and if they are entirely relative, then, to paraphrase an undergraduate philosophy professor I once had, we have nothing to talk about and might as well go home. Beyond being virtually meaningless, exclusively context-bound standards also can be difficult for students, who must negotiate their risks eventually within an institutional context that includes grades and evaluations.[42]

However, suggesting that standards cannot be entirely contingent and context-specific is not the same thing as suggesting that they can be partially contingent and context-specific,[43] and the way I try to accomplish this end is by authorizing students to legitimize their own contexts and standards. (Immediately, I see the difficulty that comes from the fact that I am the one who is doing the authorization, and at least at this point, I am not sure how to get around it.) Initially, the only criterion for authority is that a person is enrolled in the class, and then once a community begins to emerge, they assume more of the responsibility for authorizing themselves. Early on, the students and I collaboratively select the literacies that will be used, the content that is addressed, the knowledge that is produced, and the actions that are taken, all of which, according to Nan Elasser and Patricia Irvine, are ways to establish new discourse communities. Once the discourse community is established, then they begin to police (or not police) their own, and my function as authorizing agent diminishes accordingly. The more students authorize themselves, the less I serve as a monitor, and the more I function as a participant.

When I reflect upon our classroom practices, I can see two ways that students are authorized—through constructing the classroom and through assessment. As is the case with constructing literacies, one of my functions is to use theories of literacy and learning to justify the practices of individual classrooms, as well as generating practices from theories about legitimacy, authority, and literacies.[44] Previously, I described how students construct the classroom through co-teaching a generative theme (though the level and extent of their involvement depends upon a number of variables, many of which I have no control over.) Besides socially in groups, students also have the option to participate in constructing the classroom through a practice of participating in the planning of the day to day progress that I have appropriated from Shor as a way of justifying the practice of students in co-teaching the classroom. In his explanation of the origins of what he calls the After-Class Group, he indicates that it "was to be a formal structure invested with an ongoing responsibility to review and revise the syllabus and learning process . . . an option that required student volunteers to bring it into existence" (When 118).[45] Similar to Shor's After-Class Group, this practice in my classrooms invites "direct feedback about what was working and not working" in the day's class (123), yet unlike Shor, I hold this after-class class in cyberspace, which, in keeping with its function, seems more democratic and less determined and more fluid where students can come and go—can participate or not—as they please.[46] This mitigates some of the biases inherent in Shor's version, which, as he acknowledges, privileges those who have time and interest. In practice, I send an email message after each class, sometimes inquiring about something that happened specifically in class, sometimes inviting a general response, and then students can respond or not whenever they want and in whatever ways seem most appropriate. Some times, students' responses provide the co-teachers and me with feedback on the class's activities, as this one from a first-year student does: "I find that skits and other alternative ways of learning are helpful. They help you learn because you have to apply the information you learned. It makes it so you don't just memorize the info., you have to know how to use it."⁴⁷ Other times, students' responses engender independent conversations, as this one did:

From: Chris
To: English 101 (11 a.m.)
Subject: after-class class (11 a.m.)

As many of you probably realize, the co-teaching during our semester works in a number of ways. For my part, I have used some of the themes as places where we experiment with the ways that writing and reading help us to think in general, and, at the same time, I have used other themes as places where we consider issues that are more specific to academic discourses, such as rational discourses and elaborate codes.

I'm interested in hearing your response to the ways that I have used my part of the co-teaching to help you learn more about writing and learning, both inside and outside the academy.

From: Morgan
To: Chris
Subject: after-class class (11 a.m.)

the coteaching has in many ways been an aid to me as a student and also a confusing part of my learning. the themes seem to go back and forth between the two goals within a class period or a week. it seems sometimes that you aren't sure which one you want to focus on and if you don't know then how are we as co-teachers or students supposed to know either?

From: Chris
To: Morgan
Subject: after-class class (11 a.m.)

but why can't we focus on both? why must we always focus on one?

From: Morgan
To: Chris
Subject: after-class class (11 a.m.)

I didn't mean to imply that we needed to focus on just one in fact you need to focus on both to make the subject whole and maybe there are even more that would make the subject even more understandable, the problem occurs when there is no transitions between the two, when in one sentence it is about academic literacy and the next it is not.

From: Chris
To: Morgan
Subject: after-class class (11 a.m.)

but isn't that what it means to *read*, or make sense of a situation—to make connections in order to make meaning? in the chaos, students have to make their own *readings* of the semester, which is what I'm striving towards. what do you think? how could I do that more effectively?

From: Morgan
To: Chris
Subject: after-class class (11 a.m.)

If it is your goal to make students have to overcome the chaos of the situation you are presenting in order to make connections, then I congratulate you . . . seriously I do because you have met that goal. I didn't know that was one of your main objectives though, I thought that we were supposed to be following your train of thought the entire semester and so I have gotten lost many times . . . but see that is what we have all been taught, A lot of us are on the banking mode, some more than others. I think that I have actually started to get out of that more now that I have been through your class because you don't allow for the banking method. Thank you. I know that I have grown a lot while in your class, my writing style as started to develop more. Things are starting to make more sense to the reader if I can find a good solid warrant about a topic that is relevant but not to personal to me.

Sometimes, students negotiate alternatives to the standards that our class has established, as this student writer does in an excerpt from his response to the class's efforts to establish the contents of the portfolio:

I think today's class was both productive and not productive . . . it allowed us to express our frustrations, but I think we are all still stuck. I would like to propose my own, independent portfolio thing. I decide what goes in, etc. I want it to be a theme on Southerness, or however you spell it" and "We need more class discussion. And to clarify—I know I said that I might not want my portfolio graded by a classmate . . . after the example you gave me in class, I'm not so sure. Now I feel I need to have it evaluated by a peer. Don't ask why, I just do.[48]

As the previous excerpts indicate, the second way that students are authorized is through assessment practices.[49] Similar to Shor (and Elbow), I use learning contracts to assess students' performances, and I encourage students to participate in the negotiation of these contracts. Unlike Shor, the contracts that I offer have spaces built into them to accommodate discourses and literacies other than those of the academy, thereby establishing the classroom as a zone of difference both that legitimizes other discourses and that, as Hephzibah Roskelly points out, enables students to name their alienation from the conventional discourses and literacies of the academy (145). For example, here is a version of a learning contract from a second semester composition course:

What follows are the initial terms for the contracts. In response, you have three options: to accept, by signing, the proffered contract; to amend the proffered contract, either individually or as a group, which you will then sign; or to negotiate a new contract as to what constitutes average, good, and excellent performances in the classroom:

To earn an **average evaluation**, or a **C**, students must do everything that is expected of them, nothing more and nothing less:

- All of their cumulative assignments must incorporate readings and/or class activities.
- Their portfolios may contain conventional academic writing, no experimental pieces, and the portfolio itself must earn an average evaluation.
- In order to earn a C, students are allowed to miss up to, but no more than, the number of classes specified by the College.
- Also, they need to engage in at least one identifiable dialogue with their readings or writings, with others or themselves, or with the professor per each theme.
- Students cannot arrive to class without having completed their homework more than twice per theme.

- Students must write a passing final exam.

In order to earn what the college identifies as a **good evaluation**, or a **B**, students must go beyond the minimums specified in the syllabus in these ways:

- All of their cumulative assignments must integrate most of the readings and class activities.
- Their portfolios must contain at least one piece of experimental writing, or writing that brings together competing discourses, and overall, the portfolio must earn a good evaluation.
- Students cannot miss more than four classes in a MWF class or three classes on a TR class.
- Also, they need to engage in a minimum of two identifiable dialogues, in whatever forms, per theme, and they must demonstrate discernable leadership throughout the semester.
- Students cannot arrive to class without having completed their homework more than once per theme.
- Students must write a passing final exam.

Finally, students who aspire to earn an **excellent evaluation**, or an **A**, must achieve excellence in the classroom, which amounts to going well beyond the minimums specified in the syllabus:

- All of their cumulative assignments must incorporate all of the readings and all of the relevant classroom activities.
- Their portfolios are experimental, insofar that they integrate competing discourses in multiple texts throughout the portfolio, and overall, their portfolio must earn an excellent evaluation.
- Students cannot miss more than two classes in a MWF class or one in a TR class.
- Also, they need to engage in a wide range of dialogues throughout every theme, and they must assume co-responsibility for classroom activities and discussions.
- Students cannot arrive to class without having completed their homework more than twice over the course of the entire semester.
- Students must write a passing final exam.

Obviously, anything below the standards specified for an average evaluation will earn a **below average** or **failing** evaluation. As you should know, you must earn a C or higher in order to complete the general education requirement for this course. Anyone who aspires to a D or an F should reconsider why they're in here, because not only are they wasting their time but they are also wasting our time. As a result, I refuse to specify what it takes to earn lower than an average evaluation because I expect that anyone who aspires to perform less than average should probably find somewhere else to be. (Which is not to say that you cannot earn a D or an F but which is to say that, at the outset, you shouldn't *aspire* to being "below average" or "failure," as defined by the *College Catalog*.)

In producing this initial contract, I used the description of the course in the college catalogue, the college's policy on attendance, and my own expectations about effective learning to establish minimal expectations, which are contingent, at least in part, upon institutional and disciplinary contexts in which the class was situated. Though some students that semester renegotiated their learning contracts, either partially or, in some cases, totally, in ways that reread and rewrote what I had called average, or a C, as above average or even, in rare cases, superior, they had to justify their renegotiations, which required that they reread and rewrite the function of first-year writing classrooms or the purpose of education. At the same time, by defining above average and excellent—the college's terms—as experimental and risky, I tried to establish provisional standards that nonetheless reflected the contingency of individual students, each of whom, in accepting the original contracts and aspiring for a B or an A, had to demonstrate how, for them, their portfolios were risky and experimental, a condition that differed for individual students depending upon their histories, their experiences with literacies, and a number of other variables.

In addition to contracts that recognize the legitimacy of competing literacies and that seek to be contingent and specific, a second way that students are authorized in our classrooms is through their participation the practice of assessment. As co-teachers, students have the option of collaborating with me on responding to cumulative assignments, and at the end of the semester, students evaluate their own and a peer's portfolio, which may be incorporated into the final evaluations. For example, some co-teachers elect to use plus and minus columns in which they describe their responses to students' submissions since cumulative assignments are not formally evaluated unless they appear in the portfolio, and some classrooms have elected to use their evaluations of themselves and their peers as one-fifth of the overall portfolio grade, which leaves three-fifths of the evaluation for me. Nevertheless, some co-teachers elect not to respond to the cumulative assignments, and some classrooms decide not to use their evaluations of themselves and each other as part of their grades. At the same time, some never feel authorized or see their peers as legitimate, as this excerpt from a student's course evaluation of an American literature survey suggests:

As the class approached an end, Mr. Schroeder encouraged the students to evaluate each others work with this evaluation being factored into the final grade. I strongly disagree with this concept. There is a level of knowledge and skill required in assigning grades. With no disrespect intended to anyone, as students we have not acquired this level of knowledge or skill required to assign grades. While we were able to discourage student evaluations, we did have to evaluate ourselves with the self-evaluation factoring into our final grade. Again, this is not a policy I am comfortable with. If I don't have the skills required to evaluate someone else's work, I surely don't have the skills required to evaluate my own.

Others agree, at least in principle, yet struggle with the practices we use or want more explicit direction, as Nayla's reflections suggest:

From: Nayla
To: Christopher Schroeder
Subject: the evaluation process

Chris:
I realize that in your attempt to create authentic learning you have to remain a little unorganized in your methods, but once again, as was seen last semester, you have created too much confusion.

Last semester you and I had a talk in which we discussed the balance of chaos and organization. You explained to me why you choose to teach the way that you do. You said something like true learning takes place when chaos is involved, and that it is not necessary to be an expert or to understand all aspects of what you were teaching because through chaos you learn critical thinking and awareness.

Now maybe I just came to that conclusion on my own, or maybe that is what you said, it was last semester and for my brain that was a long time ago. So if I have misunderstood, please let me know.

But , anyhow, my point is that I agree that a certain amount of chaos is necessary to make students think for themselves, but we have to keep in mind the fact that too much chaos will only cause frustration and eventual turn-off. This is not the goal that you have. I understand your goals for the most part, but I don't think most of my fellow class-mates do.

My recommendation to you is to continue along the same path as far as criteriaand cirriculum is concerned, but be a little more upfront about what your doing when you do it.

For example, the discussion of the evaluations on Monday began in the middle, instead of the beginning. I also understand that may have been on purpose, but regardless, on a subject like evaluations it's okay to start at the beginning.

Perhaps begin by saying that you are going to allow us to pick out some of the criteria for evaluation. Then continue by stating that there are a few guidlines you want to follow, but besides them (and state what they are directly!!) the rest is up for vote.

It may not sound very different to you, but to a class full of people who have never had you it will help to make sense. I remember last semester when you began to talk about the evaluation process you confused me to frustration. Luckily, for me, I asked you privately to explain yourself more clearly-and you did-and I got it.

Perhaps an explanation of your teaching methods in laymans terms right off the bat would assisit in easing the tension. I think you can get the main idea, here. Be more clear and direct. I know it goes against your principles, but try. I think you'll find it helps.

Later, Nayla

For these two, and others like them, escaping histories that legitimize top-down, authoritarian practices in which the teacher calls the shots and directs the entire show becomes too overwhelming, and dialogic and collaborative classroom practices never completely authorize them as legitimate participants in the process of teaching and assessing, or maybe the ways that I struggle to negotiate institutional expectations with dialogic and collaborative classroom practices fails to authorize them. While students and I struggle with the same dangers of dialogues and collaborative learning—class, gender, and ethnic privileges reinscribed within classrooms—that everyone who uses collaborative learning must face,[50] and while we are never able to overcome the fundamental inequalities that exist, almost by definition, between their discourses, and them, and my discourses, and me,[51] they are afforded, through the practices of constructing the literacies of our classroom, the opportunity to assume legitimate positions of authority from which they do participate in the construction and evaluation of our classrooms. Besides struggling to negotiate authority and legitimacy through co-teaching and through collaborative assessments, the students and I also examine institutional and social limitations, such as grades or gender biases, upon collaboration and dialogue and, consequently, legitimacy and standards, thereby acknowledging the institutionalized inequalities and struggling within them to negotiate alternatives.

Even those students who cannot, for whatever reasons, fully assume positions from which they participate in constructing literacies, must, in their efforts to read and write what for them are the failures of our classrooms, consider issues of authority, legitimacy, and standards for literate performances, and ultimately themselves, as Jack attests. As I indicated earlier, Jack used the after-class class to negotiate an alternative content for his portfolio (viz., Southerness) and to change his mind about participating in the collaborative evaluation of his portfolio, and yet in the process of reading and writing his experiences in his evaluation of himself and his semester, he has rewritten himself and the classroom once again:

> As a class, expository writing was a confusing ordeal. I do not like the direction it took (the experimental bent). Majority shouldn't rule in the classroom—the instructor should. While I appreciate to some degree the instructor's emphasis that this class was negotiable, this class was not negotiable as I understand the meaning of the word. I saw the negotiation going on as a sham.
>
> The method used for instructing this class does not work. Sure, it provides a good and entertaining discussion, but no more so than my drunken friends and I trying to ponder the meaning of the universe on a slow Saint Augustine Friday night. I would be lying if I said I have no anger for this course. I would also be lying if I said that this anger does not prejudice my evaluation of it—but this is life, and this is who I am. I have resisted terribly. I do not support this method of teaching/learning. I have not grown as a writer in this course. I have had to draw from other courses in order to complete my assignments, at times. This class taught me nothing I didn't really already know or believe.
>
> There are two principle problems:
> * To allow students to evaluate themselves is a tricky business. We are not all objective. Those of us who have high self-esteem will bestow upon ourselves an A. Those of us who have low self-esteem (no matter how good the work or product may be) will grant ourselves a lower grade. Yes, the grade ultimately rests with the instructor, but what real use is it when to have us as peers evaluate each other if our judgment can be superseded by said instructor?
> * The instructor needs to define clearly (and I mean crystal-clearly) how this interpretation of negotiation will work in the classroom. He needs to make it understood that the ultimate power rests in his judgment, and that a student's judgment can always be usurped, while at the same time delivering this news delicately.

Also, without wishing to offend anyone, I am not paying tuition dollars in order for my classmates to directly instruct me. Yes, I agree that the learning I can get from my peers is some of the most valuable education I will ever receive, but the education from them that I do gather is secondary to the knowledge I hope to attain from my instructor. Group work is not a good thing. I don't even yet hold a bachelor's degree! The most credentials I have are a diploma from a school in rural Ohio and some tutoring experience.

It comes down to this: if I cannot trust what a course stands for, if I am constantly weary and apathetic, if I feel consistently uncomfortable with a course, I am not as apt or open to learning. Okay, go ahead and challenge my notions about literacy and writing, but do not offend me in the process. You will only turn me off.

In my cover letter I stated that I believed in the pieces I wrote, and I stand by this assertion. I think they are quality items and are an accurate representation of my experiences in the South; however, I believe that I would feel even more strongly about them if I had also felt more passionately about this course.

As Jack explains, he and I had been debating the meanings of dialogue and negotiation, as well as authority and institutional limitations, all semester long. In class, he had been unable to collaborate easily or successfully. Either he assumed a position of complete authority, such as when he wanted himself and his peers to co-teach their theme without my intervention or consultation or when his evaluation, and not his peer's', could only be legitimate, or he wanted a position of little to no authority, such as when he argues that teachers, alone, should "rule" or when he recognizes the legitimacy of my credentials and not those of his peers or his own. A third position—an excluded middle or an excluded third or a contradiction—in which we participated in a give and take, back and forth dialogue[52] —was never an option for him. During our discussions of the evaluation process, he and his peers expressed concern that personal grudges from peers might influence the evaluation he received on his portfolio. In response, I suggested that perhaps I should reserve the authority to discard any assessments that were not justified from materials in the portfolio and from experiences during the semester. Though his peers believed that this option would prevent potential abuses of their authority, Jack read it as an attempt on my part to "usurp" his authority in spite of his assertion, later in his narrative, that I, alone, possess the most authoritative credentials. Though Jack insists that "[t]he method used for instructing this class does not work" and implies that these practices left him "weary and apathetic," he did manage to produce texts that he "believed in," and as his after-class class comments and his evaluation suggest, he was able to participate in the construction of the semester, neither of which can be a total loss. What I was unable to do, though, was to enable him to recognize his responsibility in his perceived failures and, in so doing, to authorize him in a way to construct a classroom that he "felt more passionately about."

At the same time, there are those who manage, even within Jack's failed classroom, to sort through their confusion to a place where they can assume positions of authority and collaborate on constructing classrooms of legitimacy, as Emma, a classmate of Jack's, indicates:

From: Emma
To: Christopher Schroeder
Subject: Re: generative theme (ENG 311)

Chris-I just wanted to tell you how interested and much I look forward to this class. You're way of teaching is so unique and beneficial. I love the way the class works-it has really opened up a lot of closed doors for me. I just wish that I could focus more attention on the class. This semester has been the busiest one yet. I wish I had more time to delve into the drafts and my responses-to expand more on my ideas or thoughts. I'm not trying to kiss ass-but, I just wanted to give you some input on how I feel about the class. Next semester, I would love to take another one of your classes, however, I don't think that there is one offered above this. Or is there? Also, I think that a lot of the class is confused about how you run the class simply because we've never had a class quite like this-it's so different-I think that they just have to adjust to the dramatic change. Love the class. Thank You for offering it.
    Emma

For these students, something about the semester is different, perhaps their educational histories or their abilities to engage or to live with uncertainty, and they manage to assume control over their experiences and to make them relevant and specific to themselves and for themselves. Whatever the reason, the difference lies in students and with students, as Jack's and Emma's shared contexts suggest—both are English majors at the same point in their undergraduate educations, and each attending the same classes in the same room at the same time during the same semester. Clearly, Emma and others who find ways to engage deserve the credit for their successes. For whatever the reason, these students are able to assume positions of authority and legitimacy in the classroom, and from these positions, they collaborate upon the standards we will use to assess their literate, and educational, performances. In assuming positions of authority and establishing legitimate standards for assessing their performances, these students construct their own literacies through constructing their own classrooms. At the same time, these students, in learning to read and write their own words, discover how to read and write their own classrooms and, in so doing, read and write their own words.

And, as for the legitimacy of these classrooms and these literacies, you don't have to take my word(s) for it.

From: Jerry
To: Christopher Schroeder

Chris,

Sorry it took me so long to get back to you but my schedual this semester is beyond busy and I just have not had the chance to respond. In regards to what I think would be relevant, well, here we go. I dont know exactly what you are expecting to hear from me. You said this is a book on teaching, and when I look back on our class, we did a lot of things right. In my opinion, what had made our classes so enjoyable (at least I found them enjoyable. Honest.), was the discussions we held. What I find discouraging about many classes today, is the regergitation of the same ideas over and over. Yes our class did attack some fairly general topics, but I feel we were really able to make them more interesting. I have always found writting classes a tad disturbing. The teachers expect us to enlighten them with new ideas. This is not as easly as it sounds. when we held our group discussions, we were able to take our ideas and bounce them off one another to recieve numerous view points which can hopefully then be further developed in our own writtings. As I tried to say in my writtings during the class, the classroom should work as a forum for ideas. Make sense?

Last semester was the first time I had ever been introduced to the idea of a generative theme. At first I was skeptical and felt rather intimidated because it seemed like so much work. However, in the end it proved to be one heck of a learning experience. Working on the theme forced us to take our subject and really pick it apart. We had to look at it from different angles and then research those angles so that we could teach them. When I think about it, it is as though through teaching we learn the most. We had to be familair and well versed in our topics. that's about all for now. If you want me to get more elaborate, please let me know. I am late for class.

jerry

What more could I write? Except: thanks, Jerry. As you went to your class that day, carrying around thoughts about your experiences, and I went to mine, carrying thoughts about your comments, you were still able, even from a thousand miles away, to teach me about constructing literacies.

INTERLUDE
Read(Writ)ing Constructed Literacies With Colleagues

MAKING POSTMODERNISM AND CRITICAL THINKING
DANCE WITH EACH OTHER

From: Peter Elbow
To: Chris Schroeder

Dear Chris,

Thanks for the invitation to respond to your interesting book. I think I have something to contribute to your project of seeking an alternative literacy that is more constructed and constructive than what now seems disappointing. For what strikes me as most eloquent in your book is your picture of students alienated from the rewards of literacy—and the more muffled tale of your own sour after taste after being such a loyal servant of literacy.

I build on four of your central terms: postmodernism, critical thinking, interlude, and constructed. That is, I think I'm talking about postmodernism and critical thinking, but I'm doing so obliquely by way of a dancing *play* ("interlude" means play sandwiched between other things) that is *constructed* (that builds rather than takes apart).

Let me begin the play by being very metaphorical. I propose to make postmodernism and critical thinking dance with each other in such a way that both are shaken up. By dancing with each other, they create a rhythm that violates the habitual rhythms each has become used to.

Am I questioning postmodernism? Lots of people do; you do—sort of. Postmodernism shouldn't complain since it celebrates questioning. Critical thinking also celebrates questioning, but no one seems to question it—not you, not radicals, not conservatives.

Yes, you make fun of the homage that textbooks pay to critical thinking (for example in chapter one). And you criticize what you see as the goal or destination or dream behind critical thinking: a kind of enlightenment era, universal, homogenized, essentialized rationality. But you never question critical thinking itself. I want to question critical thinking itself; but I want to affirm its goal—or at least its goal as we might describe it more charitably and more concretely than you do.

Let me change metaphors from dancing to driving. I want to drive the *vehi-cle* of postmodernism toward the goal or destination of critical thinking. Let me explain. The vehicle of postmodernism is play, game, fun. But instead of driving it towards its usual deconstructive destination of detachment, skepticism, and alienation, we can hijack the playful vehicle of postmodernism in the direction of critical thinking. Not toward the abstract dogmatized goal of critical thinking (an essentialized universal rationality) but rather toward the more humanly concrete goal of critical thinking: helping people assess new ideas and get unstuck from what they take for granted, thereby becoming more intellectually flexible. This is one of *your* main goals too. Interestingly, it's also a goal of postmodernism, but is largely unrealized.

What I'm interested in here—to be more blunt about my own agenda—is *the believing game*. And I'll get down to cases: the concrete condition of your students. You complain (like so many others) that they assume too much; they take too much for granted; they don't question things. This sounds like a problem of "credulity." Lack of critical thinking. The traditional cure is more crit-ical thinking, more questioning: the doubting game. This sounds logical.

But let's pause. There's an important difference here that gets overlooked. On the one hand, there's *not questioning*; on the other hand, there's *actually trusting, believing, or entering in*.

Yes, students may not question what they take for granted. But that doesn't mean they really trust or believe or enter into what they take for granted. They *don't* really trust or believe it, they just take it for granted.

This is why the traditional cure—asking them to be distrustful and detached from what they take for granted—produces the traditional response: ho hum. They resist and get bored.

What's hard for students is belief, investment, trust, entering in, inhabiting. They may be great at *leaving* themselves in (taking things for granted), but that's not the same as *putting* themselves in—especially into what's new. So the literacy practice that I'm suggesting consists of push-ups in trusting, putting self in, caring, and believing. It's a playful practice, but it goes directly against the tendency of postmodernism to make people feel that nothing is worth trusting or caring about. And it speaks to the most difficult goal of critical thinking: to pry people out of what they take for granted.

Here are the paradigm steps for the believing game:

1. Start from some issue that people disagree about, feel confused about, or want to understand better. Ideally it's an issue that feels "real" to students—that is, not an issue students feel as "merely a teacher issue."

2. Invite everyone in the room to do some private freewriting to explore their responses to this issue. It's fine to invite low stakes, off the cuff writing ("Just follow your first thoughts and immediate responses"); or else to push harder for connected thinking ("Try to think your way through to some genuine conclusions"). Either way, people need at least ten or fifteen minutes of writing to let their thinking and responding develop. (This process can be accomplished through speaking rather than writing, but writing is much more effective—especially for the first few sessions with the believing game. People need a chance to explore their responses in private without fear of "getting it wrong" or "sounding stupid.")

3. Now go around the group and hear each person briefly give his or her main thought or a central thought. A couple of sentences at most. *No one may respond*. We are just listening. And help everyone realize that the goal is to hear the widest variety of responses.

    The *final* step is to play the believing game with all the positions or responses that emerge, but there may be a need for intermediate steps because of too many views and too little time. (If the issue is important, though, the game should stretch over a number of class sessions.)

4. Intermediate step: select those positions or responses that seem most promising or useful or interesting to explore. The opinions of participants play a role here, but everyone needs to know that the whole spirit of the believing game is to work *against* the tyranny of majority rule. When most people are annoyed or dismissive of one person's strongly held view, this is often just a situation where that view needs to kept in the pot. As teacher, I sometimes jump in and pick the most diverse and interesting positions. When in doubt, choose those that are least like "common sense" or "orthodoxy" or "what's sensible." In a sense we are looking for views that are hardest to believe—though only if someone cares about them.

5. Playing the believing game itself. It's important to be explicit about rules and goals: we're outlawing all criticizing in order to foster two neglected intellectual activities: listening and entering in. I could call it the moral imagination game.

    Work with one position at a time. Start with the person who stated this view—who believes it. Get that person simply to talk more about how he or she sees things through the lens of this belief.

Most people can't do this well unless we're scrupulous about enforcing the no-criticizing rule. Then invite others to join in and help flesh out and enrich this view or position by "putting on" this lens and trying to see the world through it and telling what insights emerge. Others often have fresh insights that the originator never thought of. It can help for people to pretend to *be* someone who holds this view. This kind of role taking serves as leverage for seeing differently. When people try to enter into a view they find alien, they sometimes fall into a kind of playful and unrealistic exaggeration. This can be fruitful if done in a supportive spirit. But try to avoid hostile or parodically "positive" versions of the view in question. One sometimes has to interrupt participants when they instinctively start to criticize or object to thoughts they experience as a nutty or dangerous.

6. Then simply repeat the process with the next position or response. The process of playing the believing game with a position or point of view doesn't always have to take too long.

Needless to say, this can be a scary game for some students—and for many intellectuals in our culture. There is a fear of entering into or believing wrong or noxious beliefs. The crucial thing to remember is that the believing game involves a promise of intellectual mutuality—a contract: "You have to do your best and try to enter in or believe the views of others, but in payment, others have to try to enter into your point of view." We may have to try to enter into views we find noxious, but *everyone* has to agree to play it with views counter to those noxious views.

The nitty gritty question is this. What's so awful about having to try to enter into a racist, sexist, or violence-loving view—when in fact *everyone* in our culture is already awash in those thoughts, and feelings? Those thoughts and feelings may be *unstated*—especially in our classrooms. But for that very reason, students tend to experience those views as hovering and powerful—yet nevertheless difficult to see or analyze very clearly. The payoff is that everyone has to play the believing game with views that are *counter* to racism, sexism, violence-loving—to hear and try to enter into the world as it is experienced by someone who is hurt or bothered by racism, sexism, violence—and actually try to enter into the intellectual and felt experience of such persons.

Let me close by calling attention again to the link between my use of the believing game and your goals. We are both seeking to engender a constructed literacy. The believing game can help students get unstuck from the views they take for granted (but aren't even all that invested in), and to enter into views that are different from their own. Even more important, we are both trying to help students get unstuck from the very stance or mood of alienation, distrust, and fear of commitment that currently traps so many of them.*

---

* I've written at length about the believing game:

"Appendix Essay. The Doubting Game and the Believing Game: An Analysis of the Intellectual Process." In *Writing Without Teachers*. Oxford University Press, 1973.

"Methodological Doubting and Believing: Contraries in Inquiry." In *Embracing Contraries: Explorations in Learning and Teaching*. Oxford University Press, 1986.

"The Believing Game: A Challenge after Twenty-Five Years." In *Everyone Can Write: Essays Toward a Hopeful Theory of Writing and Teaching Writing*. NY: Oxford University Press, 2000.

To: Victor Villanueva
From: Christopher Schroeder

Here's what I'm thinking about now—maybe it's a good place to start.

I've been rewriting the introduction, talking about the conditions of literacy in society, particularly in light of GWBush's recent call for a Republican response to what he says is a pervasive literacy crisis. What I'm suggesting is that _ReInventing_ doesn't pretend to do away with any cultural hegemony, as if cultural hegemonies can be effaced, but wants to participate in the process of re-establishing a new cultural hegemony within the academy, one that is local and context-specific, one that reflects collaboration among students, teachers, and institutions, one that constructs itself out of the conflicts between the cultural capital of the academy and of the worlds of students and teachers.

What say you to that?

To: Christopher Schroeder
From: Victor Villanueva

okay—

what i have to say i'm saying right off the top: no revisions, giving myself five minutes to type and then give this closure for now (since i've been home about two hours after having been gone for a week). two things occur to me—

naming the global. (maybe not, but hear me out.) i'm thinking of _st. martin's guide to writing_, in which critical thinking—defined in universal-scientistic terms—is explicitly linked with economic, social, and personal success on the second page! as i'm reading these textbooks, there is an implicit connection between the universal and the global, insofar that global tropes and universal strategies are virtually indistinguishable (e.g. critical reading).

and what about a contingent cultural hegemony? and conversations among local-public intellectuals?

sorry about being so complicated—actually, my students make the same accusation, and i tell them that it's life, not me, that's complicated and that i'm merely talking about what is already complicated. i'm not sure they buy my response, but at least they don't complain again.

so what do you want to do about your interlude? i've been thinking that it might be interesting for you to do a reading of the book from the context of gramsci and hegemony, sort of a deconstruction or a problematization of the book itself as part of the book, as a way of continuing the conversations and a way of resisting closure and monologic proclamations.

what are your thoughts?

the deadline i've been given to finish isn't until mid summer, so there is some time.

hope the semester is concluding well for you.

From: Victor Villanueva
To: Christopher Schroeder

Well, Chris, I have finally made it through your revised manuscript. And it's quite a revision. I like the way you've situated stuff (even if I don't think that folks tend to relate "literacy crisis" with not doing well in college; literacy crisis means not getting an option to go to college). I enjoyed reading and marveled at the gutsy way you allow for folks to disagree with you. Thanks.

So let's continue our interlude, though I should say that while I'm always troubled by those who criticize what I write and say by what I didn't write or say, in some sense that's what I want to do here. I want to say something about what isn't really said—and that is that your theoretical stance leans more to the left than you allow or might even recognize. It is clear from reading your book that the ideas that most catch your fancy are those written by folks who lay claim to marxisms (like Jameson or Bourdieu or in some sense James Berlin), are labeled as marxists (like Giroux or Freire), or who have argued for composition studies to come to grips with marxisms (like Berlin or Bizzell). Yet it's equally clear that you don't know that stuff really well yet (with your labeling Berlin as "neo-Marxist" as the dead giveaway), that maybe because of the trends in composition studies and literary studies, you're more comfortable in po-mo. But I'd say as time and curiosity allow, you should get immersed in that discourse. If nothing else, the turns of discussion are interesting and are tied to discussions of discourse and thereby to rhetoric, and if to rhetoric then to composition studies and pedagogy. What you're doing in your classrooms wouldn't change much, keeping all its troubles and its successes, still struggling with rearticulations of power and agency, but given a sharper understanding of contemporary marxisms in particular, you'd be able to work from a more thoroughly articulated body of theories.

Marxisms: classical, orthodox, neo, and post. There are revisionists (like Kaustky), radicals (like Rosa Luxemberg), and Austro-Marxists (like Max Adler)—all of whom are German Social Democrats. There are the Russians like Trotsky and Lenin or Bukharin (who Kenneth Burke seemed interested in in *A Rhetoric of Motives*). There's Frankfurt (the ones usually labeled as "neo"). And there's France. There are existentialists and revisionists and struc-turalists and poststructuralists among the French marxists. Perhaps the most recognized among North American marxists is Stanley Aranowitz, and he's tied to Henry Giroux, though Giroux, somewhere, declares that he's not a marxist. And I'm not even going to mention the Latin and South Americans (except Ernesto Laclau, though his theories are more French than Latin American) or the Indian Subcontinent or Angola or Southern Africa. Enough. You get the idea. Marxisms are rich and varied, a lot more than rantings about proleteriats and bourgeoisie and shouts that quote Eisenhower as if he were Lenin in pointing to the military-industrial complex.

Within this huge mix of the marxist and the marxian there is Gramsci and his revisionists. Somewhere along the way, a dozen years back or so, I got into a study group with folks in Northern Arizona. We read *The German Ideology* and then the group broke down. But by then I wanted to know more. The more I learned, the more I was convinced that that word—*hegemony*—was being misused (or under-understood). Besides that, I was taken by Gramsci, for reasons I published about a while back now: it made sense, insofar as ideology as "false consciousness" never did resonate (as one subject to ideology but aware of the things I was subject to); the distinction between base and superstructure (now more and more described as political economy as separate from cultural studies) seemed false (given the indisputable ties between being of color and being poor); class as the overarching societal principle had problems (in that class ascendancy doesn't negate racism or sex-ism). Gramsci messed with all of those assumptions yet maintained the kind of cultural critique that was necessary for understanding certain things—like power positions in classrooms, say.

Gramsci was/is suggestive. So others have taken his ideas and tried to cast them in this time—the time of worldwide capitalism. Those who tried to "fix" Gramsci are the folks I find myself most interested in at the time (at least in coming to understand ideology; there's another group I look to for understanding the whole idea of worldwide capitalism, a group that comes under the head of World Systems (or World-Systems, with a hyphen) Theory). The one immediately recognized for working with Gramsci's not-fully articulated theories is Louis Althusser, of course. But you start to get at the other one who recasts Gramsci—Pierre Bourdieu. The main difference between Althusser and Bourdieu is that while Althusser tries to situate Gramsci with a large structuralist framework, Bourdieu tries to workout the large within the small— the *glocal* as my student, Azfar Hussein would put. Now, I've already written more than a mere interlude here, and I'm getting dangerously close to becoming a condescending jerk, but I'd ask that you get immersed in his *Outline of a Theory of Practice.* That book is loaded with stuff you're struggling with: *habitus*, those ways in which we are situated with internalized norms that are reflected in particular practices, the rules we follow without being aware of the rules (*critical unconscious* in Bourdieu's tems). That's what you are struggling against in your dissatisfaction with academic discouse. That's what your students are struggling with in your dismantling of your role as authority. *Heterodoxy*: the way in which you try to create a new orthodoxy of constructed classroom discourses, and the way the attempt has to deal with *doxa*—your own authority (even in asserting a breakdown on the authority). *Field* (though that might be *Sociology in Question* and surely in *The Field of Cultural Production*)—competition within social and institutional relations, a competition that functions under its own logic. Surely, you're rubbing up against this and sr are your students. And that puts you in a contradictory location (which recall the Gramsci-influenced work on class by Erik Olin Wright). So though you'e right to try to lessen what Bourdieu calls the "symbolic violence" that aris es in the attempt to negotiate cultural capital, the stuff's really complicated, since students will leave your office only to be subjected by others' assumption of cultural capital as the students try to attain the symbolic capital of whatever field the students decide to enter into. Got that?

Now, having said all that, let me point to one other pair of theorists I am sure would light you up and cause you to continue to problematize the kinds of issues surrounding political economy (like your objection to *The St. Martin's Guide*) and culture. And that pair would be Ernesto Laclau and Chantal Mouffe. They fall under the head of "post-marxists," insofar as they don't give the same kind of almost essentialist attention to social or economic class that classical, orthodox, and neo-marxists, in all of their various manifestations do. I know you'll like them because they argue that universal discourses are no longer tenable, that the very idea of "society" is an untenable universal discourse, that new social movements must be localized to deal with problems that continue despite class politics—movements concerning anti-racism, feminism, rights of sexuality, ecology, and the like. Laclau and Mouffe begin with Gramsci (the one book that I'm still grappling with but which is so very compelling, to the degree that I would even claim to "get it," is *Hegemony and Socialist Strategy*)—they begin with Gramsci, incorporate, explicitly, the most meaningful concepts of Derrida and others of that ilk, making for a marxism that addresses our more pressing concerns (or at least mine—bigotry of all sorts) while arguing the need for focussing attention on the micro-social.

And there are others. So though you said in one of our first exchanges that you are not thinking in terms of countering the hegemonic, your book flirts with contemporary leftist writers. Get this book out. But know it's almost prewriting to ideas I would invite you to explore. And once explored, I'd also invite you to keep the conversation going with me. That would be fun.

EPILOGUE

There must be a way to go about doing our jobs in some traditional sense and meeting some of the potential inherent in our jobs, the potential for social change, without inordinately risking those jobs. Utopianism within pragmatism; tradition and change.

Victor Villanueva, Jr.
Bootstraps

Concentrating on the question of what changes are possible or desirable for those employed in the academy, I look in detail at past efforts to reform educational practice. And, perhaps because I am keenly aware of the ways in which my own circuitous route through the academy has brought me to this project, I have made every effort in what follows to stress how profoundly local educational practices and possibilities are shaped by local constraints. For this reason, I have not set out to reveal some master pattern in the deep structure of the past that inexorably expresses itself across in time in movements to reform the academy; nor have I argued for a national revision of standards, modes of assessment, or plans for teacher training that can and should be applied here as well as there; nor finally have I suggested some ludic approach that will allow us all, à la Dr. Strangelove, to stop worrying and start loving the contradictions afforded by bureaucratic life. Critical research on education and calls for educational reform tend to sound the battle cry in these ways, but as the history of educational reform amply illustrates, a mountain of similarly hortatory educational tracts have left no real traces in the world beyond the paper on which they were written.

Richard E. Miller
As If Learning Mattered

Thanks, in part, to a coalition of forces that have been loosely called postmodernism, we, as a profession and as a society, have become more aware of differences in our classrooms, as well we should. Between 1960 and 1980, the admission of 8.5 million additional students brought the total enrollment in American colleges and universities in 1980 to 12 million, of which slightly more than 6 million were female students and well over 2 million were minority students.[1] By 1990, the enrollment in American colleges and universities had risen to 13 million students, who represented 32.5 percent of all white 18-24 year olds, 25.4 percent of all African-American 18–24 year olds, and 15.8 percent of all Hispanic 18-24 year olds.[2] At least demographically, college classrooms are much less homogeneous than one might expect, and so is the world. If the world were shrunk into a village of 100 people with all of the human ratios remaining consistent, this village would have 57 Asians, 21 Europeans, 14 from the Americas, and 8 Africans; 70 would be non-white and 30 white; 70 would be non-Christian and 30 Christian; 50% of the world's economic wealth would be held by 6 people, all of whom would be U.S. citizens; 70 people would be unable to read; 50 would suffer from malnutrition; 80 would have inadequate housing; and only one would have a college education.[3]

Despite what the literacies of the academy might suggest, our classrooms, and the communities in which they exist, can be defined much more easily by differences than they can by similarities. And if the traditionally aged students in our classroom represent less than a third of white teens and young adults and just over a fourth of African-American and less than a fifth of Hispanic counterparts—all of whom, if they graduate, will become part of that one percent of the world population with a college degree—then we, as educators, must recognize the legitimacy of these differences in our practices if we are preparing students, in fact, to read and write their worlds in the twenty-first century.

To assume the subject positions and narratives of constructed literacies, teachers must be capable of crossing boundaries that often challenge the con- tact zones that they recognize as legitimate in order to legitimize competing literacies and competing cultures in classrooms. These boundaries are the fault lines that Richard Miller describes,[4] and whether or not we can traverse them depends, at least in part, upon where we are situated, or where we situate our- selves, as outsiders and insiders.

There is something of a history of these literacy narratives in English studies, such as Keith Gilyard's and Victor Villanueva's, as well as challenges to conven- tional academic discourses and academic literacies, such as those by Lillian Bridwell-Bowles and Derek Owens.[5] Though I am oversimplifying the complex- ities of these growing traditions, I still want to suggest that they, too, struggle with an institutional legitimacy. Many of these literacy narratives, including those of Villanueva and Gilyard, are told by narrators who had originally been constructed as outsiders to the academy, which, as Villanueva and Gilyard sug- gest in *Bootstraps* and in *Voices of the Self,* generally resists the legitimacy of their cultural experiences. As such, the purported functions of these narratives are to reread and rewrite the narrators into the culture of the academy and to question this culture that excludes them. In a related way, the challenges to conventional academic discourses and academic literacies, such as Bridwell-Bowles's and Owens's, are often limited to the process of textual production for individual students or the boundaries of individual classrooms, and, as such, their potential for challenging the institutional formations that authorizes, and is authorized by, academic culture(s) emerge relatively intact.

What I am trying to do in effect is to extend the best of these traditions to collaboratively reinvent the university. In other words, I want to use the legitimacy that already exists in both, by being an insider working alongside others who have authorized personal literacy narratives and by relying upon potential inscribed within the scattered challenges to conventional academic discourses and literacies, in order to expand these challenges beyond the level of the individual to includes larger social and cultural dimensions. Like Bartholomae, Elbow, and other insiders, I, too, am working from the inside out. Unlike Bartholomae, I am calling for students and teachers to reinvent the university, and unlike Elbow, I want to extend these challenges beyond individual classrooms to the larger social and cultural contexts of the academy. In other words, I am calling for students and teachers to move beyond constructing contingent classrooms and to reread and rewrite academic institutions through the literacies that they generate in their classrooms, versions of literacy and education that seek to connect the work of Bartholomae, Elbow, and other insiders to the work of outsiders toward educational, and cultural, reform. What I have tried to do is exploit the legitimacy that I have to authorize students' struggles to acquire and/or learn academic literacies and academic cultures—the struggles of all students and not just the obvious outsiders to the academy. I have tried to do so by authorizing my own struggles, as an insider, to appropriate, and to be appropriated by, the literacies and the cultures of the academy and by collaborating with students, supervisors, and practicing professionals in producing this text. Such efforts require assuming precarious positions, positions that, however, become less precarious the more that we legitimize them though both conventional ways, such as publishing and student evaluations, and unconventional ways.

Lately, however, I have been questioning the legitimacy of educational and cultural reform, particularly in light of recent criticisms of such reforms, such as Richard Miller's *As If Learning Mattered* and Bill Readings's *The University in Ruins*. Looking back on *ReInventing*, I would reread Miller as arguing that such reforms are not easy, not that such reforms are limited to local practices, such as "training teachers to think differently about the assumptions underlying the idea of native intelligence" or "participating actively in hiring decisions" (212). Instead of the failures of Matthew Arnold and the Great Books campaign or the Open University and ethnographic methodologies, I would offer the National Writing Project and the Writing Across the Curriculum movements. Both of these have had relative success at the national level, in part, perhaps, because they have emphasized the importance of the local and the specific and because they have been willing to reread and rewrite their definitions of success in response to these experiences. Both the NWP and WAC did this, I believe, in recognizing the legitimacy of transformations in teachers, as well as in students. And I would suggest that Readings only has part of the picture when he suggests that we "abandon the notion that the social mission of the University is ineluctably linked to the project of realizing a national cultural identity," which involves relinquishing our status as intellectuals and resigning our claims of service to society, in favor of versions of academic communities "without recourse to notions of unity, consensus, and communication" (90, 20). Though I agree that we should abandon the connection between education and **a national identity**, I do not think that it is necessary to abandon the social function of universities in our efforts to "to think about a community in which communication is not transparent, a community in which the possibility of communication is not grounded upon and reinforced by a common cultural identity," to insist "that *the position of authority cannot be authoritatively occupied*," to reinvent classrooms as sites that are informed by "an obligation to the existence of otherness" and that, among other implications, interrogate disciplinarity (185-91, original emphasis). Unlike Readings, I believe that these functions can be reread and rewritten within local contexts that acknowledge the differences of the public and the private. In fact, a legitimation of constructed literacies can be found, I believe, in Richard Rorty's private irony and liberal hope that simultaneously invokes individual acts of self-perfection and social acts of redescription, a justification that endorses the contingency of literacies and education.[6]

For what are we about if we're not about meeting the intellectual and cultural needs of the people and the communities in which we work?

As I was finishing an early draft of this manuscript, I became a father, six and a half weeks before I expected. As I was trying to think through cultures and literacies, I watched the first seventeen days of my daughter's life initially from outside her isolette and later from outside her transparent crib. Sometimes I would watch the monitors attached to her tiny chest and to her even smaller foot; they blinked her heart rate, her respirations, her oxygen saturation in reds, blues, and yellows, and I would ask the nurses to explain, once again, that the Special Care Nursery was not the NICU and that she was doing well and would be coming home with us soon.

During those three weeks when, first, my wife was in the hospital, and then—when she was discharged—my daughter had to remain in the hospital, and while we were hastily preparing to move and before my daughter came home, I inexplicably seemed to have more than enough time on my hands. It was the end of the week before finals, which meant that the semester quickly ground down to a crawl, and though I remember those days as exhausting, I somehow had hours where I couldn't sleep and couldn't rest, so I tried to keep working on this manuscript. I remember trying to work out my critique of Berlin's foundationalism as I sat in the hospital cafeteria, barely tasting the half of the rubbery hamburger I had managed to eat. And yet no matter how hard I tried, I was unable to remain focused on anything but my daughter.

Which is understandable, I guess, though not for the reasons you might expect. For the first time in my life, I became aware, almost suddenly and at a visceral level, of the prevalence of cultural biases in American society. Sure, I had been privy to them before. While at a crawfish boil in south Louisiana, I watched over the fence as the neighbors openly held a Klan wedding, replete with white and red robes and burning crosses—which were quickly doused so as to prevent an apple tree from burning. I listened to a white student with a shaved head from an advanced writing course explain to me, after an hour of trying to understand the warrants of his essay on the social merit of institutionalized slavery for African-Americans, how his parents always told him that he should be a lawyer because he never lost an argument, and now not even to a teacher. In fact, I didn't even have to go to the South in order to see it. Though I had lived in St. Louis, a moderate-sized city with purportedly northern sensibilities, I still witnessed acts of prejudice.

What was different was that I never had experienced it, or at least hadn't been aware of any, for myself. By the time I got married, I had returned to St. Louis, and my wife and I were selective about the people with whom we spent time. Nevertheless, she would tell me how, for example, as she was walking down a crowded street, a man chased her, arms flailing, yelling for her to "go home." Occasionally, she would tell stories of when she was a little girl growing up in a rural Nebraska town.

"Hell," I'd say, "even I'd get discriminated against in a rural Nebraska town." And I'd go on about my day in what was for me a blissful ignorance.

Which is not to say that I didn't love my wife. It is to say that, although I love her more than anything, I could do nothing more than empathize with her and then theorize about cultural biases in classrooms and in society toward what I thought was a more socially responsible teaching.

Until I became a father.

You see, Rani, my wife, happens to be a Pacific Islander, a Filipina with skin the color of café mocha and hair that is blacker than ink. Which means that my daughter, who was now lying alone in her isolette, is Filipino-American.

As I think back, I cannot understand why I didn't have a better sense of prejudice, especially after getting married. I mean, I prided myself on my own enlightened sensitivities, and Rani, well, she cannot hide her difference. Though she moved to Chicago with her family when she was two, her difference is written in her skin and on her face, and if you know her well or listen to her, you can see Filipino cultures and hear traces of Tagalog in her utterances. In my defense, I think I might have been oblivious because she is a strong woman who comes from a family of strong women. "The Philippines is a matriarchal society," she sometimes says in jest. (Or I *think* she's joking.) As such, I could never imagine a time when she might be discriminated against simply because of the way she looks or the way she sounds.

My daughter, however, was another story. Already, her helplessness as a newborn was accentuated by the NG tube that enabled her to eat without an tiny IV or the colored knit cap she had to wear to help her stay warm. And suddenly I realized that I would have an additional responsibility—a responsibility to help my daughter move among competing cultures, the same cultures that I had struggled, and still struggle, to understand, and the emergent culture of our home, which brings together these differences in more or less productive ways. In no way am I trying to suggest that, by virtue of being married to a woman of color, I know what a minority life experience is like. What I am trying to suggest, though, is that, gradually, living with Rani has made me aware of how contingent my world is upon a whole host of cultural assumptions about language, meaning, and life, and that she has helped me to see the ways that competing cultures almost define our existence rather than serve as occasional conflicts.

As I sat in various spots in that hospital, waiting for the next time that we could wake our daughter, Mahal, to talk to her, to try to feed her, or to simply hold her close and whisper of when we'd take her home instead of leaving her behind in her glass bed, this manuscript gradually began to develop another dimension, a dimension that, for whatever reasons, I couldn't have seen or understood if I hadn't become a father before I finished it. (Maybe there is something to the connections between becoming a father in the U. S. and a growing awareness of competing cultures—at least I learned later that Keith Gilyard's efforts to understand his own cultural experiences in *Voices of the Self* were motivated, in part, by the birth of his son (10-11).) I'd thought I had always valued other literacies and discourses because of the ways that these have enabled me to talk differently about my world, to understand my experiences and to envision the world in ways that were less confined by the literacies and cultures in which I was raised. Over time, I came to believe that competing literacies and discourses can produce more satisfying experiences in the academy for students and teachers alike. Now, however, in addition to all the other personal and professional reasons I was writing this book, it had also become a place where I could envision classrooms that would celebrate our daughter's differences rather than deny them. The book had become a place where I was trying to describe classrooms and schools where I would want Mahal—someone who, by now, evinces obvious signs of competing cultural heritages—to learn and to grow. (In Tagalog, *mahal* means *love* and *expensive*, and since the SPN was $2,000 per day, she earned both halves of her name.) Since then, I've become much more aware not only of the cultural differences, even in our own home, but also of the ways that strangers' countenances suddenly change when they see me join Rani and Hali in a restaurant or at the grocery store, or the looks I receive when someone asks me to explain my daughter's "exotic" looks or strange name. Fortunately for her, the sidewalks and streets of our new neighborhood are filled with children of Hispanic parents and South American parents and Asian-American parents and African-American parents and Indian parents, a community in which, even in her differences, she is more alike than different.

As I look back on the book that you have just finished reading, even before you've read it, I can see how this new purpose is consonant with constructed literacies. As such, I suppose that one way of understanding classrooms of constructed literacies is as places where Mahal's obvious cultural differences, not to mention the less obvious and yet still powerful cultural differences—gender, class, geography, etc.—of students who are less apparently blended than she, will give rise to practices and to curricula, even into the very structures and strictures of academic institutions themselves, in a context in which her literacy needs can be, and will be, met. Not only her needs for the discourses of power in American society, but also her needs to understand her personal history and her cultural heritages in all their textuality. In the end, such a test—whether Hali, and others who are more and less like her, can get her intellectual needs met—might be a legitimate standard by which I can judge how well I have facilitated my students' efforts to construct their own literacies and their own worlds.

I wonder what would happen if teachers were evaluated on the basis of whether their students were getting their cultural and intellectual needs met. I wonder what, then, would happen to these crises of literacy and education that critics clamor so much about.

In shifting the focus of classrooms and education from context-free literacies to the negotiated literacies of contact zones, constructed literacies do not pretend to escape legitimizing narratives. As many have pointed out, escaping narratives, or attempting to escape them, is itself a narrative—that the constraints of narratives can be dissolved by absolute truth—and, I would add, it is one of the problems of conventional literacies. Rather, constructed literacies acknowledge their contingency, even as they ask students and teachers to legitimize them within this contingency through a provisional authority, one that has its basis in both traditional and nontraditional appeals. Instead of an external literacy to import into the classroom and to impose upon students, constructed literacies acknowledge the ways in which discursive practices are contingent upon contexts and are negotiated within cultural conflicts. In these classrooms, students have an authority by virtue of their proficiencies in literacies in which teachers may never be literate—legitimate literacies that can allow for different kinds of intellectual work. At the same time, teachers have an authority that arises not only from their own experiences but also from their backgrounds, their training, and their expertise.

By foregrounding the contingencies of literacies and classrooms, constructed literacies release an agency that enables students and teachers to reread and rewrite their own worlds through the ways that they reread and rewrite their classrooms. And, in so doing, constructed literacies reread and rewrite what have been called the crises in literacy and education, thereby legitimizing themselves through the ways that they respond to the needs of students, teachers, and institutions. Which is not to suggest that tradition has no place in these classrooms, but which is to suggest that tradition is contextualized and, as such, can be seen both for what it enables students and teachers to do and what it prevents them from doing.[7] At the same time, tradition can be challenged to change in the face of difference, not only to minimize its exclusivity but also to enhance its productivity, its ability to account for experiences and the world in new and different ways.

Admittedly, and not surprisingly, constructed literacies can be overwhelming for both students and teachers, for they ask both to live with and in the chaos and uncertainty of contingency as, together, they construct the literacies of their classrooms and their worlds. At the same time, they must be conscious of how their other literacies, as well as those of the discipline and of the institution, are situated in relation to those of the readers and writers with whom we work. In the process, teachers must be aware of institutional expectations and must look for ways to legitimize their classrooms and the work that students and they do together in ways that can be institutionally recognized.

If, however, the literacies of the classrooms that we construct have political and aesthetic value[8] and enable students to construct their own, then we have fulfilled the promise of education. As such, constructed literacies offer teachers the materials through which and by which they can construct classrooms of hope or hopelessness, of potential or problems, even of intellectual life or death, for students and for ourselves, and in so doing, these classrooms respond to the anxieties of the contemporary crises in literacy and education in the United States. In practice, constructed literacies foreground the politics of discursive practices within particular historical and social contexts and the means through which readers and writers can resist the sanctioned literacies of the academy in favor of versions that speak and write and read to the intellectual needs of students and teachers, both within them and beyond them. As such, constructed literacies, I hope, can serve as one of the voices in the ongoing dialogue over the nature of English studies, as well as of what it means to be literate, in America.

ENDNOTES

1. E.g. Ohmann, *Politics* (217) and Trimbur (280).
2. For example, Jeff McQuillan's recent book *The Literacy Crisis*, which has, as its subtitle, *False Claims, Real Solutions*, opens with a chapter in which he professes to dispel what he calls the seven myths about literacy in the United States, and yet Lori Olszewski cites a federal report which claims that almost one-half of adult Americans—90 million—struggle with basic reading, math, and reasoning skills. At the same time, Larry Bleiberg claims that there is no literacy crisis and that what is being identified as a literacy crisis reflects a shift in terms of what it means to be literate, that writing and reading are no longer enough to be considered literate, and yet Anthony Brandt argues that the literacy crisis has less to do with the educational system and more with changing public values.
    3. Qtd. in Giroux, "Literacy" (1) in *Literacy: Reading the Word and the World.*
4. Ohmann, "Literacy" (217).
5. Twenty years ago, 40.8 percent of first-year students indicated that their primary goal was attaining a financial security while 82.5 percent identified that their primary goal was developing a personal philosophy. Interestingly, this tendency has had a historical momentum with students' interests in income peaking in the 1980s and then decreasing a bit in the 1990s before rising again in the latest survey. For more, see Bronner ("College").
6. See ACT, Inc. ("New").
7. See ACT, Inc. ("Trend").
8. See Bonner (14) and Edmundson ("As Lite Entertainment").
9. For example, Neil Postman suggests that the problem is that contemporary education in America lacks effective narratives: "The point is that, call them what you will, we are unceasing in creating histories and futures for ourselves through the medium of narrative. Without a narrative, life has no meaning. Without meaning, learning has no purpose. Without a purpose, schools are houses of detention, not attention" (7).
10. See Habermas ("Modernity" 9).
11. See Althusser ("Ideology").
12. Althusser (141 ff).
13. Scollon and Scollon (41 ff).

14. See, for example, Gee (*Social Linguistics and Literacies* and *Social Mind*).

15. And Gale's connections between crises in China and the United States suggests that perhaps these conditions are not limited to American schools (*Teachers* 39).

16. Harkin and Schilb (3).

17. In *The University in Ruins*, Bill Readings argues that the irrelevance of the nation-state and the modernist notion of culture to "an increasingly transnational global economy" have significant implications for academic institutions, whose historical function has been the socialization of a national culture in a nation-state (12).

18. Gale, too, links these crises of legitimacy to authority (*Teachers*).

19. Berlin, *Writing* (58-60).

20. For more on the historical origins of English studies, some good places to being are Eagleton, Horner, Williams, et al.

21. See, for example, Berlin (*Reality* 25-31 and *Rhetorics* xi-xxi).

22. Halloran, "From."

23. See Miller (*Textual*).

24. See Schilb (*Between* 59).

25. See Readings (15 ff).

26. Villanueva, *Bootstraps* (137).

27. For more on this disillusionment, see Faigley (*Fragments* 53 ff).

28. See, for example, Brandt.

29. See, for example, Bleiberg.

30. See, for example, Gee (*Linguistics* 26) and Daniell (404).

31. In "Arguing," Patricia Bizzell elicits the hidden agendas of these versions of literacy.

32. See, for example, Berlin ("Literacy"), Bizzell ("Arguing"), Bizzell and Herzberg ("Inherent"), and Knoblauch ("Literacy").

33. See, for example, Kozol (*Illiterate*).

34. E.g. Knoblauch ("Literacy" 78-79).

35. Susan Jarratt makes similar critiques of expressivist theories of composition ("Feminism").

36. See Carroll ("Pomo Blues").

37. E.g. Herndl (275).

38. For more on this process, see Gee (*Linguistics* 39 ff).

39. See Faigley (*Fragments* 151).

40. Many, such as Althusser and Gramsci, make this distinction when discussing hegemony.

41. Donna LeCourt's critical WAC model, for example, considers the ways that students could use expressivist practices to resist social positions.

42. In all instances, I have reproduced students' utterances without editing.

43.   In, for example, *Empowering Education,* Shor explores a catalogue of resistances that students offer to critical pedagogies (72 ff).

44.   See Gee ("Literacy").

45.   In using these terms, I do not want to suggest essentialist versions of literacy. Rather, I am borrowing designations that are used to distinguish among the literacies into which people are initially socialized, such as the home (i.e. primary literacies), and are contrasted with secondary literacies, or literacies that are acquired and learned through direct instruction. In a similar way, popular literacies are literacies, external to the classroom, that can carry no legitimacy within the classroom walls. For more on these distinctions, see, for example, Gee (*Social* 137 ff) and Willinsky (256).

46.   See Hourigan (*Literacy* 66).

47.   Originally, the contact zone was defined by Mary Louise Pratt as "social spaces where cultures meet, clash, and grapple with each other, often in contexts of highly asymmetrical relations of power . . ." (34) though Richard Miller's understanding comes much closer to my own: places "where the central activity is investigating the range of literate practices available to those within asymmetrical power relationships" ("Fault" 399).

48.   I want to thank Richard Miller for showing me the importance of practices ("Composing").

49.   As Patricia Harkin suggests, the practices of classrooms actually legitimize theories rather than theories legitimizing classroom practices ("Postdisciplinary").

50.   I have appropriated this distinction between aesthetic and social forms of postmodernism from Fredric Jameson's "Postmoderism and Consumer Society" (124-25).

CHAPTER ONE

1.   In this section, I have relied extensively upon Nespor, Collins, Williams, Susan Miller (*Textual*), Berlin (*Rhetorics, Reality,* and *Writing*), Winterowd, and Richard Miller ("Composing").

2.   Nevertheless, Williams is quick to point out that the conditions for the emergence of this understanding of *literary* had been developing since the Renaissance (45).

3.   For more on the similarities and differences of modernism and romanticism, see Flynn (542 ff) and Crockett (742).

4.   Hourigan does a good job at providing an overview of these debates (15 ff).

5.   This editor has asked that I protect his anonymity.

6.   For example, Xin Lu Gale and Fredric G. Gale have recently edited a collection of essays entitled *(Re)Visioning Composition Textbooks: Conflicts of Culture, Ideology, and Pedagogy,* which supplements previous research done by Connors ("Textbooks"), Faigley (*Fragments*), Ohmann (*English* and "Use"),

Perrin ("Textbook"), Rose ("Sophisticated" and "Speculations"), Welch ("Ideology"), Wilson ("Writing"), Winterowd ("Composition"), and others.

7.   See, also, James Zebroski (232).

8.   See Readings (15 ff).

9.   See Schilb (*Between* 59).

10.   Bizzell elaborates on the presuppositions behind the privileging of vocabulary terms (*Academic* 134).

11.   Lest I be accused of the same neglect of "scholarly integrity" that Libby Miles cites the authors of *(Re)Visioning*, let me cite her essay, which supplements the works cited in this survey (Miles 762 ff) though, as Bizzell points out, one of the characteristics of hybrid discourses is offhanded refutation ("Hybrid").

12.   In "The 'Full Toolbox' and Critical Thinking," Xin Lu Gale limits her analysis to *The St. Martin's Guide to Writing* whereas, in this section, I attempt to consider the scope of academic literacy, as defined by the best-selling textbooks in composition.

13.   See, also, Kleine (139).

14.   Except for *The Elements of Style*, which opens with a series of contradictory "Elementary Rules of Usage" and "Elementary Principles of Composition," a mechanistic version of writing that amounts to making the right choices (15, 33).

15.   I.e. exemplification, division-classification, process analysis, comparison-contrast, cause-effect, and definition.

16.   In addition to providing an entire section on these writing strategies in the latter part of its text, *The St. Martin's Guide* also disguises them within a functional approach in the first section.

17.   See Kleine (139-40).

18.   See, for example, Crowley (*Standard*) and Smitherman (*Talkin*).

19.   See, for example, Hourigan (*Literacy*).

20.   Ohmann (*English* 143), Bizzell (*Academic* 134), Faigley (*Fragments* 133), and others have commented upon what textbooks can and cannot tell us. In some ways, I believe that textbooks might be more revealing, insofar that, while they do not necessarily reflect classroom practices, they do reveal what textbook writers, teachers, and the discipline desires to be at the center of classroom practices.

21.   See, also, Faigley ("Going" 46).

22.   See Connors ("Static" 289-92).

23.   See Larson (183 ff).

24.   See, for example, Bazerman ("What").

25.   I suppose it is worth noting that, over lunch with Pat Bizzell last December at MLA in Chicago, I agreed to use *Negotiating Difference* to see whether it

could address the concerns that I had (have) about what has been billed as the literacy crisis, so my assessment of *ND*, unlike most of the others, comes from (recent) first-hand experience.

26. To be fair, Bizzell has recently begun exploring what she calls hybrid discourses, which, similar to what I will later explain as constructed literacies, recognize the legitimacy of integrating competing discourses (e.g. article in *Composition Studies*).

27. Although *ND* repeatedly acknowledges its contingency and provisionality (e.g. viii), such disclaimers cannot resolve the problems of legitimacy.

28. Elsewhere, I have considered how a contextualization of Toulmin's substantive reasoning can foreground some deficiencies in the approach ("Knowledge").

29. For more on the institutional expectations for first-year composition classrooms, see Schilb (*Between* 59).

30. In what follows, I have applied James Paul Gee's observations about discourses, in general, to the discourses of the academy. For more, see Gee (*Linguistics* 122 ff).

31. See, for example, Lakoff (*Talking* 141ff).

32. In *The Social Mind*, Gee explores the ways that discourses lead to the formation of "appropriate folk theories" or "certain ways of making sense appropriate and satisfying" (104).

33. Mary Louise Pratt elaborates on this condition in more detail ("Contact").

34. I.e. Viacom, which is the parent company of Simon and Schuster, Prentice Hall, and Allyn and Bacon (Mortensen 219).

35. I.e. Harcourt General, which is the parent of Harcourt Brace College Publishers (Mortensen 219).

36. In "The Tie that Binds: Towards an Understanding of Ideology in the Composition and Literature Classrooms (and Beyond)," Patricia Comitini also extends these cultural problems beyond institutions to pedagogies (294).

CHAPTER TWO

1. See Flynn ("Rescuing") and Crockett for more on the totalization and unity of modernist projects.

2. In *Between the Lines*, John Schilb describes some of the conflicts between modernist and postmodernist perspectives on epistemology, artistic practices, and social conditions (85 ff, 107 ff, 129 ff).

3. See Faigley for an explanation of the relationship between historical dominance and the current authority ("Going" 46).

4. See Richard Miller (*As If Learning Mattered*).

5. See Gale for an analysis of Bizzell's classroom of authority (*Teachers* 51-52).

6. See North (23 ff).

7. See Gale (*Teachers* 51-52). What is interesting, I think, is that Bizzell reports that she resorts to the similar criteria that Shor, too, uses to establish his authority in the classroom. Perhaps the similarities between these two thinkers' efforts suggests that, in many ways, it is impossible to escape these appeals.

8. See Gale (*Teachers* 23 ff).

9. In addition identifying class, Freire acknowledges additional cultural variables, such as gender, in his later work (e.g. *Pedagogy of Hope* 67 ff).

10. See Shaull (14).

11. See *Oppressed* (17 ff, 68 ff).

12. As many have pointed out, much of Freire's literacy efforts have occurred outside of formal schools. For more on the differences between Socratic and Freirean dialogues, see Ward (100 ff). For more on the praxes of critical literacy, see *Oppressed* (52 ff).

13. See McKerrow ("Theory" and "Postmodern").

14. See Hariman ("Critical") and Charland ("Finding").

15. See Berlin ("Literacy"), Giroux ("Difference"), and McLaren and Lankshear ("Critical").

16. Irene Ward makes this case, specifically, against Ira Shor in response to his early work (Ward 102 ff) though I would extend it to Shor's later work, as well, and I would include others, even those who merely call their practices critical pedagogies.

17. In "Popular Literacy and the Roots of the New Writing," John Willinksy argues that the emphases on the social dimensions of writing, on expression as opposed to correctness, and on self-publication represent the influences of popular literacies on contemporary composition theories. While I would agree that composition studies has been willing to appropriate some of the practices of popular literacies, I would also argue that, in doing so, it denies the source of these appropriations due to a number of political reasons that, in part, relate to composition's status within academic institutions. In exchange for being able to incorporate the practices of popular literacies, teachers of composition must agree, I believe, either to pretend that these practices are somehow inferior to those of the academy or that the appropriate function of these practices is to facilitate the acquisition and/or learning of academic literacy practices. Either way, teachers ultimately deny the legitimacy of these alternative literacy practices in, for example, identifying which practices that will earn students what grades.

18. See, for example, "Literacy" (226).

19. Though Berlin acknowledges the presence of teaching assistants' experiences, he seems to imply that these "shared experiences" are limited to the alternative composition course (*Poetics* 116).

20. Compared to his description of reading in literature classrooms, his explanation of writing practices in these classrooms is neglected almost to the point that he almost reinscribes the very biases he professes to resist.

21. See also Bizzell ("Beyond" 272).

22. See *Oppressed* (52 ff). Ward makes this same criticism of Ira Shor, C. H. Knoblauch, and other practitioners of radical pedagogies (121 ff).

23. See Ward for a general assessment of authority and collaborative learning in classroom settings (81 ff).

24. Throughout *Critical Teaching and Everyday Life* and *Empowering Education*, Shor briefly describes various literature and composition classrooms, yet he devotes an entire book—*When Students Have Power*—to describing "a sophomore/junior English elective called 'Literature and Humanities'" on utopia societies (*When* 31).

25. However, Shor explains that the reason why he "accept[s] these students buying out of the process and forcing [him] into a traditional position" is that he does not "know what else to do with them," which he justifies by suggesting that "[s]tudents cannot be compelled to be nontraditional" and that "they have a right to compel [him] to be traditional towards them," which seems to mitigate the positions of resistance to his own classroom practices (*When* 77).

26. To the degree that Shor is successful in this literature classroom, his practices would respond, at least in part, to Ward's criticism that he leaves social institutions relative intact. Even in the early work that Ward cites, Shor does allude to his efforts toward social change (e.g. *Critical* 203), which Ward suggests that he does not.

27. See Ward (106, 128 note 4).

28. In "Writing and Empowerment," Richard Ohmann describes how he has resituated Shor's tendency to exploit students' discourses within historical and social contexts, to much different results, I would say.

29. Using Richard Rorty's distinction between normal and abnormal discourse, Gale makes a related argument about the importance of students' experiences with conventional academic discourses throughout *Teachers, Discourses, and Authority in the Postmodern Classroom*.

30. See Lu ("Redefining" 327).

31. See Gilmore for more on these behaviors in early classrooms.

CHAPTER THREE

1. See, e.g., Freire ("Foreword" ix) and Ward (91 ff).

2. For more on speaking for students, see Min-Zhan Lu ("Symposium") and Xin Liu Gale (*Teachers* 52).

3. Part of the problem, I believe, was that the group of co-teachers included several who expected this semester to be the same as last and several who had never worked with me before.

4. I have experimented with using textbooks and not using textbooks, and I have found strengths and weaknesses of both approaches. Using a textbook facilitates the experience of shared readings though it is often difficult, as it was this semester, to integrate one into context-specific literacies. I cannot say that I actually have a preference.

5. Both of which appear in Bizzell and Herzberg's *Negotiating Difference*, which was the textbook that we were using.

6. Bizzell has written lucidly upon the dangers of foundationalism and antifoundationalism (see "Beyond"). For a linguistic account of experientialism provides a legitimate option to objectivism and subjectivism, see Lakoff and Johnson (226).

7. Unlike Belenky et al., I understand constructed knowing not as the conjunction of intuitive knowledge and the knowledge learned from others (134) but as the confluence of competing knowledges, all of which have both social and individual dimensions.

8. It is possible, I believe, to read the ways that Pratt and Bizzell have each written about the arts of the contact zone as suggesting that, for example, producing ethnographies or storytelling have a legitimacy that transcends contexts, which, if so, makes them no different from the conventional practices of academic literacies. In identifying the discursive practices of specific contact zones, what I students and I have had to do is to consider what discursive practices represent the competing cultures within each specific zone.

9. See Camitta for more on mosaic, patchwork, embedding, and blending ("Adolescent").

10. See, for example, Bizzell ("Marxist") and McComisky (116).

11. Not unlike what Thomas Kent calls triangulation (see *Paralogic* 89-93). For more on how dialogue can enable the construction of order and meaning, see Bohm ("On").

12. E.g. Owens ("Composing").

13. See, for example, Gee (*Social* 144) on using one discourse to critique another.

14. See, for example, Worsham ("*Ecriture*").

15. In *Social Linguistics and Literacies*, James Paul Gee describes the ways that changes in discourse patterns give rise to changes in identity and that different uses of language endorse different ways of knowing (59 ff).

16. Gee asserts that school-based literacies, in general, limit difference and possibility (*Linguistics*), and to the degree that textbooks participate in these literacies, these limitations are evident in literature and composition classrooms.

17. For more on the impact of encouraging students to "philosophize" about their experiences and to "experientialize" their philosophies, see Shor and his description of the third idiom (*Empowering* 255 ff).

18. As I write, I am reminded of similar rereadings and rewritings that Pat Bizzell et al. have made of Thomas Farrell's Great Divide theories of literacy (e.g. "Arguing" 242).

19. One way of justifying the ways that constructed literacies enable students to reread and rewrite their subject positions and versions of the world are Bakhtin's dialogism and phenomenological materialism (see, for example, Bernard-Donals) and the rhizomatic epistemologies of (see Vitanza, "Three" 151 ff).

20. Pat Bizzell makes an important distinction between a position of opposition, or simple rejection, and resistance, or self-reflective noncompliance ("Marxist" 59-63). Though teachers must respect both choices, many of us would consider one to be much more legitimate than the other.

21. In "On Dialogue," David Bohm suggests that dialogues have no "rules," only "certain principles," which are learned through participation, that facilitate the dialogic process (30). Similarly, the problems with collaboration are not unique to our classrooms or to constructed literacies. For more on the problems of consensus, difference, and collaborative learning in composition classrooms, see Meyers ("Reality") and Trimbur ("Consensus"). For more on problems of social inequality and collaborative learning, see Jarratt ("Feminism").

CHAPTER FOUR

1. See Labov (xiv).

2. See Pratt (*Speech-Act*).

3. Harkin and Schilb (3).

4. Shirley Brice Heath makes a similar argument in *Ways with Words* (344).

5. In *Between the Lines*, John Schilb offers a multifaceted description of postmodernism in America comprised of these three dimensions. In articulating additional cultural values, I have drawn extensively from his descriptions of these three dimensions (86-89, 108-09, and 131-32).

6. These features are similar to the conditions that Freire calls for in his descriptions of teaching and learning. For more, see Daniell (401-03).

7. Readings, too, recognizes the importance of what he calls dialogism, to which he attributes to Bakhtin (154 ff). In my estimation, Ward's synthesis is much more productive.

8. In *Empowering*, Shor theorizes the contingency classrooms informed by what he calls the third idiom (256), yet, as I suggested previously, his classrooms fail to authorize this contingency in legitimate and productive ways.

9. These provisional standards for ethical discourse come from James Paul Gee, who has appropriated Wittgenstein's forms of life (see *Linguistics* 19-20 and "Postmodernism" 292-93).

10. One needn't turn far to find theoretical justification for constructed literacies. For example, the contingency of constructed literacies is the contingency of self, language, and community that informs Richard Rorty's liberal irony. For more, see Rorty (*Contingency, Irony, and Solidarity*, especially 96 ff).

11. Readings, too, points out the importance of listening (165).

12. By Carolyn's account, her last response to Amy was lost.

13. See Shor for a theoretical account of this process (*Empowering* 254 ff).

14. See Gee (*Linguistics* 89).

15. See Shor (*Empowering* 254 ff).

16. See McComiskey (*Teaching*) and Trimbur ("Composition") and Comitini ("Tie").

17. See Bizzell (*Academic* 3 ff, 277 ff).

18. See "'Contact'" (741) and "Marxist" (56).

19. See "When" (168 ff), "Foundationalism" (203 ff), "'Contact'" (739, 741), "Marxist" (65), "What" (222), "When" (168), and "Introduction" (16).

20. See "Beyond" (262).

21. See "Afterword" (291-92) and "Beyond" (274).

22. See "Afterword" (281).

23. See "Afterword" (280).

24. See "'Contact'" (738-39).

25. See "Afterword" (281 ff).

26. See "Marxist" (61, 65).

27. Villanueva, *Bootstraps* (130, 123).

28. Bizzell, "Afterword" (288, 292).

29. See, for example, Gale (*Teachers* 51-53).

30. Bizzell, "Afterword" (293).

31. Patricia Bizzell, email to the author, 19 June 2000.

32. Villanueva, *Bootstraps* (131).

33. Villanueva, *Bootstraps* (132).

34. I am relying upon Daniel Maltz and Ruth Borker's "A Cultural Approach to Male-Female Miscommunication" as the source of the differences between masculine and feminine discourse.

35. The handwriting that follows is not Jerry's, which, by his own admission, is fairly illegible. Though I regret not using his own handwriting, I hope that changing to a "handwriting" font will have the same, or similar, effect.

36. See, for example, Jarratt ("Feminism"), Ward (*Literacy*), and Gale (*Teachers*).

37. See Cushman (12-13, 18).

38. See Fox, Tom (90). Miles cites Fox, and also Hillocks and Richard Miller, in what she calls "the importance of individual agency within institutions" (760-61).
39. See, for example, Rorty (*Contingency*).
40. I have since then moved again, and yet Jerry and I have still continued our conversations about constructing literacies.
41. Jerry, email to the author, 22 September 1999.
42. I need to credit this point to an on-going conversation that Pat Bizzell and I are having (emails to the author, 23 September 1999 and 28 September 1999).
43. See, for example, Rorty ("Solidarity")
44. In "The Postdisciplinary Politics of Lore," Patricia Harkin offers a justification for lore as antiessentialist theories that refuse to be reductive, an approach that challenges conventional ways of producing knowledge (134 ff). In other words, she offers a version of theory as contingent and specific in which practices and problems provide a legitimacy for theories rather than the other way around.
45. In *When Students Have Power*, Shor describes, in detail, the history of his first After-Class Group, which, in his own words, "became an experience that changed my teaching life" (119). For more on Shor's After-Class Groups, see *When* (116 ff).
46. Though critics argue about the existence of the digital divide, the institutions in which I work provide students with access to cyberspace, as, I suspect, do most, if not all, institutions, through personal email accounts, access to the WWW, and the option to use other software.
47. Michael O'Rourke, email to the author, 31 October 1999.
48. Email to the author, 17 November 1999. To be fair, this student changed his mind about the assessment practices after the final exam. In his portfolio, he cites several problems that he believes student assessment has. See below.
49. Allow me to make the point, again, that it is the practices of constructed literacies that legitimize the theories. This distinction is necessary to make the literacies that emerge from classrooms contingent and specific.
50. See, for example, Hourigan (*Literacy*) and Ward (*Literacy*).
51. See, for example, Gale (*Teachers*).
52. See the physicist David Bohm's "On Dialogue" for a lucid explanation of this contingent and context-specific practice.

EPILOGUE

1. See Kerr (xiv; qtd. in Gale, *Teachers* 159).
2. See Hourigan (*Beyond*, 185; qtd. in Gale, *Teachers* 159).
3. See Gorgue.

4. See Miller ("Fault").

5. As for other literacy narratives, see, for example, Elbow ("Illiteracy"), hooks (*Talkin*), Rodriguez, Rose (*Lives*), Lu ("From"), and others, and as for other explicit and implicit challenges to conventional academic discourse(s) and academic literaci(es), see Anzaldúa, Bizzell ("Hybrid"), Elbow ("Native"), Gale (*Teachers*), Helen Fox (*Listening*), Lippi-Green, Meisenhelder, Smitherman, Severino, Guerra, and Butler, Tompkins ("Me"), and others.

6. See Rorty (*Contingency*).

7. Gale also writes of the importance of the traditional alongside the radical (*Teachers* 152 ff).

8. I have stolen these criteria, with his permission, from an email from Victor Vitanza.

WORKS CITED

ACT, Inc. "New Low for College Graduation Rate, But Dropout Picture Brighter." Press Release. Iowa City, IA. 1 April 1998.

———. "Trend of Increases in ACT College-Entrance Scores Continues." Press Release. Iowa City, IA. 13 August 1997.

ADE. "Doctorate Recipients from United States Universities in English and American Language and Literature, 1998–99." website: http.www.ade.org/facts/PHD_ade.htm.

Althusser, Louis. "Ideology and Ideological State Apparatuses." *Lenin and Philosophy and Other Essays.* Trans. Ben Brewster. New York: Monthly Review Press, 1971.

Anzaldúa, Gloria. *Borderlands/La Frontera: The New Mestiza.* 2nd ed. San Francisco: Aunt Lute Books, 1999.

Arp, Thomas R. *Perrine's Literature: Structure, Sound, and Sense.* 7th ed. Fort Worth: Harcourt Brace College Publishers, 1998.

Axelrod, Rose B., and Charles R. Cooper. *The St. Martin's Guide to Writing.* 5th ed. New York: St. Martin's Press, 1997.

Bakhtin, M. M. *The Dialogic Imagination: Four Essays By M. M. Bakhtin.* Ed. Michael Holquist. Trans Caryl Emerson and Michael Holquist. Austin: University of Texas Press, 1981.

———. "Discourse in the Novel." Bakhtin 259–422.

Bartholomae, David. "Inventing the University." Villanueva 589–619.

Barton, Ellen L. "Literacy in (Inter)Action." *College English* 59 (1997): 408–37.

Bazerman, Charles. "What Written Knowledge Does: Three Examples of Academic Discourse." *Landmark Essays on Writing Across the Curriculum.* Eds. Charles Bazerman and David R. Russell. Davis, CA: Hermagoras Press, 1994. 159–88.

Belenky, Mary Field, Blythe McVicker Clinchy, Nancy Rule Goldberger, and Jill Mattuck Tarule. *Women's Ways of Knowing: The Development of Self, Voice, and Mind.* New York: Basic, 1986.

Berlin, James. "Literacy, Pedagogy, and English Studies: Postmodern Connections." Lankshear and McLaren 247–69.

———. *Rhetoric and Reality: Writing Instruction in American Colleges, 1900–1985.* Carbondale, IL: Southern Illinois University Press, 1987.

———. *Rhetorics, Poetics, and Cultures: Refiguring English Studies*. Urbana, IL: National Council of Teachers of English, 1996.

———. *Writing Instruction in Nineteenth-Century American Colleges*. Carbondale, IL: Southern Illinois University Press, 1984.

Bernard-Donals, Michael. "Mikhail Bakhtin: Between Phenomenology and Marxism." Farmer 63–79.

Bialostosky, Don H. "Liberal Education, Writing, and the Dialogic Self." Farmer 187–96.

Bishop, Wendy, ed. *Elements of Alternate Style: Essays on Writing and Revision*. Portsmouth, NH: Boynton/Cook Publishers, 1997.

Bizzell, Patricia. *Academic Discourse and Critical Consciousness*. Pittsburgh: University of Pittsburgh Press, 1992.

———. "Academic Discourse and Critical Consciousness: An Application of Paulo Freire." Bizzell 129–52.

———. "Afterword." Bizzell 277–95.

———. "Beyond Anti-Foundationalism to Rhetorical Authority: Problems Defining 'Cultural Literacy.'" Bizzell 256–76.

———. " 'Contact Zones' and English Studies." Villanueva 735–42.

———. "Hybrid Discourses: What, Why, How." *Composition Studies* 27 (1999): 7–21.

———. "Marxist Ideas in Composition Studies." Harkin and Schilb 52–68.

———. "What Happens When Basic Writers Come to College?" Bizzell 164–74.

———. "What Is a Discourse Community?" Bizzell 222–37.

Bizzell, Patricia, and Bruce Herzberg. " 'Inherent' Ideology, 'Universal' History, 'Empirical' Evidence, and 'Context-Free' Writing: Some Problems in E. D. Hirsch's *The Philosophy of Composition*." Bizzell 51–74.

———. *Negotiating Difference: Cultural Case Studies for Composition*. Boston: Bedford Books, 1996.

Bleiberg, Larry. " 'Literacy Crisis' Called Overblown, A Matter of Changing Definitions." *The San Diego Union-Tribune* 29 April 1994: A30+.

Bohm, David. *On Dialogue*. Ed. Lee Nichol. London: Routledge, 1996.

Bourdieu, Pierre. "The School as a Conservative Force: Scholastic and Cultural Inequalities." *Contemporary Research in the Sociology of Education*. Ed. J. Eggleston. London: Methuen, 1974. 32–46.

Brandt, Anthony. "Literacy in America." *The New York Times* 25 August 1980, late city final ed: A23.

Bridwell-Bowles, Lillian. "Discourse and Diversity: Experimental Writing Within the Academy." *College Composition and Communication* 43 (1992): 349–68.

Bronner, Ethan. "College Freshman Aiming for High Marks in Income." *The New York Times* 12 January 1998, late edition: A14.

Camitta, Miriam P. "Adolescent Vernacular Writing: Literacy Reconsidered." Lunsford, Moglen, and Slevin 262–68.

Carroll, Lee Ann. "Pomo Blues: Stories from First-Year Composition." *College English* 59 (1997): 916–33.

Charland, Maurice. "Finding a Horizon and Telos: The Challenge to Critical Rhetoric." Quarterly Journal of Speech 77 (1991): 71–74.

Chiseri-Strater, Elizabeth. *Academic Literacies: The Public and the Private Discourse of University Students.* Portsmouth, NH: Boynton/Cook Publishers, 1991.

Clifford, John. "The Subject in Discourse." Harkin and Schilb 38–51.

Cochran-Smith, Marilyn. "Blind Vision: Unlearning Racism in Teacher Education." *Harvard Educational Review* 7 (2000): 157–90.

Collins, James. "Hegemonic Practice: Literacy and Standard Language in Public Education." Mitchell and Weiler 229–54.

Comas, James. "War and the Anima of Criticism." *Rhetoric Review* 16 (1998): 188–225.

Comitini, Patricia. "The Tie that Binds: Toward an Understanding of Ideology in the Composition and Literature Classrooms (and Beyond)." Robertson and Smith 279–96.

Conners, Robert J. "Static Abstractions and Composition." Tate, Corbett, and Meyers 29–93.

———. "Textbooks and the Evolution of the Discipline." *College Composition and Communication* 37 (1986): 178–94.

Crockett, Andy. "Unity." Enos 156–57.

Crowley, Tony. *Standard English and the Politics of Language.* Urbana, IL: University of Illinois Press, 1989.

Cushman, Ellen. "The Rhetorician as an Agent of Social Change." *College Composition and Communication* 47 (1996): 7–28.

Daniell, Beth. "Narratives of Literacy: Connecting Composition to Culture." *College Composition and Communication* 50 (1999): 393–410.

Dean, Terry. "Multicultural Classrooms, Monocultural Teachers." Tate, Corbett, and Meyers 105–18.

Donald, James. "How Illiteracy Became a Problem (And Literacy Stopped Being One)." Mitchell and Weiler 211–27.

Douglas, Wallace. "Rhetoric for the Meritocracy: The Creation of Composition at Harvard." Ohmann, *English in America* 97–132.

Eagleton, Terry. *Ideology.* New York: Verso, 1991.

———. *Literary Theory: An Introduction.* Minneapolis: University of Minnesota Press, 1983.

Edmundson, Mark. "On the Uses of a Liberal Education: I. As Lite Entertainment for Bored College Students." *Harper's Magazine* September 1997: 39–49.

Elasser, Nan, and Patricia Irvine. "Literacy as Commodity: Redistributing the Goods." *Journal of Education* 174 (1992): 26–40.

Elbow, Peter. *Essays Toward a Hopeful Theory of Writing and Teaching Writing.* New York: Oxford University Press, 2000. 323–50.

———. "Illiteracy at Oxford and Harvard: Reflections on the Inability to Write." Elbow 5–27.

———. "Inviting the Mother Tongue: Beyond 'Mistakes,' 'Bad English,' and 'Wrong Language.'" *Essays Toward a Hopeful Theory of Writing and Teaching Writing.* New York: Oxford University Press, 2000. 323–50.

———. "Re: dialogue and evaluation." Email to the author. 9 January 1999.

Emerson, Ralph Waldo. *The Works of Emerson.* Roslyn, NY: Black's Readers Service Company.

Enos, Theresa, ed. *Encyclopedia of Rhetoric and Composition: Communication from Ancient Times to the Information Age.* New York: Garland, 1996.

Evans, Henry L. "An Afrocentric Multicultural Writing Project." Severino, Guerra, and Butler 273–86.

Faigley, Lester. *Fragments of Rationality: Postmodernity and the Subject of Composition.* Pittsburgh: University of Pittsburgh Press, 1992.

———. "Going Electronic: Creating Multiple Sites for Innovation in a Writing Program." *Resituating Writing: Constructing and Administering Writing Programs.* Eds. Joseph Janangelo and Kristine Hansen. Portsmouth, NH: Boynton/Cook, 1995. 46–58.

Farmer, Frank, ed. *Landmark Essays on Bakhtin, Rhetoric, and Writing.* Mahwah, NJ: Hermagoras Press, 1998.

Fishman, Andrea R. "Becoming Literate: A Lesson from the Amish." Lunsford, Moglen, and Slevin 29–38.

Flynn, Elizabeth. "Rescuing Postmodernism." *College Composition and Communication* 48 (1997): 540–55.

Foster, Hal, ed. *The Anti-Aesthetic: Essays on Postmodern Culture.* Port Townsend, WA: Bay Press, 1983.

Foucault, Michel. "The Discourse on Language." *The Archaeology of Knowledge and the Discourse on Language.* New York: Pantheon Books, 1972. 215–37.

Fox, Helen. *Listening to the World: Cultural Issues in Academic Writing.* Urbana, IL: National Council of Teachers of English, 1994.

Fox, Tom. *Defending Access: A Critique of Standards in Higher Education.* Portsmouth, NH: Boynton/Cook-Heinemann, 1999.

Freire, Paulo. *Education for Critical Consciousness.* New York: Continuum, 1973.

———. Foreword. *An Unquiet Pedagogy: Transforming Practice in the English Classroom.* By Eleanor Kutz and Hephzibah Roskelly. Portsmouth, NH: Boynton/Cook, 1991. ix–x.

———. *Pedagogy of Hope: Reliving Pedagogy of the Oppressed.* New York: Continuum, 1994.

———. *Pedagogy of the Oppressed.* New York: Continuum, 1970.

Gale, Xin Liu. *Teachers, Discourses, and Authority in the Postmodern Composition Classroom.* Albany, NY: State University of New York Press, 1996.

Gale, Xin Liu, and Fredric G. Gale, eds. *(Re)Visioning Composition Textbooks: Conflicts of Culture, Ideology, and Pedagogy.* Albany, NY: State University of New York Press, 1999.

Gee, James Paul. "The Narrativization of Experience in the Oral Style." Mitchell and Weiler 77–102.

———. "Postmodernism and Literacies." Lankshear and McLaren 271–95.

———. *Social Linguistics and Literacies.* 2nd ed. Bristol, PA: Falmer Press, 1996.

———. *The Social Mind: Language, Ideology, and Social Practice.* New York: Bergin & Garvey, 1992.

———. "What is Literacy?" Mitchell and Weiler 3–11.

Gilmore, Perry. " 'Gimme Room': School Resistance, Attitude, and Access to Literacy." Mitchell and Weiler 57–73.

Gilyard, Keith. *Voices of the Self: A Study of Language Competence.* Detroit: Wayne State University Press, 1991.

Giroux, Henry. Introduction. *Literacy: Reading the Word and the World.* By Paulo Freire and Donaldo Macedo. Westport, CN: Bergin & Garvey, 1987. 1–27.

———. "Literacy and the Politics of Difference." Lankshear and McLaren 367–78.

———. "Paulo Freire and the Politics of Postcolonialism." *Journal of Advanced Composition* 12 (1992): 15–26.

Gorgue, Jay. "Food for Thought." Letter. *Family and Community Services Connections.* July 1998.

Habermas, Jürgen. "Modernity—An Incomplete Project." Foster 3–15.

Hacker, Diana. *A Writer's Reference.* 4th ed. Boston: Bedford/St. Martin's Press, 1999.

Halasek, Kay. *A Pedagogy of Possibility: Bakhtinian Perspectives on Composition Studies.* Carbondale, IL: Southern Illinois University Press, 1999.

Halloran, S. Michael. "From Rhetoric to Composition: The Teaching of Writing in America to 1900." *A Short History of Writing Instruction: From Ancient Greece to Twentieth Century America.* Ed. James J. Murphy. Davis, CA: Hermagoras Press, 1990. 151–82.

Hariman, Robert. "Critical Rhetoric and Postmodern Theory." *Quarterly Journal of Speech* 77 (1991): 67–70.

Harkin, Patricia. "The Postdisciplinary Politics of Lore." Harkin and Schilb 124–38.

Harkin, Patricia, and John Schilb, eds. *Contending With Words: Composition and Rhetoric in a Postmodern Age.* New York: Modern Language Association, 1991.

———. Introduction. Harkin and Schilb 1–10.

Harmon, William, and C. Hugh Holman. *A Handbook to Literature.* 7th ed. Upper Saddle River, NJ: Prentice Hall, 1996.

Heath, Shirley Brice. *Ways with Words: Language, Life, and Work in Communities and Classrooms.* New York: Cambridge University Press, 1983.

Herndl, Carl G. "Freire, Paulo." Enos 274–75.

Hodges, John C., Winifred Bryn Horner, Suzanne Strobeck Webb, and Robert Keith Miller. *Harbrace College Handbook.* 13th ed. Fort Worth: Harcourt Brace College Publishers, 1998.

hooks, bell. *Talking Back: Thinking Feminist, Thinking Black.* Boston: South End Press, 1989.

———. *Teaching to Transgress: Education as the Practice of Freedom.* New York: Routledge, 1994.

Horner, Winifred, ed. *Composition and Literature: Bridging the Gap.* Chicago: University of Chicago Press, 1983.

Hourigan, Maureen M. *Literacy as Social Exchange: Intersections of Class, Gender, and Culture.* Albany, NY: State University of New York Press, 1994.

Jacklosky, Rob. "The ComPosition-ing of *Culture and Anarchy:* Recovering a Cultural Conflict in Arnold's Serene Text." Robertson and Smith 313–36.

Jameson, Fredric. "Postmodernism and Consumer Society." Foster 111–25.

Jarratt, Susan C. "Feminism and Composition." Harkin and Schilb 105–23.

Johnson, Lemuel. 22 August 2000 <http://www.westafrica review.com/war/vol1.2/vol1.2a/lemuel.html>.

Johstone, Barbara. *The Linguistic Individual: Self-Expression in Language and Linguistics.* New York: Oxford University Press, 1996.

Kennedy, X. J., and Dana Gioia. *Literature: An Introduction to Fiction, Poetry, and Drama.* 7th ed. New York: Longman, 1999.

Kent, Thomas. *Paralogic Rhetoric: A Theory of Communicative Interaction.* Lewisburg, PA: Bucknell University Press, 1993.

Kerr, Clark. *The Great Transformation in Higher Education, 1960–1980.* Albany, NY: State University of New York Press, 1988.

Kleine, Michael W. "Teaching from a Single Textbook 'Rhetoric': The Potential Heaviness of the Book." Gale and Gale 137–61.

Knoblauch, C. H. "Literacy and the Politics of Education." Lunsford, Moglen, and Sleven 74–80.

Kozol, Jonathan. *Illiterate America.* New York: Doubleday, 1985.

Labov, William. *Language in the Inner City: Studies in the Black English Vernacular.* Philadelphia: University of Pennsylvania Press, 1972.

Lakoff, George, and Mark Johnson. *Metaphors We Live By.* Chicago: University of Chicago Press, 1980.

Lakoff, Robin Tolmach. *Talking Power: The Politics of Language.* New York: Basic Books, 1990.

Lankshear, Colin, and Peter L. McLaren, eds. *Critical Literacy: Policy, Praxis, and the Postmodern.* Albany, NY: State University of New York Press, 1993.

Larson, Richard L. "The 'Research Paper' in a Writing Course: A Non-Form of Writing." Tate, Corbett, and Meyers 180–85.

LeCourt, Donna. "WAC as Critical Pedagogy: The Third Stage?" *JAC: A Journal of Composition Theory* 16 (1996): 389–405.

Leki, Ilona. "Twenty-Five Years of Contrastive Rhetoric: Text Analysis and Writing Pedagogies." *TESOL Quarterly* 25 (1991): 123–43.

Levy, Clifford J. "Citing a Crisis, Bush Proposes Literacy Effort." *The New York Times* 29 March 2000, national ed.: A1+.

Lippi-Green, Rosina. *English With an Accent: Language, Ideology, and Discrimination in the United States.* London: Routledge, 1997.

Lu, Min-zhan. "From Silence to Words: Writing as Struggle." *College English* 49 (1987): 437–47.

———. "Redefining the Legacy of Mina Shaughnessy: A Critique of the Politics of Linguistic Innocence." Tate, Corbett, and Meyers 327–37.

———. "Symposium on Basic Writing, Conflict, and Struggle, and the Legacy of Mina Shaughnessy." *College English* 55 (1993): 894–903.

Lunsford, Andrea A., Helene Moglen, and James Sleven, eds. *The Right to Literacy.* New York: Modern Language Association, 1990.

Lyons, Scott. "A Captivity Narrative: Indians, Mixed Bloods, and the 'White' Academy." *Outbursts in Academe: Multiculturalism and Other Sources of Conflict.* Eds. Kathleen Dixon, William Archibald, and Jane Varley. Portsmouth, NH: Heinemann, 1998.

Lyotard, Jean-François. *The Postmodern Condition: A Report on Knowledge.* Trans. Geoff Bennington and Brian Massumi. Minneapolis: University of Minnesota Press, 1984.

Maltz, Daniel N., and Ruth A. Borker. "A Cultural Approach to Male-Female Communication." *Language and Social Identity.* Ed. John J. Gumperz. Cambridge: Harvard University Press, 1982. 196–216.

McComiskey, Bruce. *Teaching Composition as a Social Process.* Logan, UT: Utah State University Press, 2000

McKerrow, Raymie E. "Critical Rhetoric: Theory and Praxis." *Communication Monographs* 56 (1989): 91–111.

———. "Critical Rhetoric in a Postmodern World." *Quarterly Journal of Speech* 77 (1991): 75–78.

McLaren, Peter, and Colin Lankshear. "Critical Literacy and the Postmodern Turn." Lankshear and McLaren 379–419.

McQuillan, Jeff. *The Literacy Crisis: False Claims, Real Solutions.* Portsmouth, NH: Heinemann, 1998.

Meisenhelder, Susan. "Redefining 'Powerful' Writing: Toward a Feminist Theory of Composition." *Journal of Thought* 20 (1985): 184–95.

Meyer, Michael. *The Bedford Introduction to Literature: Reading, Thinking, Writing.* Boston: Bedford/St. Martin's Press, 1999.

Meyers, Greg. "Reality, Consensus, and Reform in the Rhetoric of Composition Teaching." Villanueva 415–38.

Miles, Libby. "Disturbing Practices: Toward Institutional Change in Composition Scholarship and Pedagogy." Rev. of *Ways of Thinking, Ways of Teaching*, by George Hillocks Jr., *Defending Access: A Critique of Standards in Higher Education*, by Tom Fox, and *(Re)Visioning Composition Textbooks: Conflicts of Culture, Ideology, and Pedagogy*, by Xin Liu Gale and Fredric G. Gale, eds. *College English* 62 (2000): 756–66.

Miller, Richard. *As If Learning Mattered: Reforming Higher Education*. Ithaca: Cornell University Press, 1998.

———. "Composing English Studies: Towards a Social History of the Discipline." *College Composition and Communication* 45 (1994): 164–79.

———. "Fault Lines in the Contact Zone." *College English* 56 (1994): 398–408.

Miller, Susan. *Textual Carnivals: The Politics of Composition*. Carbondale, IL: Southern Illinois University Press, 1991.

Mitchell, Candace, and Kathleen Weiler, eds. *Rewriting Literacy: Culture and the Discourse of the Other*. Westport, CN: Bergin & Garvey, 1991.

Morris, Paul J., II, and Stephen Tchudi. *The New Literacy: Moving Beyond the 3Rs*. San Francisco: Jossey-Bass, 1996.

Mortensen, Peter. "Of Handbooks and Handbags: Composition Textbook Publishing after the Deal Decade." Gale and Gale 217–29.

Nadell, Judith, John Langan, and Linda McMeniman. *The Macmilian Reader*. 5th ed. Boston: Allyn and Bacon, 1999.

Nespor, Jan. "The Construction of School Knowledge: A Case Study." Mitchell and Weiler 169–88.

North, Stephen M. *The Making of Knowledge in Composition: A Portrait of an Emerging Field*. Portsmouth, NH: Boynton/Cook Heinemann Publishers, 1987.

Ohmann, Richard. *English in America: A Radical View of the Profession*. Hanover: Wesleyan University Press, 1996.

———. *Politics of Letters*. Middletown, CN: Wesleyan University Press, 1987.

———. "Use Definite, Specific, Concrete Language." Tate, Corbett, and Meyers 310–18.

Olszewski, Lori. "U.S. Strains to Cope with Literacy Crisis." *The San Francisco Chronicle* 17 September 1993, final ed.: A1.

Owens, Derek. "Composing as the Voicing of Multiple Fictions." *Into the Field: Sites of Composition Studies*. Ed. Anne Ruggles Gere. New York: Modern Language Association, 1993. 159–75.

Perrin, Robert. "Textbook Writers and Textbook Publishers: One Writer's View of the Teaching Canon." *Journal of Teaching Writing* 7 (1988): 67–74.

Postman, Neil. *The End of Education: Redefining the Value of School*. New York: Random House, 1995.

Pratt, Mary Louise. "Arts of the Contact Zone." *Profession* 91 (1991): 33–40.

———. *Toward a Speech Act Theory of Literary Discourse.* Bloomington: Indiana University Press, 1977.

Readings, Bill. *The University in Ruins.* Cambridge: Harvard University Press, 1996.

Robertson, Alice, and Barbara Smith, eds. *Teaching in the 21st Century: Adapting Writing Pedagogies to the College Curriculum.* New York: Falmer Press, 1999.

Rodriguez, Richard. *Hunger of Memory: The Education of Richard Rodriguez.* New York: Bantam, 1982.

Rorty, Richard. *Contingency, Irony, and Solidarity.* New York: Cambridge University Press, 1989.

———. "Solidarity." *Contingency, Irony, and Solidarity.* New York: Cambridge University Press, 1989. 189–98.

Rose, Mike. *Lives on the Boundary: A Moving Account of the Struggles and Achievements of America's Educationally Underprepared.* New York: Penguin, 1989.

———. "Sophisticated, Ineffective Books: The Dismantling of Process in Composition Texts." *College Composition and Communication* 32 (1981): 65–74.

———. "Speculations on Process Knowledge and the Textbooks' Static Page." *College Composition and Communication* 34 (1983): 208–13.

Roskelly, Hephzibah. "The Risky Business of Group Work." Tate, Corbett, and Meyers 141–46.

Schilb, John. *Between the Lines: Relating Composition Theory and Literary Theory.* Portsmouth, NH: Boynton/Cook Publishers, 1996.

Schroeder, Christopher. "Knowledge and Power, Logic and Rhetoric, and Other Reflections in the Toulminian Mirror: A Critical Consideration of Stephen Toulmin's Contributions to Composition." *JAC: A Journal of Composition Theory* 17 (1997): 95–107.

Scollon, Ron, and Suzanne B. K. Scollon. *Narrative, Literacy, and Face in Interethnic Communities.* Norwood, NJ: Ablex, 1981.

Severino, Carol, Juan C. Guerra, and Johnnella E. Butler, eds. *Writing in Multicultural Settings.* New York: Modern Language Association, 1997.

Shaull, Richard. Forward. *Pedagogy of the Oppressed.* By Paulo Freire. New York: Continuum, 1994. 11–16.

Shor, Ira. *Critical Teaching and Everyday Life.* Chicago: University of Chicago Press, 1980.

———. *Empowering Education: Critical Teaching for Social Change.* Chicago: University of Chicago Press, 1992.

———. *When Students Have Power: Negotiating Authority in a Critical Pedagogy.* Chicago: University of Chicago Press, 1996.

Smitherman, Geneva. *Talkin and Testifyin: The Language of Black America.* Detroit: Wayne State University Press, 1977.

Soliday, Mary. "The Politics of Difference: Toward a Pedagogy of Reciprocity." Severino, Guerra, and Butler 261–72.

Sosnoski, James J. "Postmodern Teachers in Their Postmodern Classrooms." Harkin and Schilb 105–21.

Stewart, Donald C. "Composition Textbooks and the Assault on Tradition." *College Composition and Communication* 29 (1978): 171–75.

Stuckey, J. Elspeth. *The Violence of Literacy.* Portsmouth, NH: Boynton/Cook, 1991.

Sullivan, Anne McCrary. "Notes from a Marine Biologist's Daughter: On the Art and Science of Attention." *Harvard Educational Review* 7 (2000): 211–27.

Tate, Gary, Edward P.J. Corbett, and Nancy Meyers, eds. *The Writing Teacher's Sourcebook.* 3rd ed. New York: Oxford University Press, 1994.

Tompkins, Jane. "Me and My Shadow." *Feminisms: An Anthology of Literary Theory and Criticism.* Eds. Robyn R. Warhol and Diane Price Herndl. New Brunswick, NJ: Rutgers University Press, 1991. 1079–92.

Trimbur, John. "Consensus and Difference in Collaborative Learning." Villanueva 439–56.

———. *The Call to Write.* New York: Longman, 1999.

———. "Literacy and the Discourse of Crisis." *The Politics of Writing Instruction: Postsecondary.* Eds. Richard Bullock and John Trimbur. Portsmouth, NH: Boynton/Cook Publishers, 1991. 277–95.

Tompkins, Jane. "Pedagogy of the Distressed." *College English* 52 (1990): 653–60.

Troyka, Lynn Quitman. *Simon & Schuster Handbook for Writers.* 5th ed. Upper Saddle River, NJ: Prentice Hall, 1999.

Villanueva, Victor, Jr. *Bootstraps: From an American Academic of Color.* Urbana, IL: National Council of Teachers of English, 1993.

———, ed. *Cross-Talk in Comp Theory: A Reader.* Urbana, IL: National Council of Teachers of English, 1997.

Vitanza, Victor. Email to the Pre-Text list. 8 December 1997.

———. "Three Countertheses: Or, A Critical In(ter)vention into Composition Theories and Pedagogies." Harkin and Schilb 139–72.

Ward, Irene. *Literacy, Ideology, and Dialogue: Towards a Dialogic Pedagogy.* Albany, NY: State University of New York Press, 1994.

Weathers, Winston. "The Rhetorician." *Rhetoric Review* 16 (1997): 92–104.

Weil, Danny K. *Towards a Critical Multicultural Literacy: Theory and Practice for Education for Liberation.* New York: Peter Lang, 1998.

Welch, Kathleen E. "Ideology and Freshman Textbook Production: The Place of Theory in Writing Pedagogy." *College Composition and Communication* 38 (1987): 269–82.

Williams, Raymond. *Marxism and Literature.* Oxford: Oxford University Press, 1977.

Willinsky, John. "Popular Literacy and the Roots of the New Writing." Mitchell and Weiler 255–69.

Wilson, Matthew. "Writing History: Textbooks, Heuristics, and the Eastern Europe Revolutions of '89." *College English* 54 (1992): 662–80.

Winterowd, W. Ross. "Composition Textbooks: Publisher-Author Relationships." *College Composition and Communication* 40 (1989): 139–51.

———. *The English Department: An Institutional and Personal History.* Carbondale, IL: Southern Illinois University Press, 1998.

Worsham, Lynn. "Writing Against Writing: The Predicament of *Écriture Feminine* in Composition Studies." Harkin and Schilb 82–104.

Yee, Marian. "Are You the Teacher?" *Composition and Resistance.* Eds. C. Mark Hurlbert and Michael Blitz. Portsmouth, NH: Boynton/Cook, 1991. 24–30.

Zavarzaden, Mas'ud, and Donald Morton. *Theory as Resistance: Politics and Culture After (Post)structuralism.* New York: Guilford Press, 1994.

Zebroski, James Thomas. "Textbook Advertisements in the Formation of Composition: 1969– 1990." Gale and Gale 231–48.

INDEX

ABOUT THE AUTHOR

Christopher Schroeder lives, writes, and teaches in New York, where he continues to explore literacies and education in a postmodern United States. Currently, he coordinates the Writing Across the Curriculum program at the C. W. Post campus of the Long Island University where he also teaches undergraduate and graduate courses in rhetoric, composition, linguistics, and literature. With Helen Fox, he is working on a collection of essays about alternative academic discourses as alternative forms of intellectual work.